Top Federal Tax Issues for 2020 | CPE Course

Jennifer Kowal, J.D.
Greg White, CPA

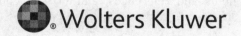
Wolters Kluwer

Contributors

Contributing Editors . . . . Jennifer Kowal, J.D.

Greg White, CPA

Technical Review . . . . Lorraine Zecca, CPA

Production Coordinator . . . . Mariela de la Torre; Jennifer Schencker;

Ranjith Rajaram

Production . . . . Sharon Sofinski; Anbarasu Anbumani

This publication is designed to provide accurate and authoritative information in regard to the subject matter covered. It is sold with the understanding that the publisher is not engaged in rendering legal, accounting, or other professional service. If legal advice or other expert assistance is required, the services of a competent professional person should be sought.

ISBN: 978-0-8080-5240-1

SUSTAINABLE FORESTRY INITIATIVE

Certified Sourcing
www.sfiprogram.org
SFI-01681

No claim is made to original government works; however, within this Product or Publication, the following are subject to CCH Incorporated's copyright: (1) the gathering, compilation, and arrangement of such government materials; (2) the magnetic translation and digital conversion of data, if applicable; (3) the historical, statutory and other notes and references; and (4) the commentary and other materials.

Do not send returns to the above address. If for any reason you are not satisfied with your book purchase, it can easily be returned within 30 days of shipment. Please go to *support.cch.com/returns* to initiate your return. If you require further assistance with your return, please call: (800) 344-3734 M-F, 8 a.m. – 6 p.m CT.

Printed in the United States of America

Introduction

Each year, a handful of tax issues typically require special attention by tax practitioners. The reasons vary, from tax legislation, a particularly complicated new provision in the Internal Revenue Code, to a planning technique opened up by a new regulation or ruling, or the availability of a significant tax benefit with a short window of opportunity. Sometimes a developing business need creates a new set of tax problems, or pressure exerted by Congress or the Administration puts more heat on some taxpayers while giving others more slack. All these share in creating a unique mix that in turn creates special opportunities and pitfalls in the coming year and beyond. The past year has seen more than its share of these developing issues.

Top Federal Tax Issues for 2020 CPE Course identifies those recent events that have developed into the current "hot" issues of the day. These tax issues have been selected as particularly relevant to tax practice in 2020. They have been selected not only because of their impact on return preparation during the 2020 tax season but also because of the important role they play in developing effective tax strategies for 2020 and beyond.

This course is designed to help reassure the tax practitioner that he or she is not missing out on advising clients about a hot, new tax opportunity; or that a brewing controversy does not blindside their practice. In addition to issue identification, this course provides the basic information needed for the tax practitioner to implement a plan that addresses the particular opportunities and pitfalls presented by any one of those issues. Among the topics examined in the *Top Federal Tax Issues for 2020 CPE Course* are:

- The New World of Depreciation under Tax Reform
- *Tax Cuts and Jobs Act:* Accounting Method Changes
- Maximizing Itemized Deductions under the New Law
- New Final Sec. 199A Regs for the Qualified Business Income Deduction
- Choice of Entity & Tax Issues Entity Formations
- Sale of Closely Held Businesses
- *Tax Cuts and Jobs Act:* Impact on Reasonable Compensation for S Corp Shareholder-Employees

Study Questions. Throughout the course you will find Study Questions to help you test your knowledge, and comments that are vital to understanding a particular strategy or idea. Answers to the Study Questions with feedback on both correct and incorrect responses are provided in a special section beginning at ¶ 10,100.

Final Exam. This course is divided into two Modules. Take your time and review all course Modules. When you feel confident that you thoroughly understand the material, turn to the Final Exam. Complete one, or both, Module Final Exams for continuing professional education credit.

Go to **cchcpelink.com/printcpe** to complete your Final Exam online for immediate results. My Dashboard provides convenient storage for your CPE course Certificates. Further information is provided in the CPE Final Exam instructions at ¶ 10,300. **Please note, manual grading is no longer available for Top Federal Tax Issues. All answer sheets must be submitted online for grading and processing.**

Note: The material contained in this publication was current at the time it went to print.

October 2019

PLEDGE TO QUALITY

Thank you for choosing this CCH® CPE Link product. We will continue to produce high quality products that challenge your intellect and give you the best option for your Continuing Education requirements. Should you have a concern about this or any other Wolters Kluwer product, please call our Customer Service Department at 1-800-344-3734.

COURSE OBJECTIVES

This course was prepared to provide the participant with an overview of specific tax issues that impact 2019 tax return preparation and tax planning in 2020. Each impacts a significant number of taxpayers in significant ways.

Upon course completion, you will be able to:

- Determine the best depreciation method for real estate improvements
- Identify which cost recovery method is best in specific client situations
- Apply the more widely available rules for *de minimis* expensing and for expensing real property under the TCJA
- Describe the depreciation recapture rules that apply to bonus depreciation, Section 179, and the *de minimis* rules
- Determine when a rapid method of cost recovery should not be used
- Recognize effective years for qualified property placed into service that is not eligible for bonus depreciation based on the new TCJA provisions
- Identify the maximum depreciation for passenger automobiles placed in service after December 31, 2017
- Determine how to apply the two new types of inventory methods for small business taxpayers:

    —The "raw materials" method

    —The "book conformity method

- Differentiate which clients can switch to the cash method
- Determine how to treat costs of self-constructed assets under the Tax Cuts and Jobs Act of 2017 (TCJA)
- Identify and apply the *de minimis* rules as affected by the TCJA
- Determine which clients are "tax shelters" and therefore unable to use the new accounting methods
- Recognize which Code Section can help solve the problem of double-counting income that results from a business switching to the cash method of accounting
- Describe Revenue Procedure 2004-34
- Recognize how to maximize itemized deductions under the TCJA
- Identify the new standard deductions as a result of the TCJA
- Identify how donor-advised funds and qualifying charitable distributions can maximize deductible charitable contributions at a minimal cost
- Recognize and apply case law and administrative guidance to increase the deduction for tax preparation fees
- Understand home mortgage interest deductibility, including the refinancing rules
- Identify and apply tax regulations to derive benefit from investment advisory fees

- Recognize and apply elections to increase the deduction for taxes on investment property
- Identify the basic calculation of the qualifying income business deduction (QBID)
- Recognize and apply the safe harbor as it relates to rental real estate
- Differentiate between proposed 2018 regulations and the final regulations issued for 2018 returns
- Identify what is included within qualified business income (QBI)
- Identify the QBID for various filers
- Recognize and apply correct principles relating to aggregation
- Describe which type of individual would likely be included in the "specified service trade or business (SSTB) classification, based on the final regulations
- Identify the business advantages and disadvantages of various business entity structures
- Identify the tax advantages and disadvantages of various business entity structures
- Recognize the treatment of formation transactions for C corporations, S corporations, LLCs, and partnerships
- Describe potential current and future pitfalls of forming each entity type
- Differentiate tax treatment between stock sales and asset sales
- Identify when a Code Sec. 338(h)(10) election should be made and describe its consequences
- Describe how earnouts and other contingent purchase price transactions are treated under tax rules
- Identify special rules regarding taxation of intangible assets
- Recognize the business consequences of a stock sale
- State which Internal Revenue Code section states that the buyer and seller shall allocate the purchase price in the manner prescribed in Code Sec. 338(b)(5)
- Identify which asset class is allocated last with respect to a purchase price allocation as required by Internal Revenue Code Sec. 1060
- Recognize how to determine "reasonable compensation" for S corporation shareholders
- Identify and apply the reasonable compensation rules in specific settings
- Recognize characteristics of the new QBID deduction
- Explain how to maximize S corporation shareholders' QBID
- Name the factors the courts have taken into account in determining reasonable compensation
- Identify the steps in calculating the cost of lost Social Security benefits
- Describe planning strategies with regard to reasonable compensation for S corporation shareholders

---

Contents

MODULE 2: DEVLOPMENTS IMPACTING BUSINESS ENTITIES
4 New Final Section 199A Regulations for the Qualified Business Income Deduction

5 Choice of Entity and Tax Issue Entity Formations

6 Sale of Closely Held Businesses

7 The Tax Cuts and Jobs Act: Impact on Reasonable Compensation for S Corporation Shareholder-Employees

MODULE 1: DEVELOPMENTS IMPACTING TAX RETURN PREPARATION—Chapter 1: Lightning Fast Depreciation: The New World of Depreciation under Tax Reform

¶ 101 WELCOME

On the heels of the tangible property regulations, the Tax Cuts and Jobs Act of 2017 (TCJA) has made further changes to depreciation, including bonus depreciation and Section 179 depreciation. As a result, there are ways to recover the cost of property more quickly and achieve faster tax savings. This chapter offers strategies for using depreciation to achieve the best tax results on real estate and property used in business.

¶ 102 LEARNING OBJECTIVES

Upon completion of this chapter, you will be able to:

- Determine the best depreciation method for real estate improvements
- Identify which cost recovery method is best in specific client situations
- Apply the more widely available rules for *de minimis* expensing and for expensing real property under the TCJA
- Describe the depreciation recapture rules that apply to bonus depreciation, Section 179, and the *de minimis* rules
- Determine when a rapid method of cost recovery should not be used
- Recognize effective years for qualified property placed into service that is not eligible for bonus depreciation based on the new TCJA provisions
- Identify the maximum depreciation for passenger automobiles placed in service after December 31, 2017
- Recognize components that are eligible for Section 179 deduction
- Describe the "surgical" approach to tax planning
- Recognize which items are eligible for bonus depreciation in various situations

¶ 103 INTRODUCTION

All three of the fast depreciation methods discussed in this chapter have changed as a result of the Tax Cuts and Jobs Act of 2017 (TCJA), largely for the better. The methods are bonus depreciation, Section 179 depreciation, and the *de minimis* rules for expensing real property. The application of those rules is clear, especially with respect to property improvements, and they play an important role in some circumstances.

The chapter will discuss the time when property is placed in service, which is an important element, especially if property is acquired near the end of the year. There are many different rules for different types of property. The chapter will address targeting income, and how taxpayers can use these depreciation methods to get just the amount of income they want. Although that is not always possible, it is even more important with the new qualified business income deduction (QBID), also known as the 20 percent pass-through reduction.

One of these methods gives taxpayers the flexibility to change their mind. These methods will be discussed in that context, and recapture will be covered near the end of the chapter.

¶ 104 TAX CUTS AND JOBS ACT

The TCJA was signed into law in December 2017. Under the new tax legislation, there are three fast ways to write off property, particularly fixed assets that were affected by the TCJA.

- The TCJA offers 100 percent bonus depreciation for eligible property through the end of 2022. It begins to phase out between 2023 and 2026, and will end in 2027.
- Section 179 depreciation changes greatly under TCJA; it will be discussed in more detail later in this chapter.
- The *de minimis* rules provide a very quick method for expensing property. This too will be covered later in the chapter. Although the *de minimis* rule was previously established as part of the tangible property regulations, it stands on firmer ground after the TCJA.

TCJA and Bonus Deprecation

Under the TCJA, taxpayers can take 100 percent bonus depreciation on qualified eligible property acquired and placed in service after September 27, 2017. With the ability to take bonus depreciation on used property come some anti-abuse rules. For example, taxpayers cannot take bonus depreciation on unused property that they inherited, property received as a gift, or used property acquired from related parties.

Taxpayers have a little over 5 years to take 100 percent bonus depreciation—to the end of 2022—and then it starts to phase out. In 2023 the percentage is reduced to 80 percent, in 2024 to 60 percent, in 2025 to 40 percent, and in 2026 to 20 percent. Bonus depreciation will end in 2027 unless Congress acts to extend it. Also, the TCJA includes a special placed-in-service rule for "longer production period property" and certain planes.

Bonus Depreciation Percentages	
Placed in Service*	**Bonus Percentage****
9/28/17–12/31/17	100***
2018–2022	100
2023	80
2024	60
2025	40
2026	20
2027	None
* Property must also be acquired after September 27, 2017. ** Special rule applies to longer production period property and certain planes. *** Can elect to use 50 percent.	

Although there are many categories of bonus depreciation, the most common is recovery property that has a recovery period of 20 years or less (Code Sec. 168(k)(2)(A)(i)(I)). It includes the following:

- Personal property (used property qualifies under the TCJA)
  - Equipment, carpeting, drapes, cabinets (Treas. Reg. § 1.263(a)-3(j)(3) example 5 provides support for treating cabinets as personal property), etc.
- Land improvements (Code Sec. 168(c); Rev. Proc. 87–56, § 6, Asset Class 00.3)

— Fences

— Landscaping (including shrubbery near the building, but not on the property's perimeter)

— Driveways and sidewalks

EXAMPLE: Seth acquires a rental duplex on September 30, 2018 for $205,000. The duplex was originally constructed in 2002, so it was used when he acquired it. Seth gets bonus depreciation on land improvements unless he elects out of bonus depreciation, even though the duplex is used property, and he will also get bonus depreciation on personal property. It is possible that any losses on the rental property will be suspended by the passive loss rules, but even if they are, those passive losses will ultimately be freed up (e.g., once he has passive income, when he disposes of the property, if he is a real estate professional, or if the duplex is a short-term rental property). Seth will take bonus depreciation on the land improvements. The duplex's purchase price will be allocated as follows:

	Cost	Bonus
Land	$50,000	No
Building	$120,000	No
Land improvements	$20,000	Yes
Personal property	$15,000	Yes

The building does not qualify for bonus depreciation because it does not have a recovery period of 20 years or less. The improvements and personal property qualify for bonus depreciation unless Seth elects out.

The land is not depreciable. Must the value of land improvements be separately stated in a purchase and sale agreement in order to take bonus depreciation? That is, is a written allocation of the value required in the purchase document? The answer is no. Although it is a good practice to put the written allocation into the purchase and sale agreement, doing so is not required. If there is a written allocation of purchase, in almost all instances the taxpayer is bound by it. There are some rare exceptions—for example, if the other party committed fraud or there was a common misunderstanding where a taxpayer would not be bound.

In addition to property, other types of property qualify for bonus depreciation. These include:

• Software

• TV, film property, and live theatrical productions

• Certain trees and vines that are grafted or planted

However, some items do not qualify even if they otherwise would fit in one of these categories. For example, businesses that are subject to the 30 percent business interest limitation of Code Sec. 163(j) and that have floor plan financing (e.g., car, boat, or farm equipment dealers) do not qualify for bonus depreciation. Farming businesses that elect out of the interest limitations of Code Sec. 163(j) are not permitted to take bonus depreciation on property with a recovery period of 10 years or more (Code Sec. 168(g)(1)(G)). Also, certain utilities cannot take bonus depreciation (Code Sec. 168(k)(9)).

¶ 105 ALLOCATION OF COST: BUILDING, LAND, AND PERSONAL PROPERTY

The saying "Rough justice is better than no justice at all" is not just a quote from a movie; it is a concept followed by the IRS and courts. For example, IRS General Counsel

Memorandum 39838 states that "a roughly-hewn" estimate is better than no allocation at all. Applying this to the context of a building and land, and land improvements and personal property, it is better to try to get the allocation approximately right than to not allocate at all.

The first step is to allocate the property's cost between the land and improvements to the property. There are three available methods of allocation between land and improvements that are supported by case law:

- **Reproduction cost.** This method is supported by *Meiers* (TC Memo 1982–51). In that case, the IRS argued for using the "assessed" value, but the Tax Court disagreed, agreeing with the taxpayer that reproduction costs should be used. For example, if it costs $200 per square foot to construct a new building and there are 1,000 square feet in the new building, $200,000 would be allocated to the building and the balance would be allocated to land. The *Meiers* ruling is very favorable for purchasers, and relied in part upon the IRS.

- **Reproduction cost less refurbishment cost.** This method is supported by *Westory* (6 AFTR 2d 5392) and other case law. It says that while the reproduction cost is a good method for a newly constructed building, the allocation method should be different for a used building. The fair market value (FMV) of an older building equals the reproduction cost less the cost to refurbish it. For example, assume a new building would cost $200,000 to construct. If the taxpayer purchases a used building that would require $25,000 in expenditures to restore it to similar condition to a new building, the used building would be allocated $175,000.

- **Assessed value.** Despite *Meiers*, assessed value is often used if no better evidence is available. The case supporting the assessed value method is *Conroe Office Building, Ltd.* (TC Memo 1991–224). Assessed value typically tends to overstate the value of land and understate the value of improvements. Sellers typically love this method because they have no depreciation recapture on the sale of land, and they have no 25 percent tax rate for unrecaptured Section 1250 gain on the sale of land.

Cost Segregation Studies

The second step is to allocate the remaining cost (after removing the cost of land) to the improvements: personal property, land improvements, and the building. Cost segregation allows a taxpayer to classify portions of the improvements as personal property and land improvements. These components are depreciated over a shortened recovery period, usually between 5 and 15 years. After removing the cost apportioned to land, cost segregation studies are a very common way to accomplish this and are generally accepted by the IRS. However, they may be cost-prohibitive for small projects.

Just as it is incorrect to depreciate a building over 5 years, it is incorrect to depreciate carpeting and appliances over 27.5 years. Many taxpayers consider the downside of taking more deductions but fail to realize there is also a downside to not taking *enough* deductions. Nonetheless, taxpayers have the burden of supporting their deductions.

In its *Cost Segregation Audit Techniques Guide*, the IRS looked at six types of cost segregation approaches and noted one as the least reliable: the "rule of thumb" approach, using historical cost averages. According to the IRS, taxpayers should exercise caution in using this approach because it " . . . uses little or no documentation and is based on a preparer's 'experience' . . . it estimate[s] IRC § 1245 property as a fixed percent of project cost [using] 'industry averages.'" For example, if a manufacturing facility normally has 40 percent personal property, it does not do a cost segregation study; it just uses the typical 40 percent number to break out personal property. Although the IRS suggests caution in the area of "rule of thumb" cost segregation studies, it does *not* rule them out. Therefore, "rule of thumb" studies can provide useful guidance in the case of less expensive real estate purchases.

Note that sometimes the cost of a project does not justify a cost segregation study. Three options are available for smaller projects:

- **"Rule of thumb" approach.** This method, discussed earlier, uses approximate allocations based on a historical cost segregation study average.
- **Questionnaire study.** If the depreciable property portion of the purchase price is $500,000 or less, some costs segregation firms offer an online "questionnaire study." A questionnaire study requires that the taxpayer fills out a questionnaire and pays a fee (approximately $400), and the property improvements are broken out into building and land improvement and personal property.
- **Client estimates.** Clients identify Section 1245 property and land improvements and use their estimates of FMV.

The regulations do not require—nor even recommend—the use of a cost segregation study. Although there are certainly no requirements to use a cost segregation study, they are useful for taxpayers who get audited. Taxpayers and their tax preparers have the burden of proving their deductions.

The following chart shows common allocation percentages of the total cost of property improvements to the specific components of property. Practitioners sometimes use these percentages to perform their own "rule of thumb" cost segregation studies. The first step is always to break out land. *After* the cost of land is removed from the total purchase price, the percentages below are used to allocate the remaining cost to the property's components.

Aggregate Cost Segregation Numbers					
Property Type	5-Year	7-Year	15-Year	27.5-Year	39-Year
Multifamily residential (garden style)	15%	—	10%	75%	—
Office building	9%	—	10%	—	81%
Restaurant (high-end)	25%	—	12%	—	63%
Warehouse	5%	—	10%	—	85%

The table above is based upon averages. Some practitioners reduce these percentages for the following reasons:

- Reduce allocations by an allowance to be conservative.
- Reduce allocations for properties in poor condition.

Here is an example of reducing the percentage allocations of 5-year and 15-year property to be conservative or to recognize property in poor condition (e.g., old appliances, cracked driveways, etc.):

Category	Average Percentage	Adjusted Factor	Adjusted Percentage	Property Cost (Excluding Land)	Allocation
5–year	15%	75%	11.25%	$500,000	$56,250
15–year	10%	75%	7.5%	$500,000	$37,500
27.5–year	75%	N/A	81.25%	$500,000	$406,250

Observations about the use of the "rule of thumb" method include the following:

- The IRS does not rule it out.
- It follows the "rough justice" favored by the courts and the IRS.
- The taxpayer could always obtain a cost segregation study if audited, which might result in more depreciation.

¶ 106 PASSENGER AUTOMOBILES

To say that the TCJA turbocharged the passenger automobile deduction is no exaggeration. The TCJA increased depreciation for passenger automobiles used in businesses that are placed into service after December 31, 2017. The depreciation limits are shown in the following chart.

PISA 12/31/17*, Do Not Claim Bonus	Maximum Depreciation**
1st Taxable Year	$18,000***
2nd Taxable Year	$16,000
3rd Taxable Year	$9,600
Succeeding Years in Recovery Period	$5,760

* In years ending after December 31, 2017.
** Assuming 100 percent qualified business use. Indexed for inflation for vehicles placed in service after 2018.
*** $10,000 if the taxpayer elects out of bonus depreciation (Code Sec.. 168(k)(2)(F)(i)).

Note that these limitations are for passenger automobiles only; the limitations do not apply to large trucks, sport utility vehicles (SUVs), or vans with a gross vehicle weight of more than 6,000 pounds.

EXAMPLE: Taxpayer A bought a passenger auto in 2018 for $50,000. It is used 90 percent for business. If the taxpayer takes bonus depreciation, it is limited to lesser of:

- Depreciation = $50,000 × 90 percent = $45,000, or
- Code Sec. 280F limit = $18,000 × 90 percent = $16,200

If Taxpayer A does not elect out of bonus depreciation, it can take $16,200 depreciation in 2018.

EXAMPLE: Taxpayer B bought a passenger auto in 2018 for $50,000. It is used 90 percent for business. If the taxpayer elects out of bonus depreciation and takes Section 179 depreciation, it is limited to the lesser of:

- Section 179 = $50,000 × 90 percent = $45,000, or
- Section 280F limit = $10,000 × 90 percent = $9,000 (Treas. Reg. § 1.280F-2T(b)(4))

If Taxpayer B elects out of bonus depreciation, it can take $9,000 depreciation in 2018.

An unusual technical problem arose in connection with 100 percent bonus depreciation: a taxpayer who elected 100 percent bonus depreciation would get the full $18,000 the first year but then get no depreciation in years two through six. The IRS knew that this is not what Congress intended in the TCJA and therefore issued Rev. Proc. 2019-13. It provides a safe harbor that allows the taxpayer who owns a vehicle subject to the annual luxury automobile depreciation caps to claim depreciation deductions during each year of the vehicle's regular recovery period, even though the taxpayer claimed 100 percent bonus depreciation in the year it was placed in service. Without this safe harbor, the cost of the vehicle in excess of the first-year cap ($18,000 for a vehicle placed in service in 2018) is recovered at a specified rate ($5,760 per year for a vehicle placed in service in 2018) beginning in the first tax year *after* the end of the vehicle's regular recovery period.

Under the safe harbor, depreciation deductions after the first year are limited to the lesser of the applicable depreciation cap or depreciation computed using table percentages on the cost of the vehicle as reduced by the first-year cap. The safe harbor does not impact depreciation calculations until the second year of the recovery period. However, with or without the safe harbor, taxpayers who elect 100 percent bonus depreciation in 2018 can only claim an $18,000 deduction, assuming 100 percent business use. If business use dips to 50 percent or less, a portion of the first year depreciation will have to be recaptured. However, if the taxpayer can keep business use over 50 percent for the five-year recovery period, recapture will not be required.

> **EXAMPLE:** Taxpayer C bought a passenger automobile on December 30, 2018, and uses it 100 percent for business on December 30 and 31. The taxpayer uses the auto more than 50 percent for business in the next five years. Taxpayer C can write off up to $18,000 bonus depreciation in 2018 with no future recapture. The same strategy works for larger trucks and vans that have a fully loaded gross vehicle weight of greater than 6,000 pounds.

¶ 107 15-YEAR PROPERTY

One negative element of the TCJA is the elimination of almost all types of continual property, except for land improvements. Prior to the TCJA, taxpayers could take a 15-year life on qualified leasehold improvement property (QLIP), qualified restaurant property (QRTP), qualified retail improvement property (QRIP), and qualified improvement property (QIP). That has been eliminated for property placed in service after December 31, 2017. Those four types of property still can be depreciated, but now over 39, rather than 15, years (P.L. 115–97, Sec. 13204(b)(1)).

> **EXAMPLE:** Noland and Gemar LLP, an accounting firm, makes qualified leasehold improvements to its office. If the real property portion is QLIP and the firm placed those improvements in service on December 2, 2017, the property is 15-year-old property. If instead Noland and Gemar placed the property in service on February 28, 2018, the firm would get a very unusual result: those same leasehold improvements take on a 39-year life.

STUDY QUESTIONS

1. Qualified property placed in service is *not* eligible for bonus depreciation based on the new TCJA provisions if it is placed in service during what year?

    a. 2024

    b. 2025

    c. 2026

    d. 2027

2. Which of the following identifies the maximum depreciation (not including bonus) for passenger automobiles assuming qualified business use in the second taxable year after December 31, 2017?

    a. $10,000

    b. $16,000

    c. $9,600

    d. $5,760

¶ 108 SECTION 179

The TCJA made massive changes to the Section 179 expensing deduction. Some of those changes are negative. For example, beginning in 2018, QRTP will no longer qualify for the Section 179 deduction. The good news is that the positive changes are much more significant. The most important change is that QIP, which includes almost any improvement to the interior of a commercial building, now qualifies for Section 179 depreciation.

Under the TCJA, nonresidential roof replacements—which include roofs on non-residential buildings such as office buildings, strip malls, or warehouses—can now be expensed immediately under Section 179. The same is true for nonresidential heating, ventilation, and air conditioning (HVAC) equipment. These adjustments apply only to nonresidential property.

One of the changes that applies to residential personal property is that, beginning in 2018, taxpayers can take a Section 179 deduction on carpeting, window treatments, or other personal property in an apartment building or a duplex. Section 179 depreciation did not apply to land improvements before the TCJA and still does not. The only depreciation that can be taken for land improvements is bonus depreciation.

Section 179 Changes: Property		
	Placed in Service in Tax Years Beginning Before 2018	**Placed in Service in Tax Years Beginning After 2017**
Qualifying leasehold improvements	Yes	No
Qualified restaurant property (QRTP)	Yes	No
Qualified improvement property (QIP)	No	Yes
Nonresidential roofs (only if placed in service after the building)	No	Yes
Lodging personal property (apartments)	No	Yes
Land improvements	No	No

Not only was the scope of property that qualifies for Section 179 expanded under the TCJA, but also the dollar amount. The maximum Section 179 expense, formerly $500,000, is now $1 million under the new tax legislation. And now, taxpayers can place in service up to $2.5 million in Section 179 property in the current year and still take the entire Section 179 expense. Before the TCJA, they could place up to $2 million in property in a single year before the deduction began to phase out. These amounts are indexed for inflation for years beginning after 2018 (Code Sec. 179(b)(6)). There are some limitations, however. For example, the $1 million limit and the $2.5 million phaseout apply not only to individual taxpayers but also to each partnership, S corporation, and partner and shareholder in those entities (Treas. Reg. § 1.179-2(b)(3) and (4)).

EXAMPLE: In 2018, a taxpayer has $3,250,000 in Section 179 property placed in service in 2018. It has made a huge amount of purchases in 2018. The starting point for the phaseout is the full amount, the Section 179 limit of $1 million per year. Because the client has more than $2.5 million of Section 179 assets placed in service this year, the Section 179 deduction will start phasing out.

Phaseout Example			
Section 179 property placed in service in 2018			$3,250,000
Annual aggregated cost limit		$1,000,000	
Actual Section 179	$3,250,000		
Phaseout floor	($2,500,000)		
Limit reduction		($750,000)	
Maximum Section 179 expense			**$250,000**

As is true for used bonus depreciation property, there are some serious restrictions on Section 179 depreciation. Property that is purchased from a related person (there is a special definition of *family* for this purpose) cannot take a Section 179 deduction. The same is true for property received as a gift or inheritance. For Code Sec. 1031 or 1033 property, the taxpayer can apply Section 179 only to an increase in basis, not carryover basis.

Section 179 Qualified Real Property

Section 179 depreciation applies to qualified real property ("QRP"), which includes QIP, nonresidential roofs, nonresidential HVAC, nonresidential fire protection and alarm systems, and nonresidential security systems. The property must be nonresidential, which includes retail stores, warehouses, office buildings, and hotels and motels (Code Sec. 168(e)(2)(A)(ii)(I) and (e)(2)(B)). The QRP must be placed in service after the building, in tax years beginning after December 31, 2017.

> **EXAMPLE:** Taxpayer D, a calendar year taxpayer, bought an office building in 2015. In 2018, it replaced the building's roof shingles and decking. Because the property is nonresidential and the improvements were made after the building was acquired, it is considered QRP. Therefore, the taxpayer can elect Section 179 depreciation. However, if the building were an apartment building rather than an office building, Section 179 would not apply (only nonresidential property qualifies).

> **EXAMPLE:** Taxpayer E bought a retail store in 2015. In 2018, it replaced the HVAC unit on the top of the building. The building is nonresidential and the HVAC unit was placed in service after the building was bought. Because Taxpayer E did not acquire the HVAC unit with the building, the HVAC unit is considered an improvement. Therefore, this qualifies for Section 179 depreciation. However, if the taxpayer owned an apartment building instead of a retail store, replacement of the HVAC unit would not qualify for Section 179.

> **EXAMPLE:** Taxpayer F purchased a warehouse in 2017. In 2018, it installed a new fire protection system on the warehouse's exterior. Because the property is nonresidential and the fire protection system was placed in service after the building was purchased, it is QRP and the taxpayer can elect Section 179 depreciation. That would not be the case if Taxpayer F installed the same type of system on a residential duplex.

> **EXAMPLE:** Joanne bought an apartment building in 2016. In 2018, she replaced all of the carpeting in the building. This qualifies for Section 179 treatment because personal property used in connection with lodging now qualifies for Section 179 if placed in service after December 31, 2017.

> Consider the same facts as above, but instead of replacing the building's carpeting, Joann replaced the HVAC unit on top of the building. This will not qualify for Section 179 because an HVAC unit is not personal property and the building is residential.

Note that property must be used in a business in order to qualify for Section 179 expense treatment. However, triple net leases where the landlord does not supervise repairs and simply collects a check each month are not likely to meet the business standard. In contrast, if the landlord supervises repairs to the property, the property is likely to meet the business requirement.

Trading Places: QIP Section 179 and Bonus Depreciation

QIP qualified for bonus depreciation in 2017, but it does not qualify in 2018. QIP did not qualify for Section 179 depreciation in 2017, but it does qualify in 2018. Unless Congress changes the bonus depreciation rules for QIP, Section 179 is the only method for writing off QIP. To be considered QIP, three requirements must be met:

- The improvement has to be to the interior portion of the building.
- The building has to be nonresidential real property (a duplex or an apartment building does not qualify).
- The improvement has to be placed in service after the building.

Excluded from the definition of QIP are the following:

- An enlargement of a building
- Elevators and escalators
- The internal structural framework of the building

A building's internal structural framework includes all load-bearing internal walls and other internal structural supports, including columns, girders, beams, trusses, and spandrels, and all other parts essential to the building's stability (Treas. Reg. § 1.48-12(b)(3); Treas. Reg. § 1.168(k)-1(c)(3)(v)).

> **EXAMPLE:** An accounting firm owns its own office building, which was built in 2016. In 2018, the firm decides to make its building a showplace. To make additional offices for its staff members, the firm tears out some non-load-bearing old walls and builds some new ones. It also replaces all the lighting fixtures, all the pipes, all the electrical wiring, and all the ceiling tiles. In addition, the firm installs a new furnace in the building. Which of these items qualify as QIP? The answer: all (Rev. Proc. 2017–33, Sec. 4.02(5)—this provides an example of construction of a restroom that would include plumbing and electrical wiring). Note that if the firm leased rather than owned the building, the result would be the same.

STUDY QUESTIONS

3. Which of the following types of property and related treatment under Section 179 remain unchanged under the TCJA?

   a. Land improvements

   b. Qualifying leasehold improvements

   c. Non-residential roofs

   d. Non-residential HVAC

4. Which of the following identifies the maximum Section 179 expense amount for 2018 based on the revised provisions from TCJA?

   a. $500,000

   b. $1,000,000

   c. $2,000,000

   d. $2,500,000

5. A taxpayer has acquired a duplex in 2018 and has allocated the purchase price across land, building, land improvements, and personal property. Of these components, which of the following would be eligible for a Section 179 deduction?

    a. Land

    b. Buildings

    c. Personal property

    d. Land improvements

QRP Building Placed in Service First

For an improvement to qualify as QRP under Section 179, it has to be an improvement made *after* the building is placed in service. For example, if a buyer purchased a building, and that building's former owner replaced the roof before the sale was complete, the roof will not qualify as QRP for the buyer. The new roof is not the buyer's improvement; the buyer is acquiring the new roof as part of the building, and it is placed in service at the same time as the building.

The same is true for a buyer who purchases an existing commercial building. The buyer cannot expense the building's roof or lighting fixtures because they were placed in service at the same time as the building. However, if two weeks after buying an existing commercial building, the buyer replaces the entire roof (including the decking), he can elect Section 179 for QRP and expense the entire roof.

¶ 109 *DE MINIMIS* RULES

The *de minimis* rules apply to both residential and nonresidential property. There are two different *de minimis* safe harbor rules:

- The $2,500/$5,000 safe harbor *de minimis* if the taxpayer makes an election.

- The eligible building rule, the lesser of 2 percent or $10,000 if the taxpayer makes an election.

There are many restrictions on the second rule, and the limits to which it applies are quite low; therefore, this section will focus on the first rule.

Under the *de minimis* safe harbor election, an electing taxpayer that has audited financial statements can expense amounts up to $5,000 per invoice (or per item substantiated by invoice) under the *de minimis* rules. The taxpayer must also have a written policy used for financial accounting purposes and must also expense the same item on its books ("book conformity"). That means if the taxpayer wants to write off a *de minimis* asset on its tax return, it must write it off on its books.

For taxpayers without audited financial statements, the threshold is $2,500 or less; if the invoice is $2,500 or less and the electing taxpayer meets the *de minimis* requirements, the taxpayer can expense the asset immediately; it does not even have to look at the details on the invoice (IRS Notice 2015-82). The taxpayer must have an accounting policy for financial purposes, but unlike for the $5,000 rule, the policy does not have to be in writing (though having a written policy is strongly recommended). The taxpayer must also have book conformity. Even if an invoice exceeds $2,500, the taxpayer may apply *de minimis* expensing to items shown on the invoice.

    EXAMPLE: Taxpayer G does not have audited financial statements. It has an invoice for 10 desks. The invoice shows that nine of the desks cost $2,495 and the tenth cost over $2,500. Taxpayer E can immediately deduct each item that is less than or equal to $2,500 if it makes the election, meets the book conformity requirement, and has a *de minimis* policy in place. The presence of a single item of more than $2,500 does not mean that the taxpayer cannot apply the deduction to the other items on the invoice. However, the desk that cost more than $2,500 won't qualify for *de minimis* expense treatment.

There are two types of eligible expenditures under the *de minimis* rules, improvements and purchases. For example, assume a taxpayer that has audited financial statements has a $4,400 invoice for building insulation. Building insulation normally has to be capitalized. The insulation is an improvement because it materially increases the building's energy efficiency. Even though the insulation is required to be capitalized under regular tax rules, the taxpayer can write it off immediately because it falls under the *de minimis* rules.

Under the anti-abuse rule (Treas. Reg. § 1.263-1(f)(6)), a taxpayer cannot get artificially low invoices that are tailored to abuse the safe harbor rule. For example, a taxpayer who buys a truck from a dealership cannot ask the dealership to give it separate invoices for the tires, for the engine, for the trailer, and so on (Treas. Reg. § 1.263(a)-1(f)(7), Example 11). The anti-abuse rule prohibits "gaming the system."

Required Book Conformity

Book conformity is required under the *de minimis* rules. However, it is not required for bonus depreciation or Section 179 depreciation. If a taxpayer capitalizes items on its financial statement or other financial records, the taxpayer does not qualify to take the *de minimis* deduction for tax purposes.

> **EXAMPLE:** Taxpayer H owns an apartment building and replaces the cabinets. The cost of each cabinet is less than or equal to $2,500, and the cost of each is separately stated on the invoice. The taxpayer intends to capitalize the cabinets for *book* purposes, which means Taxpayer H cannot use the *de minimis* rules for tax purposes. However, the cabinets are personal property and should qualify for both Section 179 and bonus depreciation (Treas. Reg. § 1.263(a)-3(j)(3), Example 5).

Improvements and the *De Minimis* Rules

As noted earlier in this chapter, there are two ways to use the *de minimis* rules: (1) in buying discreet items, such as refrigerators; and (2) in making improvements to the property. IRS Notice 2015-82 plainly provides that improvements qualify for the *de minimis* rules. Prior to 2018, there was a bit of controversy regarding the capitalization requirements of Code Sec. 263A. Your author believes that taxpayers could apply the *de minimis* rules to improvements prior to 2018. However, beginning in 2018, it is clear that almost all taxpayers are exempt from the requirement to capitalize under Code Section 263A. The exemption applies to all taxpayers, except for tax shelters or taxpayers with trailing three-year average gross receipts greater than $25 million (Code Sec. 263A(i)). Taxpayers meeting these requirements are referred to as "small taxpayers."

Beginning in 2018, it is clear that small taxpayers may use the *de minimis* rules with respect to improvements to residential and nonresidential real property that meet the *de minimis* requirements. Section 179 depreciation applies only to improvements to nonresidential real property. In addition, the 27.5-year recovery period for real property is longer than the 20-year maximum for bonus depreciation, so such residential improvements will not qualify for bonus depreciation. Therefore, the only way to write off a residential real property improvement is under the *de minimis* rules.

The *de minimis* rules can apply to residential real property improvements as long as those improvements satisfy the *de minimis* requirements: book conformity, having a *de minimis* policy, making the election, and an invoice amount (*or* per item amount as substantiated by the invoice) of $2,500 or less ($5,000 for taxpayers with audited financial statements).

> **EXAMPLE:** John replaces every window in the apartment building he owns (100 windows in total). The invoice amount is $7,950. The cost per window, $795, is shown on the invoice. Because the windows are real property and their 27.5-year recovery period is longer than the 20-year maximum, they do not qualify for bonus depreciation or expensing under Section 179. However, they will qualify for *de minimis* treatment if John has a *de minimis* policy, makes the election, and meets the book conformity rule.

STUDY QUESTION

6. Which of the following statements with respect to *de minimis* rules is correct?
   - **a.** Taxpayers without audited financial statements must have book conformity.
   - **b.** Taxpayers with audited financial statements can elect up to $10,000 per invoice.
   - **c.** Taxpayers without audited financial statements can elect up to $5,000 per invoice.
   - **d.** Taxpayers with audited financial statements are not required to have a written accounting policy.

¶ 110 PLACED IN SERVICE

Many people believe that *placed in service* means "ready and available," but there are several different definitions of the term. First, one must distinguish what is different about depreciable property from every other category of property. A cash method taxpayer usually deducts expenses when it pays them. An accrual method taxpayer, on the other hand, typically deducts expenses when they are incurred, and when economic performance occurs. However, depreciable property is different. A taxpayer can begin writing off depreciable property when it is placed in service even if the taxpayer has not paid for it and has not incurred a liability. Depreciable property is generally placed in service when it is in a "condition or state of readiness and availability" for a "specifically assigned" function (Treas. Reg. § 1.167(a)-11(e)(1)). In addition, the taxpayer must have possession of the property (***Northern States Power***, 151 F.3d 876 (CA8)).

> **EXAMPLE:** Taxpayer I, a cash method taxpayer, owns a restaurant. The taxpayer buys a dishwashing machine on December 31, 2017 but does not take possession of it until January 3, 2018. The dishwasher is not placed in service in 2017 because Taxpayer I does not satisfy the possession test.

> **EXAMPLE:** Another cash method taxpayer that owns a restaurant, Taxpayer J, buys a dishwashing machine. Taxpayer J takes possession of it on December 31, 2017, but does not pay for it until January 3, 2018. Normally, a cash method taxpayer would not be able to deduct the expense for the washing machine until it has been paid for, but Taxpayer J can start depreciating in 2017 when the dishwasher is placed in service. The dishwasher is ready and available for its assigned function.

Different standards apply based on the type of property. For example, there is a different rule for buildings, and there are two separate rules for equipment—one rule applies if the equipment is "ready to go," and the other applies when the equipment requires some alterations to meet the taxpayer's assigned function. There is a special rule for equipment in a closed business (a business that has not yet opened its doors or has been closed for remodeling). Specific rules apply to property improvements as well. These standards are discussed in the following sections.

Buildings

According to the final regulations, a new building is placed in service when construction is complete and the building is in a state of readiness and availability (Treas. Reg. § 1.167(a)-11(e) and Rev. Rul. 76–238). Note that a building can be considered placed in service before it opens for business.

Other sources state that depreciation can begin as soon as a taxpayer has a certificate of occupancy for a building (Prop. Reg. § 1.168-2(e)(3); *Stine, LLC* [DC LA 115 AFTR 2d 2015-637, 2015]; *IRS Audit Technique Guide for Rehabilitation Tax Credits*). A certificate of occupancy is typically issued when the shell of the building is completed and the building is functional. For example, a factory building is placed in service when construction is "substantially complete." That means the building is in a condition of readiness and availability, even if the equipment it will contain is not in service, and even if the building is not open for business (Treas. Reg. § 1.167(a)-11(e); Rev. Rul. 76–238).

The taxpayer in *Stine, LLC* operated a home improvement store and received a certificate of occupancy before the end of 2008. The store received equipment (e.g., shelving), but the equipment had not yet been installed by the end of 2008, and the store was not ready to open for business. The court ruled that the building was placed in service in 2008. In response, the IRS issued Action on Decision 2017-02, arguing that the store, because it was not open for business, could not be placed in service for the purpose of starting depreciation. The IRS will likely continue to challenge this issue. Although taxpayers should be cautious, the author's position is that there is substantial authority to follow the *Stine* case and treat receipt of a certificate of occupancy as a sufficient basis for treating the building as placed in service.

This issue is important because it relates to whether a taxpayer can depreciate qualified real property under Section 179. Suppose a limited liability company (LLC) constructs a building, receives the certificate of occupancy on March 3, completes all tenant improvements on April 30, and the tenant moves in on May 1. According to the ruling in *Stine*, the taxpayer can take Section 179 depreciation for all tenant improvements because those were placed in service after the building was placed in service. However, if the IRS is right and the *Stine* ruling is wrong, there is no Section 179 depreciation. In the context of new nonresidential real estate, the *Stine* case is very important.

Ready-to-Go Equipment

Unlike the rules for buildings, there is little debate about the rules for ready-to-go equipment. As soon as ready-to-go equipment is purchased, it can be placed in service—even if it is not being used. For example, parts that are acquired and then set aside as spare parts can be placed in service the second they are acquired, even though they are not installed on the equipment (Treas. Reg. § 1.46-3(d)(2)).

> **EXAMPLE:** Farm equipment is acquired in December 2017 but, due to winter weather, is not used until 2018. Therefore, the equipment is treated as placed in service in December 2017, when it is readily available, even though it is not actually used until the following year (Treas. Reg. § 1.46-3(d)(2)).

EXAMPLE: A taxpayer purchases a sailboat. The sailboat lacks sails, and the taxpayer has not yet placed the sailboat in the water. Despite these facts, the Tax Court ruled that the sailboat was placed in service. It reasoned that the taxpayer could have borrowed or purchased sails at any time and that the sailboat itself was ready to sail, even without sails (*Hellings v. Comm'r.*, TC Memo 1994–24).

Unfinished Equipment

Special rules also apply to unfinished equipment. To be considered placed in service, unfinished equipment must be ready for its assigned purpose. Consider the case of *Michael Brown v. Commissioner* (TC Memo 2013–275). Brown was a very successful insurance salesman who many considered an insurance genius. He had a great deal of knowledge in tax law and a number of very wealthy clients. In fact, Brown wrote some insurance policies with a face value of more than $300 million and earned a commission of more than $10 million on a single policy.

Brown eventually purchased his own plane so that he could fly to meet with wealthy clients who were interested in buying insurance policies. He took delivery of his plane in December 2003, but it lacked a couple of details. Brown was not satisfied with a 17-inch display screen for the plane; he wanted a 20-inch display screen for his PowerPoint presentations. He also wanted a conference table installed in the plane. Brown asserted that those items were essential to his business.

Brown claimed to have made two business flights before the end of 2003, but the display screen and the conference table were not installed until 2004. Consequently, the IRS argued that the plane was placed in service in 2004, when the essential items were installed. Although the plane was fully operational in 2003, the Tax Court held that it was not placed in service until 2004, when it was ready for Brown's specifically assigned function.

Equipment in a Closed Business

The placed-in-service rules for equipment in a closed business are different. The rules can be illustrated with a case involving grocery store chain Piggly Wiggly. The company installed new HVAC equipment in its new stores that had not yet opened for business. Although the stores were not open, the HVAC equipment was operational. The court ruled that the equipment could not be considered placed in service until the stores opened. Therefore, Piggly Wiggly could not begin depreciating the HVAC equipment until its stores containing that equipment were open for business (*Piggly Wiggly v. Comm'r*, 84 TC 739 (TC 1985)). Note that the *Stine* case (discussed earlier) held that the "unopened business" rule applied only to equipment, and not to a building.

Improvements

Replacement improvements are generally placed in service when their cost is paid or incurred (Joint Committee on Tax, JCX–19–13, p. 36). This can be significant for cash method taxpayers who want to claim Section 179 depreciation in the current year or if the improvements are eligible for bonus deprecation. There are two narrow exceptions to this rule. "Paid or incurred" does not apply if (1) the property improvements are additions, or (2) a partial disposition loss is taken (Treas. Reg. § 1.167(a)-11(e)(1)(iii)).

EXAMPLE: A cash method taxpayer replaces all of the lighting fixtures in its office building. The taxpayer paid for the fixtures on December 31, 2018, but they are not installed until January 20, 2019. The taxpayer does not take a partial disposition loss. The fixtures are considered placed in service in 2018 when the taxpayer pays for them.

¶110

EXAMPLE: Assume the same facts as in the previous example, except the new lighting fixtures are *additions*. (The office building had only floor lamps before.) The special "paid or incurred" rule does not apply. The new fixtures must be operational to be considered placed in service.

De Minimis Expenses

There is a different placed-in service standard for *de minimis* expenses. They are deducted when paid or incurred regardless of whether they are placed in service.

EXAMPLE: Rongxiu buys four dishwashers for her apartment building. She pays for them on December 31, 2017, but has not yet picked up the dishwashers from the store. Because she did not have possession of the dishwashers in 2017, they are not placed in service in 2017 under the general placed-in-service rule. If she uses the *de minimis* rules, however, she could take a deduction in 2017 because she paid the bill in 2017, even though the dishwashers were not placed in service in that year.

STUDY QUESTIONS

7. Which of the following types of property is considered placed in service when paid or incurred?

    a. Buildings

    b. Replacement improvements if the taxpayer does not take a partial disposition loss for the disposed of property.

    c. Ready-to-go equipment

    d. Unfinished equipment

8. Which of the following types of property is considered placed in service when work is completed?

    a. Additions

    b. Buildings

    c. Ready-to-go equipment

    d. Unfinished equipment

¶ 111 WHICH BASIS REDUCTION COMES FIRST?

When it comes to basis reductions, there are ordering rules, and *de minimis* expensing comes first. The basis is then reduced under Section 179 (Treas. Reg. § 1.168(k)-1(d)(3), Example 2). The remainder is the starting point for bonus depreciation—if the taxpayer has not elected out of bonus depreciation.

EXAMPLE: A taxpayer purchases $200,000 property that is both Section 179 eligible and bonus depreciation eligible. Here is the scenario if the taxpayer does *not* elect out of bonus depreciation:

Cost of Section 179 Property (2018 placed in service)	$200,000
Portion Make Section 179 Election	($100,000)
Remaining Basis for Bonus	$100,000
Bonus	($100,000)
Net Remaining Basis	$0

If the taxpayer elects out of bonus depreciation, the regular depreciation rules apply to the remaining $100,000.

Cost of Section 179 Property (2018 placed in service)	$200,000
Portion Make Section 179 Election	($100,000)
Remaining Basis for Bonus	$100,000
Bonus (assume elect out of bonus)	($0)
Net Remaining Basis for Regular Depreciation	**$100,000**

¶112 THE SURGICAL APPROACH

How can a taxpayer use the Section 179 rules to get just the right amount of income? Bonus depreciation is not the answer. Bonus depreciation is a "blunt instrument" that results in "all or nothing." A taxpayer takes bonus depreciation for the entire recovery period—the entire class of property—or takes no bonus depreciation at all. Using bonus depreciation to target income would be like a surgeon using a chainsaw for a delicate surgery.

EXAMPLE: In 2018, Amy places in service property of $1 million. She can take bonus depreciation either on the whole $1 million or on $0. Again, opting for bonus depreciation would be akin to performing surgery with a saw rather than with a scalpel. Section 179 depreciation is more like a scalpel. Amy can choose Section 179 for all or part of the qualified property placed in service that is eligible (Code Sec. 179(c)(1)(A); Treas. Reg. § 1.179-1(a)(1)). This will give her considerable flexibility to "target" income.

To use the "surgical approach" to target income, a taxpayer should use the Section 179 approach and elect out of bonus depreciation. The taxpayer must elect out of bonus depreciation on a class-by-class basis. For example, it could elect out for five-year recovery property but not for seven-year recovery property. To elect out, a taxpayer must file Form 4562, *Depreciation and Amortization (Including Information on Listed Property)*. The form's instructions provide details on how to elect out. In addition, most types of tax preparation software have a box that the preparer can check to indicate for which classes of property the taxpayer is electing out.

EXAMPLE: George, who is married and files jointly, places in service $700,000 of Section 179 property that is also eligible for bonus depreciation in 2018. His income is $775,000 prior to any depreciation or Section 179 expense on the property. He has consistent taxable income each year. If George does not elect out of bonus deprecation, he will see the following result:

Cost of Property	$700,000
Section 179 Election	($400,000)
Basis Remaining	$300,000
Bonus Depreciation	($300,000)
Basis Remaining	$0
Total Deductions	**$700,000***
* This has negative consequences for George; his income is driven into the 24 percent and lower brackets.	

George wants to reduce his taxable income to the bottom of the 32 percent bracket. For the 2018 tax year, this means lowering his taxable income to $315,000. George decides to use the surgical approach to accomplish his goal. He will need

$460,000 in combined Section 179/regular depreciation to reduce his taxable income to $315,000:

Cost of Property	$700,000
§ 179 Election	**($400,000)**
Basis Remaining	$300,000
Bonus Depreciation (elect out)	($0)
Regular Depreciation ($300,000 × 20%)	**$60,000**
Total Deductions	**$460,000***

* This is exactly the amount of depreciation George wanted.

¶ 113 FLEXIBILITY TO CHANGE

If a taxpayer elects to use *de minimis* or bonus depreciation, he cannot revoke that choice after the extended due date for his tax return has passed. However, the Section 179 election is unique. Taxpayers can revoke all or part of their Section 179 election on an amended return, as long as the statute of limitations is open (Code Sec. 179(c)(2)). This flexibility could come in handy if a taxpayer ends up being in a higher tax bracket in the future. The taxpayer might opt to take part of the Section 179 election off the table and save those deductions for later years. The change will affect regular depreciation, so the taxpayer must file an amended return for the year for which it elected Section 179 and any intervening years for which it has already filed.

> **EXAMPLE:** In 2017, Ann is in the 15 percent tax bracket. She takes a $50,000 deduction in Section 179 expenses. In 2018, however, Ann is in the 37 percent bracket and expects to remain in the top bracket in future years. Ann can amend her 2017 Form 1040 and revoke the Section 179 election, which will increase depreciation in 2018, 2019, 2020, etc., resulting in a much greater tax benefit. Ann can also make an election after the fact—up to three years after she filed the return.

Taxpayers can also make late Section 179 elections. Although late Section 179 elections are generally made on an original return (Treas. Reg. § 1.179-5), they can be made on an amended return as long as the statute of limitations remains open (RP 2017–33, Sec. 3.02).

¶ 114 PLANNING STRATEGIES

Freezing and Thawing

Tax professionals can use flexibility to their advantage and to their clients' advantage with two strategies: freezing and thawing. The Section 179 "active business income" limit provides an opportunity to "freeze" deductions for future years at a higher tax rate. The active business income limit applies to:

- Individuals
- Partnerships
- S corporations

For example, if a partnership has lost money even before the Section 179 deduction, its 179 deduction is limited and carries over to future years. The Section 179 deduction can be "frozen" in time, and the partnership can wait until it has active business income in future. Bonus and *de minimis* depreciation do not offer the same ability; they are flushed through in the same year.

EXAMPLE: The chart below illustrates an example of "freezing" for Section 179 deduction at the partnership level.

	2018	2019
Section 179 Property Elected	$700,000	0
Section 179 expense allowed	—	$700,000*
Taxable Income (Before Section 179)	($50,000)	$1,000,000
Section 179 Allowed	0**	($700,000)
Taxable Income Reported	($50,000)	$300,000

* This is the carryover of Section 179 expense disallowed in 2018 due to the active business income requirement.
** Must also elect out of bonus depreciation (if eligible).

If bonus depreciation, instead of Section 179 depreciation, was taken in 2018, all $700,000 would have flushed through in 2018, which may have driven income down into lower tax brackets. If so, those deductions would have a very low value in 2018.

A taxpayer using the "freeze and thaw" method makes an initial Section 179 election in one year and then revokes it. This method "freezes" the bonus depreciation, and the amended return which revokes the Section 179 election "thaws" the deduction. The "freeze and thaw" approach can be used when a taxpayer has unexpectedly lower tax rates in future years. The deduction is taken on an amended return.

EXAMPLE: In 2018, State of the Art Tax LLC places in service $75,000 of Section 179 property. The LLC's income (before depreciation or Section 179 expense) is $1,000. The LLC "freezes" its deductions and elects Section 179 depreciation for $75,000. That means $1,000 of the Section 179 property is passed through (to reduce taxable income to $0) and $74,000 is carried over to 2019. The LLC's income is very low in 2019, and its members are in low tax brackets, so the LLC amends its 2018 return, revoking Section 179. As a result, the $74,000 "thaws" and bonus depreciation is allowed for 2018. The members file amended returns and take the extra $74,000 back in 2018 when they were in a higher tax bracket.

In contrast, taxpayers may also utilize a "thaw and freeze" strategy. In this case, a taxpayer takes bonus depreciation first and then makes a late Section 179 election. A taxpayer might choose this method if it is unexpectedly in a higher tax bracket in later years.

EXAMPLE: In 2018, State of the Art Tax LLC places in service $75,000 of bonus depreciation property. The LLC's income (before depreciation or Section 179 expense) is $1,000. The LLC takes bonus depreciation and no Section 179 deduction. That means $75,000 is passed through at a 24 percent tax savings. The LLC's income is high in 2019, with members in the 37 percent tax bracket. Therefore, the LLC amends its 2018 return and makes a late Section 179 election. As a result, $74,000 "freezes." The members file amended returns and take an extra $74,000 in 2019 when they are in higher tax brackets.

The 20 Percent Pass-Through Deduction

The 20 percent pass-through deduction, also known as the qualified business income deduction (QBID), allows taxpayers to deduct up to 20 percent of domestic qualified business income from a partnership, S corporation, or sole proprietorship. If the taxpayer has higher income, it needs wages/property in order to get the full benefit of the QBID. The property factor may be affected by the taxpayer's depreciation choice. Final regulations were issued in January 2019 for the QBID. Those regulations provide that neither Section 179 nor bonus depreciation affects the property factor. Therefore, taxpayers are free to select whichever method they prefer, without fear that it will impact their QBIDs.

> **EXAMPLE:** Matt buys an apartment building, which provides taxable income of $500,000 per year. He can choose Section 179 or bonus depreciation for the personal property. Because Matt uses an outside management company for his building, he pays no wages. Matt can choose either section 179 depreciation on his personal property or bonus depreciation. Doing so will not affect his "property factor" (Treas. Reg. § 1.199A-2(c)(3)).

Code Secs. 1245 and 1250 Depreciation Recapture

Taxpayers prefer capital gains to ordinary income, due to the lower tax rates that apply to capital gains. If a taxpayer takes Section 179 depreciation on qualified real property, it creates Section 1245 recapture (Section 179(a)(2)(C)). Section 1245 also applies if a taxpayer takes bonus depreciation. Bonus depreciation on personal property and qualified real property that the taxpayer expensed under Section 179 is subject to recapture as ordinary income to the extent of depreciation when the property is sold. It is not a guarantee that all of the depreciation must be recaptured. Section 1245 recapture is limited to the lesser of gain on the sale or depreciation allowed or allowable.

> **EXAMPLE:** Seth buys a retail building, and two years later he replaces the roof at a total cost of $75,000. He makes a Section 179 election for $30,000 for the roof cost. He depreciates the other $45,000 over the 39-year period. The $45,000 is treated as Section 1250 property. The $30,000 for which he elects Section 179 depreciation will be treated as Section 1245 property.

Section 1250 applies to other types of real property, including land improvements. This recapture is limited to the excess of actual depreciation in excess of straight-line depreciation. Since the building itself is depreciated using the straight-line method, there is typically no Section 1250 recapture on the portion of the gain allocable to the business.

There are three ways to compute depreciation recapture on qualified real property for which § 179 expensing was taken:

- **Pro rata method:** Allocate the selling price based on adjusted basis.
- **Gain allocation method:** All gain is allocated first to Section 179 real property.
- **Any other reasonable method.** The author believes that this includes the method described in Treas. Reg § 1.1245-1(a)(5). The following discussion of "other reasonable method" will apply the principles of Treas. Reg. § 1.1245-1(a)(5) in the computation of Section 1245 recapture.

The gain allocation method is the worst possible method. The best method by far is the "any other reasonable method." Examples of each method follow:

> **EXAMPLE: Pro Rata Method**
>
> The original cost of a nonresidential building in 2008 is $900,000. The only improvement made is a new roof in 2019, at a cost of $100,000. Section 179 depreciation is used for the entire cost of the roof. Because the taxpayer used the entire Section 179 amount in 2019, there is no carryover. The building sold for $800,000. The taxpayer allocates 10 percent of the sales price to the roof:
>
> Sales price apportioned to roof = $80,000 ($800,000 × [$100,000 ÷ $1,000,000]).
>
> The result is $80,000 in ordinary Section 1245 gain.

EXAMPLE: Gain Allocation Method

A taxpayer bought a nonresidential building in 1986 for $400,000. She replaced all of the building's HVAC units in 2018, for a cost of $100,000, and took the Section 179 election for the entire cost. The A/D in 2019 (including Section 179 depreciation) is $500,000. The taxpayer sells the building in 2025 for $100,000.

Gain on HVAC units = $100,000

Section 1245 recapture = $100,000 (All gain is first assigned to Section 179 property, then any excess is allocated to the building.)

EXAMPLE: Other Reasonable Method

The taxpayer bought a building in 2008 and replaced the roof (decking, etc.) in 2018 at a cost of $50,000. The roof's economic life is 20 years, and the taxpayer took the Section 179 deduction for the entire cost. In 2028 (50 percent of the roof's economic useful life has passed), the taxpayer sells the building.

The cost of $50,000 × 50% economic life expired = $25,000 Section 1245 gain allocated to the roof. The Section 179 recapture is $25,000.

¶ 115 BONUS DEPRECIATION VS. SECTION 179 VS. *DE MINIMIS*

The following chart summarizes some of the finer points of depreciation: when to use bonus depreciation, when to use Section 179, and when to use *de minimis*.

	Bonus	Section 179	*De Minimis*
Applies to assets outside the United States	No	No	Yes
Allowed even if taxpayer must use ADS depreciation	No	Yes	Yes
Good with cars	Great	Good	Poor
Good for residential real property improvements	No	No	Yes
Good for commercial real property improvements	No	Yes	Okay
Increases property factor for QBID 20 percent	Yes	Yes	Not clear
Applies to Code Sec. 743 step-ups (sale only)	Yes	No	No
Avoid recapture if converting to nonbusiness	Yes	No	Yes
"Surgical" approach to target income	No	Yes	Yes
Good for noncorporate lessors (personal property)	Yes	No	Yes
Covers very expensive fixed asset additions	Yes	No	Likely no
Easy for taxpayers to change their mind down the road	No	Yes	No
No requirement of active business income	Yes	No	Yes
Can "freeze" deductions at entity level	No	Yes	No
Applies to "production of income" activities	Yes	No	Likely yes
Can deduct for tax, capitalize for books	Yes	Yes	No (need book conformity)

	Bonus	Section 179	*De Minimis*
Particularly suited for certain types of property	Land improvements	Commercial real property improvements	Residential real property improvements
Good "recapture" rules when selling	Okay	Okay	Not good
Covers land improvements	Yes	No	Possible, but unlikely
Allowed to estates and trusts	Yes	No	Yes

¶ 116 SLOWING DEPRECIATION DOWN

Although this chapter has discussed methods for fast depreciation, there may be situations where a taxpayer wants to slow down depreciation. For example, if a taxpayer has "phantom income," he or she might want to depreciate more slowly. Phantom income is taxable income, but the taxpayer does not receive cash. Examples include pass-through income from an S corporation, but no distributions; and taxable gain on a property sale, but the taxpayer has little or no cash to pay tax because the proceeds are paid to the bank. (This might be caused by rapid depreciation.) Phantom income also arises when cost segregation studies are used, especially if property is heavily leveraged.

The three primary ways to slow down depreciation are:

- Do not do a cost segregation study.
- Do not take bonus or Section 179 depreciation.
- Elect slower depreciation by:
  - Electing the "alternative" 150 percent declining balance method as opposed to double declining balance (Code Sec. 168(b)(2)).
  - Electing straight-line MACRS depreciation (Code Sec. 168(b)(5)).
  - Electing alternative depreciation system (ADS) depreciation (Code Sec. 168(g)(7)).

Practitioners should discuss these options with their clients in the year the property is placed in service, especially if it is property that is heavily financed and has a short recovery period. Clients must understand that there is "no going back." They will not be able to change their mind later, except if the property qualifies for Section 179 depreciation. In that case, they should not make the Section 179 election, and elect out of bonus depreciation. They can later elect to take Section 179 depreciation as long as the statute is open. They can also elect to do a late cost segregation study in the future.

STUDY QUESTIONS

9. Which of the following statements is correct with respect to the surgical approach to tax planning?

    a. Electing out of bonus does not require electing out of all property in a class.

    b. The surgical approach entails the optimal amount of bonus.

    c. It is not possible to revoke a Section 179 election.

    d. To use the surgical approach, you must elect out of bonus if the property is bonus eligible.

10. With respect to freezing deductions and active business income, the active business income limit applies to each of the following, ***except:***

    a. C corporations

    b. Individuals

    c. Partnerships

    d. S corporations

11. Which of the following identifies a characteristic of the freeze and thaw method?

    a. It involves revoking a prior Section 179 election.

    b. You take the bonus initially.

    c. It works if you are unexpectedly in a higher tax rate in later years.

    d. It involves making a late Section 179 election.

12. With respect to bonus, Section 179, and *de minimis*, which of the following statements is correct?

    a. *De minimis* applies to assets outside the United States.

    b. Bonus is allowed even if a taxpayer is required to use ADS depreciation.

    c. Bonus depreciation is good for residential real property improvements.

    d. *De minimis* applies to Section 743 step-ups.

MODULE 1: DEVELOPMENTS IMPACTING TAX RETURN PREPARATION—Chapter 2: Tax Cuts and Jobs Act: Accounting Method Changes: Switch to Cash Method and Not Keep Inventory?

¶ 201 WELCOME

This chapter reviews the accounting method changes for small business taxpayers under the Tax Cuts and Jobs Act of 2017 (TCJA) and whether it might be better for specific clients to switch to a cash accounting method and avoid complicated inventory accounting.

¶ 202 LEARNING OBJECTIVES

Upon completion of this chapter, you will be able to:

- Determine how to apply the two new types of inventory methods for small business taxpayers:
  — The "raw materials" method
  — The "book conformity" method
- Differentiate which clients can switch to the cash method
- Determine how to treat costs of self-constructed assets under the Tax Cuts and Jobs Act of 2017 (TCJA)
- Identify and apply the *de minimis* rules as affected by the TCJA
- Determine which clients are "tax shelters" and therefore unable to use the new accounting methods
- Recognize which Code Section can help solve the problem of double-counting income that results from a business switching to the cash method of accounting
- Describe Revenue Procedure 2004-34

¶ 203 INTRODUCTION

Accounting methods are typically timing issues. They do not involve how much income or how many deductions taxpayers get over their lifetime, but rather *when* they get them. For example, if a taxpayer depreciates property over 27.5 years and switches to depreciating over 5 years, that changes the timing of the deduction. If a taxpayer switches to the cash method, that is an accounting method change because it affects the *timing* of income and deductions: instead of recognizing receipts and expenses when they are incurred, the taxpayer recognizes the income and receipts when they are received or paid for.

This chapter addresses two separate areas: (1) small business changes, including the new inventory method and the ability of more taxpayers to use cash methods as opposed to accrual methods; and (2) changes that affect larger companies, including income acceleration and prepaid income. It will also cover Form 3115, *Application for Change in Accounting Method*, and the *de minimis* rule.

As of this writing, the IRS has not released substantive guidance on the small business taxpayer accounting methods, other than an explanation of *how* to make the changes in Rev. Proc. 2018-40. It appears there will be some guidance in the future, but it is unclear when it will be issued or what form it will take.

¶ 204 CODE SEC. 481(a) ADJUSTMENTS

All of the accounting method changes, except for the completed contract rules, require a Code Sec. 481(a) adjustment. These include the following:

- Changing to the book conformity method of inventory
- Changing from the accrual method to the cash method
- Opting out of the uniform capitalization rules under Code Sec. 263A (which opens up the *de minimis* rule, discussed later in the chapter)
- Applying the new "revenue acceleration" rule

EXAMPLE: In 2017, Jill, an accountant who is an accrual method taxpayer, bills $100 for income tax preparation. That is her only transaction in 2017. Because Jill uses the accrual method, she must report that $100 as income in 2017.

In 2018, Jill changes to the cash method for the entire year. When Jill collects the receivable for $100 that she billed back in 2017, she has to report it again in 2018. Under the cash method, the $100 must be reported when it is actually collected.

Congress recognized the problem outlined in the preceding scenario and did not want taxpayers double-counting income or double-counting deductions. As a result, it enacted Code Sec. 481 to solve this problem.

EXAMPLE: Assume the same fact pattern as in the previous example. To address the double reporting of the $100 in income, Jill can take a negative Code Sec. 481(a) adjustment. Although she reported the $100 twice (including on her 2018 return tax return), she can also include in the deduction area of her return a Code Sec. 481(1) adjustment to eliminate that double accounting of income.

Code Sec. 481(a) Adjustment: Accrual to Cash		
	2017: Accrual Method	**2018: Cash Method**
Invoice for tax preparation services	$100	$100
Collect $100 from 2017 invoice		
Code Sec. 481(1) adjustment	N/A	($100)
Net income reported	$100	$0

EXAMPLE: In 2017, Bob's Bikes LLC keeps inventories and has only one financial transaction: it purchases a bike for $200. Because the company uses the inventory method for 2017, it records the $200 as inventory. Consequently, there is no gain or loss, and Bob's Bikes cannot deduct the cost of the bike in 2017.

However, in 2018, Bob's Bikes switches to an accounting method in which the company deducts the cost of inventory as it purchases the items. In 2018, Bob's Bikes cannot write off the cost of the $200 bike it purchased in 2017 because in 2018 under its new accounting method, it expenses bikes as it purchases them (and the bike was purchased in the preceding year).

In 2018, Bob's Bikes sells the bike it purchased for $200 in 2017. The company has to report that $200 as income, but it cannot write off the cost of the bike because its new accounting method is to take the expense in the year it pays for the bike. For 2018, its cost of goods sold is $0.

Now Bob's Bikes has failed to receive *any* tax deduction for the cost of that bike. It has income reported on the sale of the bike but no cost of goods sold. The Code Sec. 481(a) adjustment allows Bob's Bikes to catch up and take that deduction for inventory that it had not taken before.

Code Sec. 481(a) Adjustment: Inventory		
	2017: Keeps Inventories	**2018: Does Not Keep Inventories**
Purchase bicycle ($200)	$0	
Sell bicycle $200 (income)		$200
Cost of goods sold (2018—does not keep inventories)	$0	$0
Code Sec. 481(a) adjustment	N/A	($200)
Net income reported	$0	$0

The preceding example illustrates how Code Sec. 481 operates if a taxpayer takes a negative adjustment. But sometimes a taxpayer has to increase income. If a taxpayer has a *net* increase in income, it is generally spread over a four-year period.

EXAMPLE: Gabriel is an accrual method taxpayer. In 2017, Gabriel's only item of business is a $200 bill from his attorney, but he does not pay it until 2018. The all-events test is met, economic performance is met, and Gabriel deducts the expense. However, in 2018 he switches to the cash method of accounting.

Using the cash method, Gabriel deducts the bill when he pays it, so the $200 is deducted in 2018. The result is that he has deducted the same expense twice, once in 2017 and once in 2018. Under Code Sec. 481(a), Gabriel can spread the $200 over four consecutive years, beginning in the year he changed accounting methods, which is 2018.

Code Sec. 481(a) Adjustment: Accrual to Cash)						
	2017: Accrual	**2018: Cash**	**2019: Cash**	**2020: Cash**	**2021: Cash**	**Totals**
Receive attorney's bill	($200)					($200)
Pay lawyer's bill		($200)				($200)
Code Sec. 481(a) adjustment	N/A	$50	$50	$50	$50	$200
Net income reported	($200)	($150)	$50	$50	$50	($200)

These accounting method changes do not permanently affect income; they just affect timing. Switching from the accrual method to the cash method typically defers income. The current benefit from the accounting method change will be offset in the year a business is sold.

EXAMPLE: Suman Inc. is an accrual method taxpayer that has the following balances on December 31, 2017:

- Accounts receivable: $100,000
- Inventory: $50,000
- Accounts payable: $50,000

Suman Inc. has already reported the $100,000 of accounts receivable and has never deducted the $50,000 in inventory because it capitalized inventory. It has deducted the $50,000 in accounts payable under the accrual method.

If Suman Inc. switches to the cash method of accounting, it will take a $100,000 deduction. The company will write off accounts receivable and inventory ($150,000) under Code Sec. 481, but it must add back the accounts payable ($50,000) because it will write those off when it actually pays them in 2018. Therefore, the net adjustment is a decrease of $100,000.

The following examples are intended to illustrate the "timing" nature of Code Sec. 481. The benefit that clients receive in the year that they switch to the cash method and eliminate inventories will reverse in the later year when the business is sold.

EXAMPLE: This example illustrates the timing nature of accounting methods. Assume the same facts as in the preceding example, but that Suman Inc. does *not* change accounting methods and continues to use the accrual method. It sells its business on January 1, 2019. The results are as follows:

	Cash Flow*	Taxable Income
Accounts Receivable	$100,000	$0
Inventory (sold net book value)	$50,000	$0
Accounts Payable	($50,000)	$0
Total	$100,000	$0
* Assumes all balances same as end of 2017.		

In other words, if Suman *does not* change accounting methods (i.e., it stays on the accrual method), it will have less income in the year it sells the business because the accounts receivable can be collected tax-free (if it remains on the accrual method) and the cost of inventory can be recovered in the year that the owner retires and sells the business.

EXAMPLE: Continuing with the Suman Inc. scenario, now assume that the company *changed* to the cash method in 2018. It took a $100,000 deduction on its 2018 tax return (Code Sec. 481(a) adjustment). If the business is sold on January 1, 2019, it will essentially have to pay back all the tax savings it had in 2018. For example, it will now have to report income on the accounts receivable it collects in 2019. If it had *stayed* on the accrual method (instead of changing methods), it could have collected the accounts receivable tax-free in 2019.

	Cash Flow*	Taxable Income
Accounts receivable	$100,000	$100,000
Inventory (sold net book value)	$50,000	$50,000
Accounts payable	($50,000)	($50,000)
Total	$100,000	$100,000
* Assumes all balances same as end of 2017.		

The big picture is that if a client plans to sell its business in the next few years, it probably does not make sense to change accounting methods because the timing difference will reverse anyway. If a taxpayer makes an accounting method change in 2018 and gets a large deduction, it will have to pick it back up as income in 2019 when it sells the business.

STUDY QUESTION

1. Which Code Section can help solve the problem of double-counting income that results from a business switching to the cash method of accounting?

    a. Section 263A

    b. Section 451

    c. Section 471

    d. Section 481

¶ 205 ACCOUNTING METHODS

There are four new accounting methods available to "small business taxpayers" under the Tax Cuts and Jobs Act of 2017 (TCJA).

- Uniform capitalization rules (Code Sec. 263A)
- Simplified inventory rules (Code Sec. 471(c))
- Cash method
- Long-term contract method

To use any of these new accounting methods, a taxpayer must:

- Meet the "small business gross receipts test": have trailing three-year average annual gross receipts less than or equal to $25 million (indexed for inflation to $26 million in 2019 by Rev. Proc. 2018-57), and
- Not be a tax shelter.

Tax shelters are defined and discussed in more detail later in this chapter.

¶ 206 CASH METHOD

The cash method of accounting is probably the most important of the four new accounting methods under the TCJA. According to the legislative history, a taxpayer can use the cash method if it qualifies as a "small business taxpayer," that is, it meets the $25 million gross receipts test and is not a tax shelter. The Blue Book indicates that the cash method is available even if the purchase, production, or sale of merchandise is a material income-producing factor. Previously, such taxpayers with gross receipts of more than $1 million were required to use the accrual method and to keep inventories. This change is effective for tax years beginning after December 31, 2017.

The Blue Book, authored by the Joint Committee on Taxation, is considered "substantial authority" and supports this change (Treas. Reg. § 1.6662-4(d)(3)(iii)). It states that the "cash method of accounting may be used by taxpayers other than tax shelters, that satisfy the gross receipts test, regardless of whether the purchase, production of sale of merchandise is an income-producing factor" (General Explanation of Public Law 115-97, p. 112).

> **EXAMPLE:** A taxpayer owns a fishing vessel and catches and processes fish. The company meets the $25 million gross receipts test and is not a tax shelter. It is an accrual method taxpayer. In 2018, the taxpayer should be able to use the cash method, even though production and sale of merchandise is a material income producing factor. It will make a Code Sec. 481(a) adjustment and will need to file Form 3115, *Application for Change in Accounting Method.*

Prior to the TCJA, there were tighter restrictions on C corporations and partnerships with C corporation partners in regard to using the cash method of accounting. Generally, a C corporation with trailing three-year average gross receipts of more than $5 million had to use the accrual method. The TCJA has quintupled the trailing gross receipts amount to $25 million or less (Code Sec. 448(c)(1)).

> **EXAMPLE:** Partnership Q has a C corporation as a partner and has $12 million in trailing gross receipts. It must use the accrual method for 2017, but it can switch to the cash method for 2018.

For calendar year taxpayers, these rules are effective for the 2018 tax year.

¶ 207 AFTER THE TCJA: CAPITALIZING COSTS

The uniform capitalization (UNICAP) rules were originally enacted in 1986 and required taxpayers to capitalize many indirect costs, such as corporate overhead. Under the TCJA, small business taxpayers are no longer subject to the Code Sec. 263A direct/indirect capitalization rules. Those taxpayers can now choose either of the following methods:

- Treat inventory as "non-incidental materials and supplies" (the "raw materials" inventory method), *or*

- Use the method it used in its audited financial statements *or* in its books and records (the "book conformity" method of keeping inventory).

The "raw materials" inventory method is the first new rule. This method involves treating inventory as non-incidental materials and supplies basically means capitalizing the cost of the raw materials only, and not the cost of rent, labor, or other indirect costs (Rev. Proc. 2002-28, Example 20). This method does *not* require book conformity.

> **EXAMPLE:** Taxpayer T manufacturers lawn ornaments. It meets the $25 million gross receipts test and is not a tax shelter. When it manufactures its lawn ornaments, it can capitalize just the raw material costs; it does not need to capitalize labor, overhead, and storage costs. But if Taxpayer T previously capitalized labor and overhead storage costs and ceases to capitalize those, does that mean its inventory will be drastically reduced? The answer is yes. Taxpayer T will reduce its inventory, which will flush through a large amount of expenses through its Code Sec. 481(a) adjustment on its 2018 return if it changes accounting methods in 2018.

The second new method is the "book conformity" method. For small business taxpayers *with* audited financial statements, the primary benefit of the new rules is simplicity. Such taxpayers are not required to make book/tax adjustments.

> **EXAMPLE:** Quick Concrete Inc. makes and sells bags of concrete. The company has audited financial statements, has trailing average gross receipts of less than $25 million, and is not a tax shelter. Every year, Quick Concrete computes GAAP inventory. Then it calculates a book/tax difference applying the Code Sec. 263A UNICAP rules. However, if the company files Form 3115 and changes to GAAP for tax purposes, it will no longer have to compute the book/tax difference. It will simply also use the GAAP inventory for tax purposes.

Taxpayers switching to the book conformity method that do *not* have audited financial statements enjoy two advantages:

- Simplicity, because they do not need to go through the complicated Code Sec. 263A rules, and

- Reduced income in the year they make the accounting change.

For small business taxpayers, the more intriguing of the two options for capitalizing costs is the book conformity method for taxpayers without audited financial statements. This is also called the "QuickBooks" method. Capitalization will be simpler in the future, but such taxpayers can also flush through many expenses in the year they make the accounting change.

> **EXAMPLE:** Taxpayer D is a small business taxpayer. Its accounting procedures say no costs are capitalized into inventory. QuickBooks and its accounting records say its inventory equals $0. Can Taxpayer D use $0 for tax purposes? The *literal* language of the statute indicates that it can; it can use whatever it uses in its

books and records. The Blue Book also provides strong support for this position. Although there is no published IRS guidance that the "QuickBooks" method is acceptable, the Blue Book states the "provision exempts certain taxpayers from the requirement to keep inventories." It is not clear when or if the IRS will issue guidance on this topic, but for now, the Blue Book provides substantial authority to support this position.

Taxpayers who want to take a cautious approach should capitalize a small amount in the inventory, for example, 10 cents per pound of bulk steel product. This would fend off one possible IRS argument—the IRS might argue that the statute allows conformity. However, it does not waive the requirement to keep *some* inventory.

Although the statute does not require taxpayers to put their accounting procedures in writing, it is a good idea for taxpayers to do so to explain their inventory methods. By committing its accounting procedures to writing, a taxpayer can prove that it has procedures in place.

Prior to switching to the "QuickBooks" inventory method, taxpayers with bank loans should make sure that the bank is supportive of switching inventory methods on the taxpayer's financial statements. If the bank objects, taxpayers may be better served by adopting the "raw materials" inventory approach discussed earlier.

EXAMPLE: Bob's Salvage Inc. has a bank loan and qualifies as a "small business taxpayer." Bob wants to switch to a new accounting method, but the bank insists that the company's compiled financials use the same inventory method that was used in the past. Bob's Salvage may not be able to use the "QuickBooks" method, but it can use the non-incidental materials and supplies approach (i.e., the "raw materials" inventory method). Because there is no book conformity requirement for the non-incidental method, the company can use a different inventory method on its tax return.

¶ 208 SELF-CONSTRUCTED ASSETS

Prior to the TCJA, if a taxpayer paid a contractor to construct an apartment building, it had to capitalize the construction, incurring interest under Code Sec. 263A. In the author's view, under the current law, this capitalization is not necessary. Although the IRS has not yet issued specific guidance on this point, the plain language of the statute indicates that small business taxpayers no longer have to capitalize the interest expense of self-constructed assets.

¶ 209 THE COMPLETED CONTRACT METHOD

For contractors, under prior law there were generally two exceptions from the percentage of completion method:

- Home construction contracts, and

- Real property contracts expected to be completed within two years (this method previously required trailing average gross receipts of $10 million or less).

The TCJA raised the gross receipts threshold to $25 million or less. The real property contract expected to be completed within two years could include, for example, an apartment building or office building. A qualifying contractor does not need to make a Code Sec. 481(a) adjustment; it can simply start using this new rule for contracts it enters into after 2017.

¶ 210 AGGREGATION OF GROSS RECEIPTS

For all of these accounting method rules, to determine a taxpayer's amount of trailing gross receipts, the gross receipts from Code Sec. 52 commonly controlled businesses must be aggregated.

The aggregation rules apply to brother-sister and parent-subsidiary groups, and taxpayers also have to follow some of the pension aggregation rules; professional service organizations providing or receiving services and their related service providers must be aggregated, although this situation is fairly uncommon (see Code Secs. 414(m) and 414(o)).

¶ 211 TAX SHELTERS

As mentioned throughout this chapter, tax shelters cannot use any of the new accounting methods that have been discussed. A tax shelter is defined as follows:

- An entity whose interests are or have been offered for sale and that is required to be registered (*registration* includes a required filing of exemption from registration) with any federal or state agency (Treas. Reg. § 1.448-1T(b)(2));
- An entity that has more than 35 percent of its losses allocated to limited partners or limited entrepreneurs (Code Sec. 448(d)(3), incorporating Code Secs. 461(i)(3) and 1256(e)(3)(B), which sends readers back to Code Sec. 461(k)(4) for the definition of *limited entrepreneur*); *or*
- A *tax shelter* as defined in Code Sec. 6662(d)(2)(C)(ii)).

Estate of Wallace v. Commissioner (965 F.2d 1038, CA11) is the only case on record that analyzes the 35 percent of losses rule. Dr. Gerald Wallace was a triple threat: a successful medical doctor, a real estate developer, and an oil and gas developer. He was perhaps too successful, however, because he had a huge tax bill and needed a tax shelter.

Wallace decided to enter a feedlot agreement, in which cattle are placed into feedlots, fed a high-protein diet, and then sold. Classic feedlot agreements are simple: a taxpayer buys a large amount of feed in year 1 and writes it off, then in year 2 it sells the cattle. The taxpayer recoups the income in that year, so it creates a loss by paying for the feed in the first year and then sells the cattle in the second year, which creates a deferral.

Congress did not like rich doctors like Dr. Wallace using this type of tax shelter. Consequently, it passed Code Sec. 464, which states that if a company allocates 35 percent or more of its losses to limited partners or limited entrepreneurs (who do not "actively participate" in management), it cannot use the prepaid feed shelter—it cannot deduct the feed in year 1. This same rule was incorporated into the TCJA to determine who can use the new small business accounting methods. If a taxpayer fails this rule, it is a tax shelter and cannot use any of the new accounting methods.

The question in ***Wallace*** was whether Dr. Wallace was an active participant in the business and therefore could avoid tax shelter status. Wallace had hired an advisor as the feedlot manager and called him three to four times a week. The doctor visited the feedlots once a year and he made final decisions, such as which lender to use, when to buy cattle, which feed lot manager to use, and when to hedge the price of cattle. However, he was not actively involved in the day-to-day operation of the feedlots. The court ruled that Wallace was not involved enough in the management of this business, and that it was therefore a tax shelter. According to the legislative history (H.R. Conf. Rep. No. 1515, 94th Congress, Second Session), factors indicating active participation include:

- Participating in decisions involving operation or management of the farm, and
- Working for the business and hiring/firing employees (not just acting as a manager).

Factors indicating a *lack* of active participation include:

- Lack of control of the management and operation,
- Having authority only to discharge the manager,
- The manager is an independent contractor rather than an employee, and
- Limited liability for the business's losses.

A taxpayer is *not* treated as a limited partner or a limited entrepreneur if:

- He or she actively participates at all times in management,
- Participation of a close relative (spouse, child, parent) satisfies the test,
- He or she actively participated in management for at least five years, or
- The IRS determines that a taxpayer should be treated as active (even if the taxpayer does not otherwise qualify for active treatment). The IRS may provide this relief if the entity and the taxpayer's interest are not used for tax avoidance purposes (Code Sec. 1256(e)(3)(v)).

  — The legislative history that accompanied this provision indicated that "the Secretary must determine that the facts and circumstances in the specific case indicate that the ... exemption is not sought, nor could it be exploited, for tax avoidance purposes" (1981-2 CB, p. 513). Certainly, very few current entities are established or could be used for tax avoidance purposes. The passive activity provisions would normally prevent any abuse by inactive owners.

  — Although it is speculative, it may be that the reason for the lack of case law in this area is that the IRS has applied this waiver to taxpayers who are not involved in traditional tax shelters. Although the statute leaves this waiver in the hands of the IRS, agency actions (like this) are subject to judicial review under an "abuse of discretion" standard (***Estate of Gardner***, 82 TC 989).

Another case illustrates the third type of tax shelter. Sammy Davis Jr. was a remarkable entertainer who got involved in a coal mining tax shelter. One of the issues raised in his case (***Sammy Davis, Jr. v. Commissioner*** (TC Memo 1989-607)) was whether his coal mining endeavor met the definition of a tax shelter under Code Sec. 6661. (The case addressed Code Sec. 6661(b)(2)(C)(ii), which was subsequently relocated to Code Sec. 6662(d)(2)(C)). The court found that the business was indeed a tax shelter because it was impossible to generate a profit from it. This tax shelter was structured only for tax purposes with little or no motive for economic gain. Today, this type of tax shelter is extremely rare. It is unlikely that clients will be treated as tax shelters under this third tax shelter provision.

¶ 212 *DE MINIMIS* RULE

The change to the *de minimis* rule is not a result of a direct change in the statue. Instead, it arises from the new exemption under Code Sec. 263A. The IRS regulations have allowed the use of the *de minimis* rule since 2014. Further, there was authority to apply the *de minimis* rule to improvements (e.g., a building remodel) (Treas. Reg. § 1.263(a)-1(f) and Notice 2015-82). However, the IRS informally took the position that taxpayers who qualified for the *de minimis* rule on improvements to property under the regulations were nonetheless required to clear a second hurdle: they had to avoid capitalization under Code Sec. 263A.

The IRS's argument now generally applies only to years before 2018, and a broad waiver from Code Sec. 263A clears up this issue for most taxpayers. The capitalization requirement does not apply to small business taxpayers because they are exempted from Code Sec. 263A. Therefore, the *de minimis rule* is opened up for small business taxpayer clients.

For small business taxpayers who have audited financial statements:

- The invoice or per item amount (as substantiated by the invoice) for the improvements must be less than or equal to $5,000.
- The taxpayer must have a written *de minimis* policy used for financial accounting.
- Book conformity is required; the taxpayer must expense the improvements on its audited financial statements.
- The taxpayer must make the *de minimis* election.

For small business taxpayers who do *not* have audited financial statements:

- The invoice or per item (as substantiated by the invoice) amount for the improvements must be less than or equal $2,500.
- The taxpayer must have a financial accounting *de minimis* policy (which can be *unwritten*).
  - Even though the policy is not required to be in writing, it is recommended that taxpayers have a written policy. The IRS Audit Technique Guide, *Capitalization of Tangible Property,* directs auditors to request a copy of the written policy.
- Book conformity is required. If you want to write it off for tax purposes, you must also write it off on the taxpayers' books.
- The taxpayer must make the *de minimis* election. Most tax preparation software has a box you can check to make the election.

Treas. Reg. § 1.263(a)-1(f)(6) provides an anti-abuse rule that prohibits taxpayers from getting artificially low invoices to abuse the safe harbor.

> **EXAMPLE:** A taxpayer visits a truck dealership and buys a used truck for $6,500. The taxpayer requests four separate invoices—one for the truck chassis, one for the tires, one for the engine, and one for the trailer—so that each invoice will be less than $2,500. The taxpayer's plan is to apply the *de minimis* rule to these separate invoices, but the regulations do not allow this abuse of the safe harbor.

As mentioned, book conformity is one of the requirements for making the *de minimis* election. If a taxpayer wants to write off an item on its taxes, it must expense it on its books. See the following example.

> **EXAMPLE:** Ellen owns a duplex and is exempt from the Code Sec. 263A requirements because she is a qualified small business taxpayer. She remodels both units of the duplex in 2018. Assume that the remodeling improvements do not qualify as repairs, and Ellen must capitalize them. The details of her invoices are as follows:
>
> - One invoice is for $14,000 and is not itemized, so she must capitalize the expense.
> - The other invoices are either less than or equal to $2,500 or the invoices show items that are each less than or equal to $2,500, so she can write off those immediately, even though they are part of the big remodeling project.

The following chart details the remodeling costs for the units' kitchens. Note that Ellen does not have audited financial statements, she meets the book conformity requirement, and she makes the *de minimis* election. The invoice substantiates each of the items.

	Cost/Item	Labor—Separate Invoice	*De Minimis* Expense?
Granite slab	$2,600	$500*	No, capitalize both*
Cabinets	$750 each (6 total)	$300 each	Expense cabinets and labor
New light fixtures	$325 each (4 total)	$225 each	Expense fixtures and labor
* The author believes there is a special rule for capitalizing labor in the context of improvements; in this area, if the materials are required to be capitalized, so must the related labor.			

STUDY QUESTIONS

2. Under the Tax Cuts and Jobs Act (TCJA), the Blue Book provides that qualifying small businesses:

   a. Must use the accrual method of accounting

   b. No longer need to account for inventory (however, this method must conform to the taxpayer's books and records, and also to its accounting procedures)

   c. Must comply with the uniform capitalization requirements

   d. Are defined as those with average annual gross receipts under $15 million

3. For taxpayers with audited financial statements, which of the following is true regarding the *de minimis* election?

   a. The election applies to capital expenditures up to $2,500.

   b. The *de minimis* threshold is applied only at the invoice level.

   c. The TCJA eliminated the *de minimis* election.

   d. To make the *de minimis* election, the taxpayer must have a *de minimis* policy for financial accounting purposes.

¶ 213 INCOME ACCELERATION

Under the TCJA, if an accrual method taxpayer receives advance payments for goods before it delivers those goods, special income acceleration rules apply. These rules are effective for years beginning after December 31, 2017. Code Sec. 451(b) applies to accrual method taxpayers who have audited financial statements. If the taxpayer will recognize income sooner on its audited financial statements than on its tax return, generally it must accelerate that income on the tax return to match its financial statements.

   EXAMPLE: Taxpayer L is an accrual method fish wholesaler that has "reviewed" financial statements. Because the taxpayer does not have audited financial statements, the income acceleration rules do not apply.

However, there are many exceptions. No acceleration is required if the taxpayer uses "special methods" (e.g., completed contract method, or the installment sale rules).

   EXAMPLE: ABC Inc. is a microbrewery that has audited financial statements. The company outgrows its old plant and sells it for an installment note. For book purposes, it recognizes all the income on the plant sale in the year the sale occurs.

The sale of the plant is reported for tax purposes over time, as the proceeds of the note are collected because it uses the installment method. There is no income acceleration under the new rules because this is a special method and special methods are excepted from the acceleration rules.

Note that the income acceleration requirement does apply to original issue discount (OID) income.

EXAMPLE: Taxpayer G is an accrual method taxpayer that has audited financial statements. It reports "cash advance fees" as income on its financial statements when the fees are received. For tax returns, Taxpayer G has historically reported later, under the OID rules, but in 2018 the acceleration rule applies to OID.

The acceleration rules do *not* apply to timing differences that arise from different realization events for book and tax purposes.

EXAMPLE: ABC Inc. is a grain exporter that has audited financial statements. It enters into derivative contracts marked to market for GAAP, but not marked to market for tax. For tax purposes, the "realization" occurs when ABC closes out a contract. Therefore, ABC is not subject to the income acceleration rule because the difference in timing between books and tax arises from a difference in the "realization" event (marking to market vs. closing out the contract).

Under the new GAAP income recognition rules (ASU No. 2014-09 (Topic 606)), taxpayers accelerate some items of income for GAAP purposes and will consequently require tax acceleration. The rules apply to nonpublic companies for years beginning after December 15, 2018.

¶ 214 ADVANCE PAYMENTS

Code Sec. 451(c) "codifies" current Rev. Proc. 2004-34 with regard to advance payments. In general, the new rule requires taxpayers to report advance payments currently. However, taxpayers may elect to defer recognition of advance payments (which include advance payments for services or goods but do not include rents) no later than the end of the following year of receipt. The election is binding for all future years (Code Sec. 451(c)(2)(B)). If the taxpayer makes a change in accounting methods, it will need to make a Code Sec. 481(a) adjustment and file Form 3115. This change is effective for years beginning after December 31, 2017.

Taxpayers cannot push income back more than a year. If they receive payment in 2018, they must recognize all the income no later than 2019. The IRS is currently seeking comments on the scope of Code Sec. 451(c). The prepayment rules under Rev. Proc. 2004-34 apply to the following items:

- Sale, lease, or license of computer software
- Use of intellectual property
- Gift cards
- Online database subscriptions
- Prepayments for services
- Membership fees (Costco)

EXAMPLE: XYZ Salon is an accrual method taxpayer that has audited financial statements. XYZ has gift card sales from 2018. On its financial statements, the salon recognizes 25 percent of those sales in 2018, 50 percent in 2019, and 25 percent in 2020.

When a business sells gift cards, it receives a prepayment for future services. For tax purposes, XYZ cannot push off any income until 2020. The farthest it can push back income is to the next year (2019). It would recognize 25 percent of the gift cards sold in 2018, and 75 percent of those gift cards in 2019.

Further guidance on the prepayment rule should be issued within the next year. Until that guidance is issued, taxpayers should continue to rely upon Rev. Proc. 2004-34 and IRS Notice 2018-35. Once the IRS releases the final guidance, it should apply only to taxpayers who have audited financial statements.

Note that former Treas. Reg. § 1.451-5 allowed taxpayers to defer income from the sale of goods for more than a year. This regulation was removed on July 11, 2019, effective for tax years ending on or after July 15, 2019.

STUDY QUESTIONS

---

4. Which of the following changes under the TCJA is *not* considered favorable to small businesses?

   a. Capitalization

   b. Income acceleration

   c. Inventory

   d. Long-term contracts

5. Revenue Procedure 2004-34:

   a. Has been superseded by the TCJA

   b. Applies only to cash method taxpayers

   c. Allows accrual method taxpayers to defer the recognition of advance payments

   d. Does not cover computer software

¶ 215 FORM 3115

To adopt new "small business taxpayer" accounting methods, a taxpayer must file Form 3115. Taxpayers do not have to fill out a great deal of information to satisfy the reporting requirements; Rev. Proc. 2018-40 provides special limited disclosure rules for taxpayers making any of the accounting method changes. Several accounting methods can be included on a single form.

Both the tax preparer and the taxpayer must sign the form, and two copies must be filed with the IRS:

- One copy of the signed Form 3115 must be filed with the tax return.
- One copy must be mailed to the IRS no later than the date on which the tax return is filed.

No fee is required because all of these methods are automatic changes. Note that the IRS will not send any type of acknowledgment of the method change. If a taxpayer files a Form 3115 and the IRS does not respond, the taxpayer can assume the IRS has granted the accounting method change.

However, if Form 3115 is improperly completed or missing information, the IRS will contact the taxpayer (Rev. Proc. 2015-13, Sec. 11(01)). The IRS will allow the taxpayer 30 calendar days to respond with the corrected or missing information, and can grant an additional 15-day extension in some situations. The IRS also has the ability to deny the accounting method change, for example, if the change would not clearly reflect income or not constitute sound tax administration (Rev. Proc. 2015-13, Sec. 12.02). If the request is denied, taxpayers can request a conference to discuss the issue and later submit an administrative appeal.

¶ 216 CONCLUSION

Accounting methods are really about timing issues, such as depreciation, inventories, and cash method versus accrual method. They do not address whether a taxpayer deducted an item but rather *when* the taxpayer deducted it. Remember that the accrual to cash method changes, the inventory method, the Code Sec. 263A uniform capitalization rules, and the new rules for contractors all apply to only qualified small business taxpayers.

STUDY QUESTION

6. Which of the following statements is true regarding Form 3115 that is filed pursuant to Rev. Proc. 2018-40 (for small business taxpayers changing accounting methods)?

    a. Only one copy of Form 3115 should be filed.

    b. It allows a taxpayer to make an accounting method change only before the tax return is due.

    c. If a taxpayer files Form 3115 and the IRS does not respond, the taxpayer can assume the IRS has granted the accounting method change.

    d. As a result of the TCJA, the IRS likely will not require taxpayers to file Form 3115 to request an accounting method change.

MODULE 1: DEVELOPMENTS IMPACTING TAX RETURN PREPARATION—Chapter 3: Maximizing Itemized Deductions under the New Law

¶ 301 WELCOME

This chapter discusses how the Tax Cuts and Jobs Act of 2017 (TCJA) affects the deductions taxpayers are able to use on their tax returns. There have been many changes in this area, and by maximizing their deductions, taxpayers can ensure they get the best possible tax treatment on items affected by the TCJA reforms.

¶ 302 LEARNING OBJECTIVES

Upon completion of this chapter, you will be able to:

- Recognize how to maximize itemized deductions under the TCJA
- Identify the new standard deductions as a result of the TCJA
- Identify how donor-advised funds and qualifying charitable distributions can maximize deductible charitable contributions at a minimal cost
- Recognize and apply case law and administrative guidance to increase the deduction for tax preparation fees
- Understand home mortgage interest deductibility, including the refinancing rules
- Identify and apply tax regulations to derive benefit from investment advisory fees
- Recognize and apply elections to increase the deduction for taxes on investment property
- Recognize the amount to which property taxes are limited for married taxpayers filing jointly, under the new tax rules
- Describe an example of a prominent miscellaneous itemized deduction that has been suspended through 2025
- Differentiate correct statements regarding health savings accounts and the impacts from the new tax regulations
- Identify one of the state tax workarounds with respect to the $10,000 deduction limit
- Recognize tax deductions that have been eliminated as a result of the TCJA
- Describe an example of an unreimbursed employee expense that has been suspended from 2018 to 2025 for purposes of tax deduction
- Recognize the types of tax preparation fees that can no longer be deducted above the line

¶ 303 INTRODUCTION

This chapter will review itemized deductions under the TCJA with an eye toward planning opportunities. It will examine how to maximize tax benefits for clients.

¶ 304 STANDARD DEDUCTION AND PERSONAL EXEMPTIONS

The TCJA changes in the standard deduction have sweeping ramifications. Because far fewer people will be able to itemize in their 2018 returns than could itemize in the year before, tax planning will be affected.

For the 2018 tax year, the standard deduction for single persons is $12,000, which is almost double the amount for 2017. For heads of household, the standard deduction is $18,000, and for married taxpayers filing jointly, it is $24,000. These numbers are indexed for inflation, so, for example, in 2019 the single standard deduction will be $12,200 and the married filing jointly deduction will be $24,400.

Filing Status	Standard Deduction for 2018
Single	$12,000
Head of Household	$18,000
Married Filing Joint	$24,000

Although far fewer people will itemize their deductions for federal tax purposes as a result of these changes, because many states have not conformed to the federal changes, many people will continue to itemize for state income tax purposes even though they are not itemizing for federal.

EXAMPLE: Francis is a single taxpayer. His itemized deductions totaled $11,000 in 2018, but he will not be able to deduct $11,000 in the 2018 tax year. For 2018, deductions are capped at $10,000, and the only other deduction he has is $1,000 in charitable contributions. In 2017, he would have itemized because the standard deduction was only $6,350. However, in 2018 he has only $11,000 in deductions and will simply take the standard deduction of $12,000.

EXAMPLE: Isaac and Kayley are married taxpayers who file jointly. Their only itemized deductions are home mortgage interest of $14,000, and real estate taxes and sales tax of $8,000. In 2017, they would have benefited from itemizing. But in 2018, they will not itemize; they will just take the standard deduction of $24,000, which is greater than the amount of their itemized deductions.

EXAMPLE: Phil is a single taxpayer. His only itemized deductions in 2017 and 2018 are property taxes and income tax, which total $25,000. He also paid investment advisory fees (in excess of the 2 percent floor) of $28,000. In 2017, he would have had $53,000 in itemized deductions, which is much more than the $12,700 standard deduction.

However, in 2018, Phil will not be able to itemize his deductions; he will have to take the standard deduction. His property and income taxes are capped at $10,000, and he will not get to deduct the investment advisory fees at all, so his total itemized deductions will be only $10,000. While Phil had $53,000 of itemized deductions in 2017, in 2018 he can take only the standard $12,000 deduction.

OBSERVATION: Some taxpayers will lose ground under the new tax rules. For example, the new standard deduction will not help a married couple filing jointly with $25,000 or more in itemized deductions. Although the couple will still itemize and take their $25,000 in deductions, they will no longer get their personal exemptions because those are eliminated after 2017.

¶ 305 HOME MORTGAGE INTEREST LIMITS

The new rules for mortgage interest limits apply between 2018 and 2025; they will expire in 2026 unless otherwise extended. Under the TCJA, home equity indebtedness is not deductible. For second homes, however, there is no change; taxpayers can still deduct interest expenses on two homes.

The key change under the TCJA with regard to mortgage interest is the limitation on mortgage interest associated with acquisition indebtedness. Mortgage interest expense on acquisition indebtedness can still be deducted, but there are two limitations:

- If the indebtedness was incurred *on or before* December 15, 2017, the acquisition indebtedness cap is $1 million. Refinancing does not strip a taxpayer of this $1 million limit.

- If the indebtedness was incurred *after* December 15, 2017, the cap is $750,000 in indebtedness.

Home equity indebtedness is secured by a qualified residence. A taxpayer cannot have more than $100,000 in indebtedness. That indebtedness does not include acquisition indebtedness and does not have to relate to acquiring or improving a home. In other words, before 2018, taxpayers could still deduct interest on home equity indebtedness. Even if they borrowed on that home equity line of credit to take a vacation or purchase an expensive car, they could still deduct the mortgage interest. However, that deduction has been eliminated after 2018.

If the indebtedness is acquisition indebtedness, it is not considered home equity indebtedness and therefore the interest might be deductible. Acquisition indebtedness is incurred to acquire, construct, or substantially improve a residence. The indebtedness must be secured by that residence (i.e., it cannot be secured by a different residence) and cannot be more than $1 million beginning in 2018. For example, if a taxpayer has a home equity line of credit, if it is (1) used to acquire, construct, or remodel a residence; (2) secured by the residence; and (3) not more than $1 million (when combined with other grandfathered indebtedness), then the taxpayer can deduct the mortgage interest in full. Usually, taxpayers who finance a remodel of their residence with a home equity line of credit qualify to treat the debt as acquisition indebtedness.

EXAMPLE: Michelle bought a home in 2004 for $450,000. In 2013, she took out a home equity line of credit for $100,000 to pay off some credit card debt from her around-the-world vacation.

In 2017, Michelle could deduct the interest on the home equity loan because she could have used the money for any purpose. But in 2018, the money must be used to acquire, construct, or remodel a residence, so for 2018 through 2025 she will not be able to deduct the interest on that home equity line of credit.

EXAMPLE: Michelle bought a house in 2004 for $450,000. In 2013, she took out a $100,000 home equity line of credit to remodel her house. Even though the loan is a home equity loan, she can deduct all the mortgage interest on it because it meets the test for acquisition indebtedness (IR-2018-32).

EXAMPLE: In 2015, Seth borrowed $1,050,000 to acquire his personal residence. In 2015, he could deduct all the mortgage interest expense on that purchase. Acquisition indebtedness soaks up the home equity limit (Rev. Rul. 2010-25). In 2018, although Seth's debt is still over $1 million, he will lose part of the deduction. He can deduct mortgage interest on only $1 million of that debt.

Assume that Seth refinances in 2020, and his outstanding balance is $975,000. Seth can deduct interest on that entire amount because his mortgage was in place on or before December 15, 2017. Even though this $975,000 loan was taken out in 2020 to refinance the original loan, it is treated as if Seth took it out in 2015.

¶305

EXAMPLE: In 2015, Joanne borrowed $900,000 to acquire her personal residence. In that year, she can deduct all of the interest. In 2018, Joanne takes out a $100,000 home equity loan to remodel her home. The original loan balance is now $875,000 (after principal payments) and the $100,000 does not qualify for the grandfathering exception (because it was not outstanding on December 15, 2017), so her interest deduction is limited to $875,000 (Code Sec. 163(h)(3)(F)(i)(III)). Because the home equity line of credit was not outstanding on December 15, 2017, it does not get the benefit of the million-dollar step-up.

EXAMPLE: Joanne borrowed $700,000 in 2015 to buy a personal residence. In 2015, she could deduct all the interest on that note. She takes out a $100,000 home equity line of credit in 2018 to remodel her home. Joann has paid down the original loan balance to $675,000 (after principal payments). The home equity line of credit was not outstanding on December 15, 2017, so $75,000 qualifies for the interest deduction. Joann's interest deduction is limited to the debt of $750,000 (Code Sec. 163(h)(3)(F)(i)(III); the $750,000 limit is reduced (but not below $0) by the amount of December 15, 2017). In other words, three-quarters of the interest on the home equity line of credit will qualify for the interest deduction.

Combined Grandfathered and New Acquisition Debt	
Acquisition indebtedness limit	$750,000
Grandfathered debt (pre-December 16, 2017)	$675,000
Available for post-December 15, 2017 acquisition debt	$75,000

How is interest computed if a taxpayer has multiple loans? The 1987 committee reports (PL 100-203) stated that a taxpayer, until final regulations are issued, can use any *reasonable* method to calculate how that interest expense is deductible. The committee reports expressly stated that the first in, first out (FIFO) method is reasonable. According to IRS Publication 936, *Home Mortgage Interest Deduction*, taxpayers can use the average interest rate on mortgage debt, and this method is almost certainly reasonable according to legislative history. The following example illustrates how to apportion interest expense.

EXAMPLE: Bob bought a house on May 1, 2018. He borrowed $750,000. His loan is not considered a grandfathered loan because it was not in place on December 15, 2017. Bob does a major remodel of the house in the fall of 2018, borrowing another $750,000.

Bob has interest of $22,500 (3 percent) on the first loan and interest of $37,500 (5 percent) on the second loan. He can choose the average interest method or the FIFO method. If he uses the average interest rate, he will get a $30,000 mortgage interest deduction, but if he uses FIFO, he will get to deduct only $22,500. Therefore, the average interest method is a better choice for Bob.

	Interest Rate	Interest Deduction
Average interest method	4%	$30,000
FIFO	3%	$22,500

	Balance	Interest Rate
First mortgage	$750,000	3%
Line of credit (remodel)	$750,000	5%

If Bob were later audited, he could simply refer to the legislative history, which notes that taxpayers can choose any reasonable method. The average interest rate method is expressly reasonable according to IRS Publication 936, and FIFO is expressly provided for in the legislative history.

EXAMPLE: Liz has two residences: a house in Seattle with a mortgage of $600,000, and a vacation home in Westport, Washington, with a mortgage of $350,000. Both are grandfathered loans; both homes were purchased before December 15, 2017.

Even though Liz has two residences, she can still continue to deduct all the mortgage interest in both 2017 and 2018 because her combined debt of $950,000 is less than the $1 million cap.

Planning Considerations

With these new rules, taxpayers with large mortgages will not receive the mortgage interest tax benefits that they used to receive, so they might want to consider paying down their mortgages more than they would have in the past. Considerations to discuss with such clients include:

- The higher standard deduction is in place only through 2025.
- Low interest rate mortgages: Can the clients invest the funds (in the stock market) rather than paying down their mortgage and get a higher after-tax investment return? If so, is this a better choice, taking investment risks into account?
- Preserving enough money in savings to cover economic downturns.

Married taxpayers are limited to $1 million in combined mortgage debt (assuming the debt is grandfathered). However, for two single taxpayers the limit is $1 million each—for a combined limit of $2 million, even if they jointly own the property. So, if two clients, each with a mortgage of $900,000, plan to get married right before midnight on New Year's Eve, they might want to wait until New Year's Day. If they wait, they will receive the benefit of the $1 million limit for each single taxpayer.

Tax practitioners should consider asking clients if their mortgage debt was for buying or improving a residence. And if it was not, they should ask whether it was for some other purpose that generates deductible interest, such as a business or an investment in rental property. In some cases, these purposes produce a better result than mortgage interest.

STUDY QUESTIONS

1. Which of the following identifies the new 2018 standard deduction for head of households as a result of the TCJA?

- **a.** $12,000
- **b.** $12,700
- **c.** $18,000
- **d.** $24,000

2. Which of the following statements with respect to the new mortgage interest rules is correct?

- **a.** Home equity indebtedness is not deductible.
- **b.** Interest expense on acquisition indebtedness up to $1 million is deductible if incurred after December 15, 2017.
- **c.** Tax consequences for second homes are significantly changed.
- **d.** Acquisition indebtedness up to $750,000 is deductible for indebtedness incurred on or before December 15, 2017.

¶ 306 TRANSFORMING INTEREST EXPENSE

If a taxpayer has an interest in a pass-through entity, there is an opportunity to change the character of that interest from nondeductible to deductible (IRS Notice 89-35). Suppose the pass-through entity borrows money and distributes the refinancing or the borrowing proceeds to the owners. A portion or all of that interest expense can be deducted by the entity. How much interest expense the entity can keep deducting depends on its annual expenditures.

If the entity's total expenditures are $100,000 for the year, the most it can borrow and distribute is $100,000. If the entity has total expenditures of $200,000 a year, it can borrow another $200,000 and distribute that to the owners, and the owners can then use that to pay off nondeductible interest. The idea is to change the character of the owner's interest from nondeductible to deductible.

> **EXAMPLE:** Karen and Sue's limited liability company (LLC) owns a profitable 25-unit apartment building. Every year, their expenditures (maintenance, real estate taxes, debt service, insurance, fixed asset expenditures, etc.) for the building total $1 million. The problem is that this year they each have mortgage balances of more than $1 million, which is creating nondeductible mortgage interest. They also have credit card debt that is not deductible, so the LLC borrows $1 million and distributes it to Karen and Sue. Karen and Sue pay off their credit card debt and excess mortgage debt, and the LLC can deduct the interest expense as passive interest expense. Karen and Sue have reduced their nondeductible personal interest expense. Because the interest expense is now at the entity level, the entity can deduct it, and Karen and Sue can pay off their nondeductible interest loans (IRS Notice 89-35, Section V.B.).

> Suppose this LLC borrows $1 million, but its annual expenditures are only $800,000. Eighty percent of the interest on this new debt will be deductible. The entity takes out a $1 million loan to refinance. It distributes $1 million in cash to its owners, but its total annual expenditures—its payments for management fees, interest, the debt service, insurance, taxes, etc.—is only $800,000. Only 80 percent of that loan will create deductible interest for the LLC; 20 percent will be nondeductible at the partner level if the partners use it to pay off debts such as credit card debt. However, if the entity's total expenditures are $1,050,000, all of the interest expense may be deducted by the entity.

	Situation #1	Situation #2
Debt-financed distributions	$1,000,000	$1,000,000
Entity's annual expenditures	$800,000	$1,050,000
Amount partners must trace	$200,000	$0

This principle is not restricted to real estate entities; it also applies to other pass-through entities. For instance, a CPA firm can borrow money on a line of credit and distribute the proceeds to its owners. If they then use those proceeds to pay off excess mortgage interest and credit card debt, they convert the partners' nondeductible interest expense to deductible interest expense at the CPA firm level.

Note that this option may not be available forever. IRS Notice 89-35 states that in the future, regulations might be issued to prevent taxpayers using this option for abusive purposes, for example, if a pass-through entity is formed with the *principal* purpose of avoiding or circumventing the rules of Treas. Reg. § 1.163-8T (IRS Notice 89-35, Section III).

¶ 307 PROPERTY, INCOME, AND STATE TAXES

Under the TCJA, both married taxpayers filing jointly and single taxpayers are subject to a $10,000 limit for personal taxes. For two single individuals, the limit is $20,000, but for a married couple filing jointly, it is $10,000, which results in a bit of a marriage penalty. The following charts detail which taxes are subject to the $10,000 limit and which are not.

Taxes Subject to the $10,000 Limit	
Type	**Treatment**
Real property taxes (personal use) domestic	Subject to $10,000 cap
State/local income taxes (wages, etc.)	Subject to $10,000 cap
State/local income tax (Schedule C or Schedule E income)	Subject to $10,000 cap
State/local sales tax, if taxpayer elects to use it rather than state and local income taxes (personal use)	Subject to $10,000 cap

Taxes *Not* Subject to the $10,000 Limit	
Type	**Treatment**
Real property tax (rental)	Above-the-line
Real property tax (business)	Above-the-line
Real property tax (investment, nonrental)	Schedule A, line 6 (see below; this area is not entirely clear*)
Generation-skipping tax (GST) tax on distributions	Schedule A, line 6
Foreign income tax (if foregoing the foreign tax credit)	Schedule A, line 6
Income in respect of a decedent (IRD)	Schedule A, line 16
Business taxes imposed on pass-throughs	Reduces Schedule K-1 income reported by S corporations/partnerships
Foreign real property taxes (personal use)	Not deductible
Foreign personal property taxes (personal use)	Not deductible
* Code Sec. 164(b)(6) *exempts* investment property from the $10,000 limit, but legislative history seems to differ. The author's belief is that it is not subject to the $10,000 limit.	

Although the legislative history is inconsistent on the topic, in this author's view the statute is clear that taxpayers can deduct real property taxes on investment property (raw land) and that it is not subject to the $10,000 limit.

Taxpayers can still deduct property taxes for investment property or business property. However, in some cases they might make a Code Sec. 266 election to capitalize the expenses so that later, when they sell the property, they will have less gain. Not all property qualifies for the Code Sec. 266 election; it has to be unimproved and unproductive. If a taxpayer were renting out land as farmland, for example, the taxpayer would not be able to capitalize the taxes, since the land would be producing income. The gist is that making a Code Sec. 266 election increases basis, and that reduces gain on the sale.

State Tax Workarounds

Many states, especially those with a high tax burden, are concerned about the $10,000 limit and have been trying to develop ways to give their taxpayers more deductions. The states are adopting two approaches. The first is a state tax "credit" if the taxpayer "donates" to a state fund. The objective was to create a "donation" that would count as a charitable contribution to the state, and the taxpayer would get a credit against its state income taxes. However, the IRS believes such a "donation" is not a true donation and should be treated like a payment of tax (to the extent of the tax credit) subject to the $10,000 limit (Treas. Reg. § 1.170A-1(h)(3)(i)). An exception provides that if the state tax credit is 15 percent or less of the contribution, the taxpayer can take the charitable deduction in full (Treas. Reg. § 1.170A-1(h)(3)(iv)).

The result is that a taxpayer simply cannot make a "donation" and call it a charitable contribution. If a taxpayer gets a large tax credit on its state income taxes instead of a charitable contribution deduction, it is treated as making a tax payment, and that tax payment is subject to the $10,000.

The second state tax workaround is a state-imposed entity tax on S corporations and partnerships. Connecticut enacted this tax on May 31, 2018. Under this workaround, an S corporation owner will get an individual tax credit for 93.01 percent of the entity-level tax. Although the IRS has not yet issued a formal response, this tax is consistent with the legislative history and should be deductible.

¶ 308 CHARITABLE CONTRIBUTIONS

In theory, it is easier for taxpayers to deduct charitable contributions in 2018 because under the TCJA, the limit for cash contributions to public charities has risen from 50 percent to 60 percent. The problem, however, is that because fewer people will be itemizing, fewer will benefit from the change for charitable contributions.

The most obvious way to beat this limitation is to donate a large amount to charity in a single year rather than, for example, giving $10,000 per year for four years. Using this strategy, called "bunching," a taxpayer would make $40,000 of charitable contributions in one year and then nothing for the following three years. In the year that taxpayers "bunch" *cash* contributions, they should also "bunch" *noncash* contributions.

Planning opportunities in this area include donor advised funds and transfers from IRAs.

Donor advised funds. Fidelity, the largest recipient of charitable contributions in the United States, sponsors donor advised funds. So do many other investment firms. There is a $5,000 minimum to set up or gift to any 501(c)(3). Donors can gift appreciated stock, real estate, or mutual funds, and can "bunch" itemized deductions by making a large contribution to the donor advised fund in a single year. This creates the deduction. They can then request that the donor advised fund disperse that contribution over future years. For example, an individual can put money in a donor advised fund in year 1 and then apportion it to the local food bank over the next four or five years.

If a taxpayer just transfers over appreciated stock from its stock account into a donor advised fund, the taxpayer can get a deduction for the full fair market value of the stock but does not have to pay tax on the gain on the stock.

The following charts detail the tax benefits of different donor advised fund scenarios.

Married Filing Jointly Taxpayers: No Donor Advised Fund and No Qualified Charitable Deduction			
	2018	**2019**	**2020**
Charitable Contributions	$10,000	$10,000	$10,000
Property Taxes + Sales Tax	$10,000	$10,000	$10,000
Total Itemized	$20,000	$20,000	$20,000
Standard Deduction	$24,000	$24,000	$24,000
Comment: This couple has $30,000 in charitable contributions with *no* tax benefit.			

Married Filing Jointly Taxpayers: Advantage of Donor Advised Funds			
	2018	**2019**	**2020**
Charitable Contributions—DAF	$30,000	$0	$0
Property Taxes + Sales Tax	$10,000	$10,000	$10,000
Total Itemized	**$40,000**	$10,000	$10,000
Standard Deduction	$24,000	$24,000	$24,000
Comment: This couple has $30,000 in charitable contributions, which nets a $16,000 deduction above and beyond he standard deduction (almost $6,000 in tax benefit at 37 percent bracket).			

Transfer from IRA. This alternative is available to people over age 70-1/2. Instead of taking his or her required minimum IRA distribution (paying tax on it) and then giving it to a charity, a taxpayer can request the custodian or trustee to directly transfer money from his or her IRA account to the charitable organization. This is called a qualified charitable distribution (QCD). Each taxpayer can make up to a $100,000 transfer per year. These taxpayers can transfer part or all of their required minimum distributions directly to a charity. Such transfers reduce their required minimum distributions, thereby decreasing their taxable income.

Note that this option is available only for IRAs *other* than SEPs or Simple IRAs to which ongoing contributions are made (IRS Notice 2007-7, Q&A #36). In other words, the IRA from which the money is transferred cannot be an IRA to which taxpayers or their employers are still contributing. An acknowledgement of the transfer must be obtained, and the money sent directly from the trustee to the charity counts toward the taxpayer's required minimum distribution.

Married Filing Jointly Taxpayers over Age 70-1/2: *No* Qualified Charitable Deduction			
	2018	**2019**	**2020**
Charitable Contributions	$10,000	$10,000	$10,000
Property Taxes + Sales Tax	$10,000	$10,000	$10,000
Total Itemized	$20,000	$20,000	$20,000
Standard Deduction	$26,600	$26,600	$26,600
Required Minimum Distribution	$10,000	$10,000	$10,000
Comment: This couple has $30,000 (three years) in charitable contributions with *no* tax benefit (and they are paying taxes on their entire required minimum distributions).			

Married Filing Jointly Taxpayers over Age 70-1/2: Qualified Charitable Deduction, Required Minimum Distribution = $10,000 Per Year			
	2018	**2019**	**2020**
Charitable Contributions	$0	$0	$0
Property Taxes + Sales Tax	$10,000	$10,000	$10,000
Total Itemized	$10,000	$10,000	$10,000

Married Filing Jointly Taxpayers over Age 70-1/2: Qualified Charitable Deduction, Required Minimum Distribution = $10,000 Per Year			
Standard Deduction (+ additional > 65)	$26,600	$26,600	$26,600
Required Minimum Distribution	$0	$0	$0

Comment: Over three years, the couple has reduced their taxable income by $30,000 (since they do not have to pay tax on their required minimum distributions). Further, the loss of their charitable contribution deduction related to the QCD has no impact on their tax liability, since they will take the standard deduction.

¶ 309 MISCELLANEOUS ITEMIZED DEDUCTIONS

Under the TCJA, some miscellaneous itemized deductions are suspended between 2018 and 2025. Among the most prominent of these are unreimbursed employee expenses, investment advisory fees, tax preparation fees that relate to the personal return, and union dues.

Expenses for a trust are not treated as miscellaneous itemized deductions if they are incurred *because of* a trust. For example, most trustee fees and Form 1041 tax preparation fees are deductible. The only reason for these expenses is the existence of the trust, so they are deductible to the trust. If the trust pays investment advisory fees, those fees are not deductible and are treated as miscellaneous itemized deductions (IRS Notice 2018-61).

Unreimbursed Employee Expenses

As mentioned earlier, the deduction for unreimbursed employee expenses has been suspended from 2018 to 2025. Examples of such expenses include the following:

- Business bad debts of employee
- Dues and subscriptions related to work
- Home office
- License fees
- Meals and lodging related to employee's work
- Transportation expense
- Work-related education

However, there is a fairly easy way around this for taxpayers who have a cooperative employer. The employer can reimburse the employee for these expenses. As long as an employee has an accountable plan, he does not have to report the reimbursement as income and does not have the corresponding nondeductible amount (Treas. Reg. § 1.62-2(c)(4)). An accountable plan requires the following:

- The expense must have a business connection,
- The employee must substantiate the expense, and
- The employee must return any excess reimbursement.

An accountable plan also saves the employer money, as the employer does not have to pay FICA tax on the reimbursements.

> **EXAMPLE:** George, a CPA, is an employee at a CPA firm. He has transportation expenses for driving to attend client meetings. Historically, his mileage expenses have totaled $2,000 per year. He has not sought reimbursement for the expenses but instead deducted them on Schedule A of his tax return. For 2018,

George should consider asking his employer to reimburse him for the transportation expenses, even if that might result in a smaller pay raise to offset the reimbursement.

Tax Preparation Fees

Now that the TCJA has suspended miscellaneous itemized deductions from 2018 to 2025, the non-deductibility of tax preparation fees will result in increased after-tax costs to tax clients. Fortunately, Rev. Rul. 92-29 allows taxpayers to apportion tax preparation fees allocable to Schedule C, to Schedule F, and to Schedule E, part 1. If a partner has one or more Schedules K-1 and part of the tax preparation fee is for those, in this author's view, the partnership can also apportion the tax return preparation fee. The key is that the taxpayer can take business expenses, except for employee business expenses, above the line since a partner is considered to be in the business of the partnership (see *Arens v. Commissioner*, TC Memo 1990-241; Code Sec. 62(a)(1)).

Whether a portion of tax preparation fees for an S corporation can be deducted is less certain. There is no direct case law on apportioning tax return preparation fees in this situation, but there are some analogies. If a taxpayer buys S corporation stock, for example, Notice 89-35 indicates that interest expense related to the stock purchase is business interest. That suggests the S corporation shareholders are in the business of the S corporation and therefore the expenses can be treated as business expenses. However, two cases state that if a shareholder is *not* in the business of an S corporation, the shareholder cannot deduct those expenses above the line by putting them on Schedule E, page 2 (*Russell v. Commissioner*, TC Memo 1989-207; *Craft v. Commissioner*, TC Memo 2005-197). Another case seems to indicate that a taxpayer can deduct such expenses (*Peter Morton*, 98 Fed. Cl. 596, cf. *Steinberger*, TC Memo 2016-104). Consequently, there is no clear answer; there is some support for and some support for not deducting the expenses.

Burleson v. Commissioner (TC Memo 1994-130) involved David Burleson, a sole proprietor in South Dakota. He was a Schedule C taxpayer, and his wife also had some income. They paid a $55 fee for their tax preparation services. The tax court ruled that because the tax preparation fee was "predominately" for Schedule C, breaking out the *de minimis* portion was not necessary. Burleson could deduct 100 percent of the $55 on Schedule C.

Hobby Losses

Hobby losses are miscellaneous itemized deductions (Treas. Reg. § 1.67-1T(a)(1)(iv); *Purdey v. United States,* 39 Fed. Cl. 413; Bittker, McMahon, and Zelenak: *Federal Income Taxation of Individuals* § 13.09[5]) and therefore are nondeductible for 2018 through 2025. Note, however, the cost of goods sold *reduces* gross income. Therefore, cost of goods sold is *not* affected by this rule (Treas. Reg. § 1.183-1(e)). Taxpayers should therefore capitalize as much to cost of goods sold as possible (Treas. Reg. § 1.263(a)-1(e)(3), Example 5).

> **EXAMPLE:** Tyrell is a horse breeder who has hobby income of $20,000. In 2017, he had $3,000 in property tax and $17,000 in deductions for horse training. Prior to the TCJA, this would have reduced Tyrell's income to $0, but the TCJA eliminated this miscellaneous itemized deduction. Tyrell has no miscellaneous itemized deduction at all in 2018. His property tax might get capped at $10,000, so as a practical matter, all of his $20,000 in income is subject to tax.

¶309

	2017	2018
Hobby Income	$20,000	$20,000
Hobby Deductions: Property Tax	$3,000	$0*
Deductions	($17,000)**	$0
Net Income	$0	$20,000

* Assume already over property tax cap.
** Assume had other 2 percent deductions and not in AMT.

Tyrell suffers a significant loss by having a hobby, but remember that this does not affect the cost of goods sold. So, if instead Tyrell had sold Amway products, he could offset the cost of these products against income from the sales of Amway products.

Gambling Losses

Before 2018, a *professional* gambler could create a loss on Schedule C. But for 2018 through the end of 2025, Schedule C losses for professional gamblers have been suspended. Under the TCJA, *casual* gamblers can still take a gambling deduction, a wagering loss, but as under prior law, it is limited to wagering gains and it is below the line. So if they do not itemize, they will not get any benefit. Because many casual gamblers will no longer itemize, even wagering losses will not provide a benefit.

EXAMPLE: On June 7, Sheryl, a casual gambler, wins $10,000 playing slot machines. Later that year, on December 8, she loses $5,000 while playing the slots. Sheryl does not itemize in 2018 (the $5,000 gambling loss is her only itemized deduction). She will report the income of $10,000. She will not receive any benefit from the $5,000 loss and instead takes the standard deduction.

Shollenberger v. Commissioner (TC Memo 2009-310) is a case involving the measurement of net wagering gains by session. George and Lillian Shollenberger withdrew $500 from their bank account and went to a casino. They hit a $2,000 jackpot while playing a slot machine. They continued to play, putting *some* of their winnings back into the slot machines. They later left the casino with $1,600, which they deposited into their bank account. Their *net* wagering gains were $1,100 ($1,600 – $500) for this gambling "session." The net gains were determined by how much the couple redeposited to their bank account. The Shollenbergers had to report $1,100 on line 21 of their Form 1040 (no disallowed wagering losses).

The court found that the Shollenbergers could just report their net winnings for that gambling session. The question was not how much they made on a particular slot machine, but rather how much they made over that session. A session starts when a taxpayer walks into the casino, and it ends when they walk out. Here is an example of netting out gambling winnings on a session-by-session basis.

October 2, 2018		
Wagering gains (slots): Form 1099-G	$2,000	
Wagering gains (slots): Not on Form 1099-G	$100	
Wagering losses (slots)	($1,100)	
Net gains for session (line 21 other income)		$1,000

November 3, 2018		
Wagering gains (slots)	$850	
Wagering losses (slots)	($1,000)	
Net loss for session (no deduction unless itemize)		($150)

STUDY QUESTIONS

3. Under the new tax rules, state and local income taxes, property taxes on personal use property, etc., are limited to what amount for those taxpayers filing married jointly?

  a. $5,000

  b. $10,000

  c. $12,000

  d. $18,000

4. Each of the following is an example of a prominent miscellaneous itemized deduction that has been suspended through 2025, *except:*

  a. Unreimbursed employee expenses

  b. Investment advisory fees

  c. Casual gamblers' gambling losses

  d. Tax preparation fees

Pease Limitation

The Pease limitation has been repealed by the TCJA for 2018 through 2025. Prior to tax reform, if a married filing jointly taxpayer's adjusted gross income was over $313,800, the taxpayer had to subtract 3 percent of the difference from the itemized deductions it was claiming. The limitation did not apply to some itemized deductions (e.g., medical, casualty). This is one of the big changes from the TCJA that has not received a lot of attention.

Qualified Business Income Deduction

The qualified business income deduction (QBID), also known as the 20 percent pass-through deduction, does not reduce a taxpayer's adjusted gross income (Code Sec. 63(b)(3)); instead, it reduces taxable income. But even if taxpayers do not itemize deductions, they will get the full QBID (Code Sec. 63(b)(3)).

Medical Expense Deduction

Before the TCJA, there was a 10 percent floor before taxpayers could take a medical expense deduction. The TCJA drops that floor to 7.5 percent for 2017 and 2018, but it goes back up to 10 percent in 2019.

> **PLANNING POINTER:** If a taxpayer itemizes and has deductible medical expenses, she might consider accelerating medical expenses into 2019. For example, if the taxpayer learns she needs a shoulder replacement but does not need surgery immediately, she might want to schedule the shoulder replacement surgery in 2018 before the medical expense deduction limit goes back up to 10 percent in 2019.

¶309

Personal Casualty Losses

Personal casualty and theft losses are limited by the TCJA. For 2018 through 2025, they are deductible only if they occur in a disaster area declared by the president (under the Robert Stafford Disaster Relief and Emergency Assistance Act). That means that other personal losses will not be deductible. However, investment and business casualty losses are still deductible to the same extent they were before the tax legislation took effect.

> **EXAMPLE:** On December 31, 2017, Brett's basement flooded after a water pipe burst. He had a large insurance deductible, and his out-of-pocket losses were greater than 10 percent of his adjusted gross income. Brett itemized deductions, so he took a deduction on his 2017 tax return. However, if his basement floods in 2018, he will not be able to take a deduction because his basement flooding was not part of a presidentially declared disaster area.

Health Savings Accounts

The TCJA did not make changes related to health savings accounts (HSAs). But because fewer people will be itemizing and the medical expense floor is increasing from 7.5 percent to 10 percent after 2018, HSAs are a better deal than they used to be. HSA contributions are still deductible above the line. The taxpayer must have a "high deductible health plan" (HDHP) and an HSA account.

The benefit of getting an above-the-line deduction for medical expenses makes HSAs increasingly popular with taxpayers. In 2008, there were 1.6 million HSAs, and that number almost quadrupled by 2014.

Investment Advisory Fees

Investment advisors often charge taxpayers a fee equal to a percentage of the taxpayer's portfolio. For example, if a taxpayer has a $1 million portfolio, the investment advisor might charge .75 percent, or a fee of $7,500. Because miscellaneous itemized deductions have been suspended for the years 2018 through 2025, taxpayers can no longer take a deduction for investment advisory fees.

The primary alternative to investment advisory fees is mutual funds. Mutual funds do not have this problem because the character of income passes through to investors. Publicly traded mutual funds' expenses reduce dividends, and shareholders are treated as receiving *net* dividends (IRS Publication 550). There is no investment expense at shareholder level.

> **EXAMPLE:** A mutual fund has $501,000 in gross dividend income. It pays investment management fees of $1,000 and passes $500,000 through to its shareholders. The shareholders pay tax on the *net* dividend of $500,000. They have no investment expense and no disallowed itemized deduction.

> **EXAMPLE:** Kevin has a $2 million investment portfolio, and his investment advisor charges a fee of .75 percent. Kevin's portfolio includes $1 million in equities and $1 million in private equity funds. If Kevin invests new money directly into an index mutual fund, he will not have the large nondeductible expense that he would with an investment advisor.

Clients should be careful about selling stocks indiscriminately. They might want to move their whole portfolio to an advisor who does not charge a fee. Some advisors charge on a commission basis.

¶309

There are two ways of capitalizing investment advisory fees: (1) capitalizing into the purchase cost of stock, which is much more complicated, and (2) capitalizing into the sales price. The part of the investment advisory fees that relates to the purchase of stock is covered by Treas. Reg. § 1.263(a)-4(e). The sales portion is covered by a different regulation, Treas. Reg. § 1.263(a)-1(e). The rules are similar, and you can do one without the other. That is, you can capitalize some of the investment advisory fees into the sales portion but choose not to do it for the purchase portion. This idea is still in a formative stage; the IRS has not commented on it.

Required capitalization includes stock purchases (Treas. Regs. § 1.263(a)-4(b)(1) and (c)(1)), but capitalizing is not required. In order to capitalize, whether on the sell side or the buy side, it has to be a facilitative cost, which is defined as a cost paid in the process of investigating or pursuing a transaction.

Note that this applies to the purchase side, allocating to the stocks you buy during the year. There is a *de minimis* rule: a taxpayer can deduct facilitative costs that are less than $5,000 per transaction. However, the taxpayer can sidestep this *de minimis* rule and can elect to capitalize. The election to capitalize is made separately for each transaction. A taxpayer makes the election by treating the costs as facilitative costs, in other words by capitalizing the costs to the basis of stock purchased and reducing gains when the stocks are sold (Treas. Reg. § 1.263(a)-(e)(4)(iv)).

As already mentioned, sales transactions are much simpler. There is no *de minimis* rule and no election. If there are facilitative costs, the taxpayer must expense them. It is likely that this is not an accounting method change because it does not involve timing. Taxpayers do not need to file Form 3115.

Keep in mind that this is an emerging topic. The IRS has not issued a private letter ruling on this issue, and currently there is no case law pertaining to it.

EXAMPLE: A taxpayer is charged $10,000 in investment advisory fees. Here is a potential application:

	Number of Transactions	Percentage of Advisor's Time	Allocate	Treatment
Number of Purchase Transactions	50	40%	$4,000	Allocate to each purchase. Recover when that stock is sold.
Number of Sales Transactions	50	40%	$4,000	Reduce capital gain.
Other Services	N/A	20%	$2,000	No deduction for miscellaneous itemized.

Very large firms appear to be taking different approaches to capitalizing investment advisory fees. Anecdotally, one large firm has been capitalizing without any incident. Another says it requires a study to break out "other services." Still another thinks capitalization is not defensible.

This author's closing advice is to consider capitalizing on the sell side. A conservative approach is to file Form 8275 with the IRS. The purchase side is much more complicated because the taxpayer has to allocate it to the stocks, for example, that it purchased in 2018, and since some of those will not be sold until 2019, 2020 and 2021, a lot more accounting work will be needed.

STUDY QUESTIONS

5. Which of the following statements is correct regarding HSA accounts and the impacts from the new tax regulations?

    a. Contributions to HSAs are deductible below-the-line.

    b. Contributions are allowed after the first month entitled to Medicare.

    c. Deduction limits are the same for self-only and family coverage.

    d. An HDHP and a HSA account are required to deduct contributions.

6. Which of the following identifies one of the state tax workarounds with respect to the $10,000 deduction limit?

    a. States impose entity tax on C corporations.

    b. States provide tax credit if the taxpayer donates to a state fund.

    c. Addition of personal exemptions

    d. Doubling of 529 matching

CPE NOTE: When you have completed your study and review of chapters 1-3, which comprise Module 1, you may wish to take the Final Exam for this Module. Go to **cchcpelink.com/printcpe** to take this Final Exam online.

MODULE 2: DEVLOPMENTS IMPACTING BUSINESS ENTITIES—Chapter 4: New Final Section 199A Regulations for the Qualified Business Income Deduction

¶ 401 WELCOME

This chapter gives a detailed overview of the final Code Sec. 199A regulations for the qualified business income deduction (QBID). Among the topics covered are QBID limits for higher income taxpayers, specified service trades or businesses, wage and property caps, loss carryovers, the rental real estate safe harbor, and how to select between the proposed or final regulations for the 2018 filing season.

¶ 402 LEARNING OBJECTIVES

Upon completion of this chapter, you will be able to:

- Identify the basic calculation of the qualifying income business deduction (QBID)
- Recognize and apply the safe harbor as it relates to rental real estate
- Differentiate between proposed 2018 regulations and the final regulations issued for 2018 returns
- Identify what is included within qualified business income (QBI)
- Identify the QBID for various filers
- Recognize and apply correct principles relating to aggregation
- Describe which type of individual would likely be included in the "specified service trade or business (SSTB) classification, based on the final regulations
- Recognize which type of entity would result in all SSTB income
- Identify an area where it gets "foggy" as it relates to rental real estate

¶ 403 INTRODUCTION

In January 2019, the U.S. Treasury Department and the IRS issued final regulations for one of the most talked-about areas of taxation, the qualified business income deduction (QBID), also known as the 20-percent pass-through deduction. The final regulations finalize the proposed regulations that were issued in 2018, and a new set of proposed regulations offers guidance on several QBID topics. The final regulations may be used on 2018 returns; alternatively, taxpayers may use the proposed regulations for the 2018 tax year.

¶ 404 OVERVIEW

The regulations under Code Sec. 199A allow taxpayers to deduct up to 20 percent of domestic qualified business income (QBI) from a partnership, S corporation, or sole proprietorship. The QBID has a shelf life of eight years (2018 through the end of 2025), then it will expire unless further action is taken.

For most taxpayers, calculating the QBID is fairly simple: If a taxpayer has $100,000 of QBI, he would have a $20,000 QBID. The deduction does not apply to income from C corporations. The QBID does not reduce self-employment tax or net investment income tax (NIIT). To qualify for the QBID, the income must be "effectively connected" to the United States.

The final regulations offer clear guidance on the specific exclusions and inclusions. Excluded from the QBID are the following:

- Wages, including wages received by an S corporation shareholder
- Guaranteed payments received by partners
- Specified service trades or businesses (SSTBs)—such as lawyers, doctors, accountants, consultants, etc. However, this exclusion does not affect all taxpayers. Income from SSTBs qualifies for the QBID in the case of lower and moderate-income taxpayers.
- Investment short-term/long-term capital gain or loss (Code Sec. 1231 gain is also excluded from QBI *if* the taxpayer qualifies for capital gain treatment.)
- Dividends (except ordinary dividends from REITs and patronage dividends from cooperatives)
- Interest income on working capital (but interest income on customer accounts receivable *does* qualify as QBI)

Net operating losses (NOLs) do not reduce QBI, with the *exception* of the portion that relates to "excess business loss" under Code Sec. 461(l) (Treas. Reg. 1.199A-3(b)(1)(v)).

Items that reduce QBI include self-employed health insurance, half of self-employment tax, and retirement contributions, to the extent that gross income from the business is taken into account in the computation. Code Sec. 1231 losses, paradoxically, *do* reduce qualified business income.

¶ 405 QBID CAPS: HIGH-INCOME TAXPAYERS

Two income-dependent caps affect high-income taxpayers:

- The wage or wage and property cap (the "Wage Cap")
- The SSTB cap

These two caps are estimated to apply to only about 5 percent of American taxpayers. The Wage Cap is 50 percent of wages or, if it produces a better result, 25 percent of wages plus 2.5 percent of a property factor.

For both the Wage Cap and the SSTB cap, married taxpayers filing jointly with pre-QBID taxable income of $315,000 or less can deduct 20 percent of QBID on all of their SSTB income (subject to the 20 percent of ordinary income discussed below). For those with taxable income of $315,000 or more, the QBID on SSTB income begins to slowly phase out; at $415,000 it is entirely phased out. For non-SSTB businesses, taxpayers will begin to lose the QBID unless the business generates sufficient amounts of wages or property.

For purposes of simplicity, we will use the term "hamburger" taxpayer. A "hamburger" taxpayer is one with $315,000 of taxable income or less (married filing jointly). "Caviar" taxpayers are those with taxable income of $415,000 or more.

	"Hamburger" Threshold Limits *Do Not* Apply	Phase-In Range	"Caviar" Limits Apply *in Full*
Married Filing Jointly	$315,000	$100,000	$415,000
Single, Head of Household, Married Filing Separately	$157,500	$50,000	$207,500

A taxpayer who files married filing jointly has no Wage Cap at up to $315,000 in income and gets the full QBID for SSTB. Between income of $315,000 and $415,000, that taxpayer starts losing the SSTB. For those who file as single, head of household, or married filing separately—and estates and trusts—the limits do not apply if their income is $157,500 or less.

Roughly 95 percent of American taxpayers are in the "hamburger" category and do not have to worry about these limits; the caps do not apply to them. They can simply multiply their QBI by 20 percent.

EXAMPLE: Taxpayer AA's filing status is married filing jointly. She has $312,000 of taxable income before the QBID ("pre-QBID taxable income"). The taxpayer is considered a "hamburger" taxpayer because her pre-QBID taxable income is below $315,000. Neither of the income-based limits—the SSTB limit nor the wage and property limit—applies. Taxpayer AA can take the full QBID, subject to the 20 percent of ordinary taxable income limit that applies to all taxpayers (see discussion below).

EXAMPLE: Taxpayer BB is a married filing jointly taxpayer who has $650,000 of taxable income from a medical practice. This taxpayer's SSTB income does not qualify for the QBID.

However, suppose Taxpayer BB has income from both a medical practice and a restaurant. The result for this "caviar" taxpayer would be as follows:

	Income	QBID?
Medical Practice	$650,000	No
Restaurant	$75,000	Yes, if the taxpayer has sufficient wages/property

¶ 406 THE 20 PERCENT OF ORDINARY TAXABLE INCOME LIMIT

In addition to the SSTB and Wage Cap limits discussed earlier, there is also a third limit: the 20 percent of net ordinary taxable income limit. This limit applies to all taxpayers, including "hamburger" taxpayers. This limits the QBID to 20 percent of net ordinary taxable income. "Net ordinary taxable income" is taxable income, before the QBID and reduced by long-term capital gain and qualified dividends.

EXAMPLE: Rongxiu has taxable income before the QBID of $100,000 (which includes $20,000 of long-term capital gain and qualified dividends). Her net ordinary income will be $80,000, and her ordinary taxable income limit will be $16,000 ($80,000 × 20 percent).

¶ 407 SPECIFIED SERVICE TRADES OR BUSINESSES

Under the final regulations, taxpayers involved in a SSTB lose the ability to take the QBID if their income puts them in the "caviar" category (married filing joint, pre-QBID taxable income of $415,000 or more). A full list of the professions that are subject to the SSTB rules is included in Treas. Reg. § 1.199A-5. Included in the list are the fields of health, law, accounting, actuarial science, performing arts, consulting, athletics, financial services, investing and investment management, and brokerage services (which essentially includes only stockbrokers and mortgage brokers). Also included is income from a business where the principal asset is the skill or reputation of one or more of the owners. (However, the final regulations narrowly interpret this to include only income from endorsements, "identity" income, and fees for appearances.) Real estate brokers and insurance brokers are not subject to the SSTB rules.

Some entities have both SSTB income and non-SSTB income. If the entity has a "single business" that receives income from both SSTB and non-SSTB sources, the "all or nothing" rule applies: the income is treated as either all SSTB income or all non-SSTB income. The income will be treated as 100 percent non-SSTB income if the entity meets the *de minimis* rule, that is, it can keep the SSTB portion of its gross receipts below 10 percent. Again, even though the entity has some SSTB income, all of the income is treated as non-SSTB income.

Under the *de minimis* rule (Treas. Reg. § 1.199A-5(c)(1)(ii)), if an entity's total gross receipts are $25 million or less and its SSTB income is less than 10 percent of gross receipts, the income is treated as *entirely non-SSTB* income. The SSTB percentage drops to 5 percent if the entity has more than $25 million in gross receipts.

> **EXAMPLE:** Anita is a Code Sec. 1031 exchange facilitator who also has a separate law practice in the same entity. She bills out $50,000 per year in legal fees, and her total gross receipts (including Code Sec. 1031 facilitation fees) amount to $1 million. Dividing $50,000 by the $1 million in total gross receipts results in 5 percent SSTB income. None of Anita's income is treated as SSTB income even though a small portion of it is, illustrating the "nothing" part of the "all-or-nothing rule."

However, if the entity does not pass the *de minimis* test, if 10 percent or more of its gross receipts is from a SSTB, all of it is treated as SSTB income—even though the entity has a great deal of non-SSTB income.

> **EXAMPLE:** L&L, a single entity, provides landscaping advice (which is a SSTB under the regulations) and has a lawn care business. Only $300,000 (15 percent) of L&L's total receipts of $2 million is SSTB income from its landscaping advice services, but because that is more than the *de minimis* threshold (10 percent of gross receipts), 100 percent of L&L's income is treated as SSTB.
>
> Even if L&L has separate invoices for each side of its business, it doesn't matter; L&L is treated as a single business. This illustrates the "all" part of the "all or nothing rule."

Is it possible to have a single entity that has two businesses—that is, an SSTB and separate non-SSTB that are treated as separate businesses? In order to avoid the "all or nothing" rule discussed earlier, an entity can establish that it has two separate businesses. If an SSTB (such as a landscape design business) and non-SSTB (such as a lawncare maintenance business) have separable books *and* separate employees, they will generally be treated as two separate businesses (even if housed in the same entity). Then the "all or nothing" rule will not apply, and the entity will report separate SSTB and non-SSTB income to its owners, based upon the receipts and expenses of each business.

> **EXAMPLE:** Javier is a veterinarian who also has a dog food sales business in the same S corporation. The veterinary and dog food sales portions of the business are treated as separate business, with separate invoices and separate books and records. The dog food sales business has separate employees who work only on dog food sales. The dog food sales business is non-SSTB, whereas the veterinary

services Javier provides constitute a SSTB. Javier can treat each of the two sides of his business as a single business and break out SSTB income and non-SSTB income, even if his total income is over the *de minimis* amount.

However, to be safe, Javier could instead separate his two businesses into different entities (e.g., transfer the dog food business to a new 98-percent-owned LLC) so that he has two separate businesses.

Generally, a single business cannot be carried on by two entities. That means it is far easier to have two separate businesses if they are separated into different entities. In such cases, operating two businesses through separate entities will insulate taxpayers from the "all or nothing" rule. Planning can help. For example, assume that an S corporation operates a dermatology medical practice (SSTB) and sells skincare products (non-SSTB). Also assume that the dermatology practice and skincare products business utilize the same employees, so it is treated as a single business if operated within a single entity. If it is unable to meet the *de minimis* test, all of its income is treated as from an SSTB. If the S corporation transfers the skincare product business to a newly formed LLC (with the S corporation owning 98 percent and the S corporation shareholder owning 2 percent), the dermatology practice and the skincare products will be treated as two separate businesses, and the "all or nothing" rule will not apply.

EXAMPLE: ECG, an elder care facility, has contracted with a separate healthcare organization that provides it with doctors and nurses. The separate organization bills ECG's residents directly for the healthcare services. All of ECG's income is considered as SSTB income (Treas. Reg. § 1.199A-5(b)(3)).

The following chart summarizes the results of the situations presented in the preceding examples.

	Example	Result
Single Entity		
Single business	Landscape design/lawn maintenance	All SSTB (not *de minimis*)
Single business	Exchange facilitator (5 percent of revenues SSTB)	Nothing: No SSTB (*de minimis*)
Two businesses	Vet and separate dog food businesses	Separate SSTB and non-SSTB
Multiple Entities	Vet (S corporation) owns 98 percent of LLC (dog food business)	Separate SSTB and non-SSTB

¶ 408 QBID CAP: WAGES AND PROPERTY (THE "WAGE CAP")

Wages

For "caviar" taxpayers, the QBID is capped at 50 percent of Form W-2 wages or, if more advantageous, 25 percent of wages plus 2.5 percent of the original cost of the depreciable business property. Taxpayers with rental real estate usually pick the second option because they typically do not have wages, and the wages and property factor usually breaks out better for them. W-2 wages include *both* of the following:

- Wages to the owner: Consider bonuses to S corporation shareholder/employees (if the taxpayer has insufficient wages). It must be reasonable compensation.
- Wages to everyone else.

W-2s must be filed within 60 days of the due date; generally, if they are later than this they are not counted.

Often, a paymaster situation can arise. For example, a management company acts as the common paymaster for S corporation A, which operates a restaurant, and S corporation B, which also operates a restaurant. Those wages are treated as being paid by the common law employers, which in this case are S corporation A and S corporation B, not the common paymaster—even though the common paymaster will issue the W-2s.

Although IRS Notice 2019-11 provides three methods for determining wages, most taxpayers use the approach provided in the final regulations: Box 1 wages for all the employees (including medical insurance shown on a 2 percent shareholder's W-2) plus elective deferrals (e.g., employee contributions to a 401(k) plan, a SIMPLE IRA, etc.).

Property Factor

The regulations use the term *unadjusted basis immediately after acquisition* (UBIA) to describe the amount a taxpayer paid for tangible depreciable property, but it is also known as the *property factor*. The property portion of this QBID cap is 2.5 percent multiplied by the UBIA of tangible depreciable property. The cost is no longer counted after the *later* of the following:

- Ten years after the property is placed in service, or
- The last day of the last full year of the recovery period.

The property must be owned at the end of the year, and land does not qualify because only depreciable property qualifies. Note that bonus depreciation and Section 179 expensing do not reduce the property factor (Treas. Reg. § 1.199A-2(c)(3)(i)).

> **EXAMPLE:** Stephan is a "caviar" taxpayer who bought a building on January 15, 1997, for $1 million. (The purchase does not include land.) The building's 27.5-year life ends on July 15, 2024. Stephan's 2018–2023 property cap is calculated as $1 million × 2.5 percent = $25,000. Stephen won't be able to count the building in the property factor in 2024 (because 2024 is not a full-year recovery period). Note: If Stephan were a "hamburger" taxpayer, he would not be subject to this limit.

Code Sec. 1014 step-ups *increase* UBIA (Treas. Reg. § 1.199A-2(c)(3)(v)). The depreciable period also begins anew on the date of death of the original owner.

> **EXAMPLE:** Kayla inherits an apartment building from her great uncle. Kayla will get an increased property factor based upon the date her uncle passed away. Consequently, if her uncle paid only $20,000 for the building, but it is worth $2 million when he passes away, Kayla will get to count the $2 million in her UBIA. She will also begin counting a new 27.5-year life from the date of her uncle's death.

Section 743 Step-Ups

Code Sec. 743 basis adjustments also increase UBIA, but only to the extent that the fair market value (FMV) of the property is greater than the original cost. If a client buys a partnership interest from somebody else, the client will get an increase of the difference between what the partnership paid for the property and the FMV of the property at the time of purchase.

Section 743 step-ups usually involve a comparison of the FMV of the property to the adjusted basis. However, there is a special rule here: A taxpayer can increase the property factor only by the difference between what the partnership paid for it and what it is worth when the taxpayer buys in. The taxpayer cannot increase the property factor for the full 743 step-up (which takes into account depreciation), but only for the increase in the gross costs and the gross FMV of the property.

¶408

EXAMPLE: Bob purchases 50 percent of partnership ABC LLC for $1,200. The company's only asset is a building. When the original partnership purchased the building, 50 percent of the building cost $1,000; but when Bob buys in, 50 percent of the building is worth $1,200. Under the proposed regulations, Bob can count only the partnership's original cost, but the final regulations state Bob can count half of the FMV on the date Bob bought into the partnership. The actual 743 step-up (which takes accumulated depreciation into account) is irrelevant. Look at the FMV versus the original cost in the following chart. Under the final regulations, Bob gets an additional $200 in UBIA for the step-up ($1,000 carryover plus a $200 step-up).

| | Original Cost to the Partnership (50 percent) | Fair Market Value at Time of Bob's Purchase (50 percent) | Basis for Property Factor | |
			Proposed Regulations	Final Regulations
Building	$1,000	$1,200	$1,000 (only the carryover basis)	$1,200 ($1,000 carryover plus $200 step up)

Like-Kind Exchanges

Under the proposed regulations, the net book value of a taxpayer's adjusted basis in the relinquished property was the taxpayer's cost in the new property, or UBIA. So if a taxpayer paid $1,000 for the original property, she would take $200 in depreciation, resulting in a net book value of $800. The proposed regulations stated that the taxpayer would use only $800 in the cost factor.

EXAMPLE: Michelle trades a building for another building ("straight across"). She does not pay any cash or receive any cash. There were no liabilities before or after the transaction.

| | Relinquished Property | | | Property Factor Replacement Property | |
	Cost	A/D	Net Book Value	Proposed Regulations	Final Regulations
Building	$1,000	($200)	$800	$800 (carryover net tax basis)	$1,000 (carryover cost)

STUDY QUESTIONS

1. The new Code Sec. 199A deduction allows for a _____ percent deduction on qualifying business income.

   a. 10

   b. 15

   c. 20

   d. 25

2. Which of the following is included in QBI?

   a. Ordinary income on the sale of a partnership interest (Code Sec. 751 recapture)

   b. Guaranteed payments

   c. Wages

   d. Interest income on investment of working capital

¶ 409 WAGE AND PROPERTY CAPS: BUSINESS BY BUSINESS

Generally, the QBID Wage Cap is computed separately for each business. Both the proposed and the final regulations allow individuals to aggregate certain businesses for purposes of applying the Wage Cap. The final regulations also allow entities to aggregate businesses at the S corporation and the partnership level. Once an individual or entity elects to aggregate businesses, however, it must consistently group them unless there is a material change of facts (e.g., the entity no longer qualifies for aggregation). Note that individuals and entities are not required to aggregate all of eligible businesses; they can choose to aggregate none of the eligible businesses, some of them, or all.

Aggregating Businesses

Generally, the Wage Cap (50 percent of the W-2 wage limit, or 25 percent of W-2 plus 2.5 percent of UBIA if it produces a better result) is applied on business-by-business basis. The aggregation rules have only one function: taxpayers who qualify to aggregate businesses may *combine* businesses for purposes of the 50 percent Wage Cap limit. This frequently increases the QBID. Keep in mind that most taxpayers are not affected by these limits; "hamburger" taxpayers are not impacted by this limit. Only higher income taxpayers are affected.

Individuals who qualify may aggregate businesses. Entities can also aggregate businesses. In some cases, it might be easier for the entity to aggregate than for each shareholder or partner, especially if all the aggregated businesses use the 50 percent of wages limit (no downside), or if all the aggregated businesses use 25 percent of wages plus 2.5 percent of UBIA. In order to aggregate, each business to be aggregated must meet all five of the following requirements:

1. The businesses must be under common control (50 percent or more; 50 percent is sufficient, and it includes indirect ownership). The Code Sec. 267 definition of attribution applies. This common control must exist for the majority of the year and on the last day of the year. Any number of persons may be counted for the 50 percent or more test, as long as they own at least some interest in all the entities sought to be aggregated.

2. The businesses must report on the same taxable year (however, an exception is provided for businesses with short taxable years).

3. None of the aggregated businesses can be a SSTB.

4. The businesses must meet certain reporting requirements every year (discussed later in this chapter).

5. The businesses must meet at least two of three factors (listed after the following example).

EXAMPLE: The aggregation rules appear to provide a very broad definition of common control. Bob and Ray own interests XYZ and ABC. No other owners have interests in both entities. Bob and Ray together are treated as owning 50 percent of XYZ and 50 percent of ABC; therefore, the common control standard is met.

	XYZ	ABC
Bob	1%	49%
Ray	49%	1%
Combined ownership	50%	50%

As mentioned in the fifth item in the previous list, businesses must meet at least two of the following three hurdles in order to aggregate:

- They must have the same products, property, or services. For example, a restaurant and a food truck would meet this requirement because the product for both is food. In the alternative, this first hurdle can be satisfied if the products, property, or services are customarily provided together (e.g., a gas station and a car wash).

- They must share facilities *or* share significant centralized business elements (e.g., common personnel, accounting, legal, purchasing, human resources, IT, advertising, etc.). For example, if the restaurant and the food truck have the same accountant and the same lawyer, they should be able to clear this second hurdle.

- They must be operated in coordination with or reliance on other aggregated businesses. A classic example is a supply chain. If S corporation A manufactures widgets, and S corporation B sells the same widget, that would be an interdependency and the businesses would clear this hurdle.

Remember that the businesses need to meet at least two of these three requirements. Most planning is related to the second hurdle, significant centralized business elements.

EXAMPLE: S Corporation Z has interests in two restaurants, one directly and one indirectly. It operates one restaurant directly and owns 60 percent of an LLC that operates another restaurant. They meet the common control test, and because both businesses are restaurants, they clear the first of the three hurdles. They also share the same taxable year.

The restaurants share common management and common advertising, so they meet the requirements of the second part of the second hurdle. Therefore, S Corporation Z can choose to aggregate. It can combine the wages and QBI of the 60-percent-owned LLC and its 100-percent-owned restaurant.

Note that to get over the second part of the second hurdle, S Corporation Z's businesses must have shared business elements (note the plural). If the businesses have common management but no other shared element, they will not meet the test.

In short, aggregation is beneficial if:

- The entity has a wage limit.

- One of its businesses has excess wages, that is, more than enough to cover its own QBI.

- Another business does not have enough wages to cover its own QBI.

EXAMPLE: In this example, the taxpayer is not aggregating. Business A, an S corporation, has QBI of $500,000 and tentative QBID of $100,000, but no wages. Using the business-by-business computation, the $100,000 QBID of Business A is not allowed because there are no wages.

Business B, also an S corporation, just happened to have the same amount of income, $500,000. It has a tentative QBID of $100,000, but its wages are $400,000. The $200,000 wage limit results in much more wages than Business B needs, so it gets the full QBID.

¶409

	Business A	Business B
QBI	$500,000	$500,000
QBID rate	20%	20%
Tentative QBID	$100,000	$100,000
Wages*	$0	$400,000
Wage limit (50%)	$0	**$200,000**
QBID	$0	$100,000
* Assumes no tangible property, so the alternate formula does not help.		

With aggregation, Business A and Business B are combined into one big business that would have $1,000,000 in QBI and a $200,000 QBID. All the wages would be combined into $400,000 of wages, and the $200,000 wage limit is just enough wages to cover the QBID.

Basically, some of the excess wages of Business B are used against the QBI of Business A, which did not have any wages at all—that is the essence of aggregation.

	Business A	Business B	Total
QBI	$500,000	$500,000	$1,000,000
QBID rate			20%
Tentative QBID			$200,000
Wages*	$0	$400,000	$400,000
Wage limit (50%)			**$200,000**
QBID			**$200,000**
* Assumes no tangible property, so the alternate formula does not help.			

There is one situation in which aggregation can backfire: when one business uses the 25 percent of wages plus 2.5 percent of UBIA factor and the other business uses the 50 percent of wages factor. If the businesses do not aggregate, one business could utilize the property factor and the other business could utilize the 50 percent of wages factor. However, if the two businesses are aggregated, the combined businesses cannot "cherry-pick"—they must pick either the property factor *or* the 50 percent of wages factor for the combined business.

Disclosure on Form K-1

Individuals who wish to aggregate are required to make an annual disclosure every year. Relevant pass-through entities that aggregate are also required to make an annual disclosure. A relevant pass-through entity (RPE) is basically any S corporation or any partnership. Nongrantor trusts and estates can also be RPEs.

Each year, RPEs (including each RPE in a tiered structure) must attach an aggregation statement to each Form K-1 identifying the businesses aggregated. The statement must:

- Include a description of each business.
- Include the name and employer identification number (EIN) of each entity in which a business is operated.
- Identify businesses that were formed, acquired, ceased operations, or disposed of during the taxable year.

- Identify any aggregated business of another RPE in which the RPE holds an ownership interest.
- Contain other information required by the IRS (e.g., forms, instructions, other published guidance).

The individual disclosure is almost identical to that for RPEs (Treas. Reg. § 1.199A-4(c)(2)).

Failure to Disclose

If an RPE or an individual fails to attach the aggregation statement to its Form K-1, the IRS may disaggregate the businesses. Note that disaggregation for a reporting failure is not automatic; the IRS must affirmatively choose to disaggregate. Since most returns are not audited, it is very unlikely that the IRS will make such a choice. However, if this happens, the individual or entity will not be able to re-aggregate for the next three taxable years.

¶ 410 QBID FORM K-1 DISCLOSURE

RPEs must include information on each Form K-1 for *each* business (including aggregated businesses) engaged in directly by the RPE. The form must include:

- Each owner's share of QBI, W-2 wages, and UBIA of qualified property attributable to *each* such business, and
- Whether any of the businesses is a SSTB (Treas. Reg. § 1.199A-6(b)(3)).
- In addition, if the RPE owns an interest in another RPE (a "lower-tier" RPE), it must also report the same information reported to it by the lower-tier RPE.

The RPE must also report each owner's share of:

- Qualified REIT dividends received by the RPE (including through another RPE), and
- Qualified publicly traded partnership (PTP) income for each PTP in which the RPE has an interest.

¶ 411 LOSS CARRYOVERS

Sometimes a qualifying business loses money. Suppose an individual owns S Corporation A, which makes $100, but S Corporation B, which it also wholly owns, loses $200. The individual has a $100 net qualifying business loss (that reduces taxable income), which means it will not have a QBID for 2018. But even worse, its 2019 QBID will be affected. The net business loss in 2018 carries over to 2019 and reduces the individual's QBI in 2019. Note that is a carryover that affects only the 2019 computation of the QBID. It will not create a tax deduction in 2019.

If the same entity has another loss in 2019, it would carry that over to 2020. There is no limit on how long an entity can carry over losses.

	2018	2019
QB income or loss	($100)	$200
Carryover loss	—	($100)
Net QBI (loss)	($100)	$100
QBID (assuming no wage limit)	$0	$20

¶ 412 THE QBID AND RENTAL REAL ESTATE

Whether rental real estate qualifies for the QBID is a bit complicated. Real estate rentals qualify for the QBID if they are businesses as defined in Code Sec. 162. In *Curphey v.*

Commissioner (73 TC 766), the U.S. Tax Court held that rental of a "single piece of real property . . . [is]a . . . business." The Tax Court came to the same conclusion in several other cases. However, it has declined to hold that *all* rentals are businesses.

In contrast to the Tax Court's more generous position, the U.S. Court of Appeals for the Second Circuit has required a higher level of activity for rentals to be treated as businesses. The Second Circuit is the appellate court for taxpayers who reside in New York, Connecticut, and Vermont. Other courts have weighed in as well; see the following chart for a summary.

Rental Real Estate: Is It a Business?			
	Facts	Business	Venue/Comments
Murtaugh v. Commissioner	Two timeshares, management company had substantial activity	Yes	Tax Court/Managers' activity counts (post-*Groetzinger*)
LaGreide v. Commissioner	Inherited, single-family residence	Yes	Tax Court/Rental single-family property is a business
Hazard v. Commissioner	Single-family, taxpayer lived in different city	Yes	Tax Court/Rental single-family property is a business
Reiner v. United States	Single-family, management company	Yes	CA7/Cited *LaGreide*
Grier v. United States	Single-family, only one tenant, made repairs	No	CA2/Circuit has least favorable position.
Balsamo v. Commissioner	Inherited, no repairs, sold three months after inheritance	No	Tax Court used CA2 law, bound by *Golsen* rule because case was appealable to the Second Circuit. The Tax Court would likely have reached a different result if the case had been appealable to a different circuit.
Union Bank of Troy	Triple net lease, tenant maintained building	No	District Court of New York (cited *Grier*, appealable to CA2)
Durbin v. Birmingham	Lease of land	No	District Court of Louisiana
IRS Private Letter Ruling 8350008	Triple net lease, owned land only, tenant owned maintained building.	No	Nonprecedential administrative guidance

In this author's view, there is substantial authority in almost all cases that the rental of a single-family home qualifies for the deduction. Although this determination is a bit more difficult to come by in the Second Circuit, there is still substantial authority for a single-family rental residence being able to take the QBID.

Rental Real Estate to Commonly Controlled Entity

There are two special rules for real estate rented to commonly controlled entities.

- When real estate is rented to a commonly controlled SSTB, the rental income is *treated* as SSTB income even though rental income is technically not SSTB income.

- When real estate is rented to a commonly controlled entity, the rental income is *treated* as business income even if it does not rise to the level of a business.

EXAMPLE: A dentist rents 80 percent of his building to a wholly owned S corporation that is a dental practice. The other 20 percent is leased to other (unrelated) dentists. Eighty percent of the rental income is SSTB income, and the 20 percent rented to the other dentists is treated as non-SSTB income.

EXAMPLE: A real estate broker rents a building subject to a triple net lease to a 100-percent-owned S corporation that operates the real estate brokerage firm. The rental income is treated as QBI. The rental property is *treated* as a business whether or not it meets the requirements to establish a business under the general Code Sec. 162 principles.

¶ 413 "FOGGY" AREAS

The IRS has left many questions unanswered regarding rental real estate. Neither IRS Notice 2019-07 (the rental real estate safe harbor, discussed later in this course) nor the final regulations rule out land leases or triple net leases. The regulations state only that the determination is a "facts and circumstances" test. The IRS declines to rule that all rentals are businesses, and does not want to imply that land leases are, or are not, businesses.

The final regulations state that the relevant factors for determining whether rental real estate is a business *might* include:

- The type of rental (residential versus commercial)
- The number of properties rented
- The owner's or owner's agent's day-to-day involvement
- The types and/or significance of ancillary services under the lease
- The terms of lease (net lease versus traditional)

With regard to triple net leases, some commentators cite Code Sec. 871 cases that state triple nets do not qualify for the QBID. Some cite Rev. Rul. 73-522 and *Neill v. Commissioner* as authority. Rev. Rul. 73-522 addresses business within the "meaning of §871 of the code," and *Neill* (46 BTA 197) is a case that was decided under a prior law version of Code Sec. 871. However, rather than use the Code Sec. 871 standard, the Code Sec. 199A regulations explicitly incorporate the Code Sec. 162 definition (Treas. Reg. §1.199A-1(b)(14)). Further, Rev. Rul. 60-206 provides that a triple net lease of equipment *is* a business for purposes of the Code Sec. 513 unrelated business income definition. This revenue ruling is relevant to the QBID and rental real estate, since Code Sec. 513 uses the same definition of business that the QBID rules do, that is, they both utilize the Code Sec. 162 definition (see Treas. Reg. §§1.513-1(b) and 1.199A-1(b)(14)). Taxpayers are allowed to rely upon revenue rulings. See *Rauenhorst v. Commissioner,* 119 TC 157.

Here is the long and short of it: In this author's view, the rental of real property normally meets the definition of a business. There is some uncertainty in the area of triple net leases where the landlord merely collects a check and also in the area of land leases. Taxpayers who wish to claim the QBID for these activities should consider filing Form 8275 in order to reduce the possibility of penalties.

If an entity is claiming a QBID, it should be issuing Form 1099s (Preamble, p. 21). This is particularly applicable to real estate rentals.

STUDY QUESTIONS

3. Which of the following identifies the full phase-in amount ("caviar" level) related to the QBID for single filers?

- **a.** $157,500
- **b.** $207,500
- **c.** $315,000
- **d.** $415,000

4. Which of the following statements relating to aggregation is incorrect?

- **a.** Each operation must be a business.
- **b.** Aggregated businesses must share two of three factors.
- **c.** Service and nonservice businesses are always aggregated.
- **d.** Shareholders should always aggregate.

¶ 414 NOTICE 2019-07: RENTAL REAL ESTATE SAFE HARBOR

IRS Notice 2019-07 offers a safe harbor for when a rental real estate will qualify as a business for purposes of the QBID. It provides a safe harbor but states that rentals that do not meet this safe harbor may still qualify to take the QBID. The safe harbor applies beginning with 2018 tax returns and can be utilized by both individuals and RPEs. Notice 2019-07 applies to what are called "rental real estate enterprises." A taxpayer can treat each one of its rental properties as a separate enterprise, or it can group similar properties together and treat them as a single enterprise. However, commercial and residential rentals cannot be grouped together for this purpose.

EXAMPLE: Bob owns three residential rental homes. He can either:

- Treat each rental as a separate enterprise, or
- Group all three together as a single real estate rental enterprise.

Bob does not need to attach a statement to his tax return in order to group the homes for the safe harbor. However, Bob must have:

- Separate books and records for each enterprise
- Separate bank accounts for each enterprise
- More than 250 hours of rental services per year for the enterprise
- Contemporaneous records

Beginning for the 2019 tax year, contemporaneous records must be maintained for rental real estate. These include time reports, logs, and similar documents regarding:

- Hours and descriptions of all services,
- Dates on which the services were performed, and
- Who performed services

The 250 hours of rental services required include not just the owner's time, but that of the management company, employees, agents, and independent contractors. Rental services include the following: advertising, negotiating and leasing, verifying information in tenant's applications, collection of rent, daily operation, maintenance, repairs, management, purchase of materials, and supervising employees and independent contractors. Financial and investment activities, and planning/managing/constructing long-term improvements do not count as rental services.

> **EXAMPLE:** In the 2018 tax year, Bob owns two duplexes. He decides to group them together and treat them as one enterprise. Bob spends 100 hours of his time on the duplexes, and the management company spends 160 hours. (Remember that there is no contemporaneous time record requirement for 2018.) Bob has a separate checking account and records for duplexes, and he attaches a signed statement to his tax return. Bob should qualify for the safe harbor.

Excluded Real Estate Arrangements

Some property does not qualify for the safe harbor. For example, a vacation home that a taxpayer rents out for a portion of the year but uses for more than 14 days will not qualify for the safe harbor. Also, some triple net leases are excluded from the safe harbor. This does not mean that such rental property does not qualify for the QBID; it just means it is not covered by the safe harbor.

Triple net leases "include" leases where the tenant must:

- Pay taxes, insurance, and fees, *and*
- Be "responsible" for maintenance activities.

Ambiguity arises from the word *includes*; it implies that other types of triple net lease might also be excluded. There are two types of triple net leases:

- The landlord is responsible for (i.e., oversees) maintenance, and the tenant reimburses the landlord. It is the author's belief that this type of triple net lease is not excluded from the safe harbor.
- The tenant is responsible for maintenance. The landlord has little or no involvement, except to collect checks. It is the author's view that this type of triple net lease is excluded from the safe harbor.

Required Statement

There are no reporting requirements for the safe harbor. To qualify for it, the taxpayer simply attaches a signed statement to its tax return each year stating, under penalty of perjury, that the requirements have been met. The statement must be signed by one who has personal knowledge (e.g., the individual taxpayer or authorized representative of the individual or the RPE). See the language in IRS Notice 2019-07, Section 3.06.

The Safe Harbor: Not Much of a Concession

If a taxpayer meets the safe harbor's 250-hour test, it is very likely that its rental real estate is a business anyway, even without the safe harbor. Although the safe harbor is not much of a concession, that does not mean a taxpayer should never use it. If a client has significant rental income, the tax practitioner should at least offer this safe harbor as an option.

When to Utilize the Safe Harbor

Assume a client has $150,000 per year in rental income. If the tax practitioner does not mention the safe harbor to the client, and the client loses the QBID, there might be some finger-pointing. If the client is later audited, he or she might question why the safe harbor was never mentioned. Therefore, practitioners should discuss the safe harbor with clients that have significant amounts of rental income. Even though most clients will not be keen on contemporaneous record-keeping, it still makes sense to present them with the option.

If a client is already meeting the difficult parts of the safe harbor test (e.g., contemporaneous record-keeping), the practitioner should definitely recommend using the safe harbor. The practitioner can provide a sample statement, have the client customize and sign it, and attach it to the return.

¶ 415 ANSWERS TO COMMON QUESTIONS

Here are answers to some frequently asked questions about the Code Sec. 199A QBID.

Question: If a client is a passive investor, can he or she qualify for the QBID?

Answer: Yes. Passive status is completely irrelevant. According to the final regulations (Preamble, p. 15), an investor can be completely passive and the business can still qualify; it is the business level that matters, not the individual.

Question: If a real estate rental is a business, does the owner have to pay self-employment tax?

Answer: No. Real estate rentals are broadly exempt from self-employment tax, even if they are businesses. (However, "hotel-type" operations are subject to self-employment tax (Code Sec. 1402(a)(1).)

Question: How is income apportioned between a trust and a beneficiary?

Answer: It is apportioned based on the proportion of distributable net income (DNI). If half of the DNI goes out to the beneficiaries, half of the QBI, half of the wages, and half of the property go out to the beneficiaries too.

Question: How do fiscal year partnerships work?

Answer: They should report QBI for the fiscal year ending in 2018 on the owner's 2018 return.

¶ 416 BASIS, AT-RISK, AND PASSIVE CARRYOVERS

Basically, the regulations state that a basis limitation, an at-risk limitation, or a suspended passive loss that arose before 2018 does not reduce QBI. These carryovers are applied on a first-in, first-out (FIFO) basis (Preamble, pp. 40–41). However, this sometimes results in a limitation under the "20 percent of ordinary income limit."

> **EXAMPLE:** In 2018, a taxpayer has passive income of $40,000, but in 2017 it had a suspended loss carryover of $40,000. The passive income in 2018 allows $40,000 of suspended passive losses to be utilized. This will reduce the taxpayer's taxable income. The taxpayer will report $0 income from the activity on its tax return, but those pre-2018 carryovers do not reduce QBI in 2018.

Carryovers Originating in 2017 and Before		
	Amount	
2018: Passive income	$40,000	
2017: Suspended loss carryover	($40,000)	
Net income tax return		$0
Qualifying business income*		$40,000
* Not reduced by pre-2018 carryovers, but *will* be reduced by post-2017 carryovers. The final regulations provided that the losses are used up on a FIFO basis.		

However, if that passive loss arose in 2018, it reduces taxable income and reduces QBI. If the taxpayer has both pre-2018 and post-2017 losses, it should use up the old losses first.

Passive Carryovers *Originating* in 2018 and After		
	Amount	
2020: Passive income	$40,000	
Suspended loss carryover (*originated* in 2018)	($40,000)	
Net income tax return		$0
2020 qualifying business income (passive)*	$40,000	
Suspended loss carryover (originated in 2018)	($40,000)	
QBI		$0
* Reduced by suspended losses that originated in post-2017 years.		

¶ 417 WAGE STRATEGIES

There are some strategies "caviar" non-SSTB taxpayers can use regarding wages. (These strategies are irrelevant for "hamburger" taxpayers, since they are not subject to the wage limits.) To find the optimal amount of wages for a "caviar" taxpayer, divide the taxpayer's pre-wage income by 3.5. For a taxpayer with pre-wage income of $350,000, dividing by 3.5 results in $100,000, the optimal amount of wages. If the taxpayer pays $100,000 in combined wages to the owner and all employees, it is at the perfect balancing point. If the taxpayer pays more than $100,000 in wages, however, it ends up paying extra payroll taxes and has a reduced QBID. The $100,000 provides just enough W-2 limits so that the taxpayer qualifies for the full QBID.

Proof		
Net income (before wages)		$350,000
Optimal wages		$100,000
Net income		$250,000
QBID (net income × 20%)		**$50,000**
Wages (to owner and nonowners)	$100,000	
50% wage limit	50%	**$50,000**

¶ 418 CHOOSING BETWEEN THE FINAL AND PROPOSED REGULATIONS

For the 2018 tax year, taxpayers must choose to apply—in their entirety—either the proposed regulations or the final regulations. They cannot cherry-pick the most advantageous requirements from each set of regulations. The following charts can help different types of entities in making their choice.

UBIA: Property Factor		
Topic	Proposed	Final
UBIA increased by Code Sec. 743 adjustment	No	Partially (to the extent FMV exceeds original UBIA. Preamble, p. 35.)
UBIA "carries over" in Code Secs. 1031, 1033, and 168(i)(7) (Code Secs. 351, 721, etc.)	No (use net book value)	Yes
UBIA reduced by A/D in Code Secs. 1031, 1033, and 168(i)(7)	Yes	No

Aggregation		
Topic	Proposed	Final
Entity-level aggregation permitted	No	Yes
Aggregation "attribution" under Code Secs. 267(b) and 707(b)	No	Yes
Clarifies entity can aggregate real estate rentals with other businesses	No	Yes
Entity cannot aggregate nonresidential and residential rentals	No	Yes
Clarifies that if entity does not aggregate in 2018, it can still choose to aggregate in future year	No	Yes
Can make aggregation choice on amended return (2018 only)	No	Yes
If taxpayer fails to disclose aggregation, IRS may choose to disaggregate for three years	No	Yes

SSTBs		
Topic	Proposed	Final
"Professional advice and counsel" includes landscape design	No	Yes
Single business assisted living centers not "health" SSTB if medical billed separately by health professionals	No	Yes
Surgical center (separate billing by doctors/nurses) not "health" SSTB	No	Yes
Health: Services must be provided directly to patient	Yes	No
Engineering and architecture are not consulting services	No	Yes
"Financial services" includes arranging lending transactions between lender and borrower (appears to include mortgage brokers)	No	Yes
Commission-based sales of insurance generally not "investing"	No	Yes
"Shared expenses" *de minimis* rule	Yes	No
If 80 percent of products/services provided to SSTB under common control, 100 percent treated as SSTB	Yes	No
Clarifies single business: if SSTB income > *de minimis*, entire business is SSTB	No	Yes
Two businesses: Single entity can have SSTB and also a non-SSTB (but must be a separate businesses, which generally requires separable books and separate employees)	No	Yes

RPE Reporting		
Topic	Proposed	Final
If RPE fails to report a single item (e.g., wages), only that single item is presumed to be zero.	No	Yes
If RPE fails to report on QBI, UBIA, W-2 wages, etc., it can correct it on amended return.	No	Yes

Other		
Topic	Proposed	Final
Qualified dividends reduce the net ordinary taxable income (20 percent taxable income limit)	No	Yes
Makes clear: Irrelevant whether taxpayer is material participant	No	Yes
Electing small business trust: Both S and non-S portion of trust share a combined $157,500 amount	No	Yes
Clear statement: No reasonable compensation required for partners	Yes	No

STUDY QUESTIONS

5. Which of the following is *not* one of the requirements in order to use the Notice 2019-7 safe harbor as it relates to rental real estate?

   a. There must be separate books and records for each enterprise.

   b. There must be greater than 500 hours of rental services per year in the enterprise.

   c. There must be contemporaneous recordkeeping for taxable years beginning in 2019.

   d. There must be separate bank accounts for each enterprise.

6. Which of the following statements is false?

   a. Landscape design income is SSTB income.

   b. Assisted-living centers are not health SSTBs if medical services are billed separately by health professionals.

   c. A surgical center (separate billing by doctors/nurses) is not a health SSTB.

   d. Commission-based sales of insurance produce SSTB income.

MODULE 2: DEVLOPMENTS IMPACTING BUSINESS ENTITIES—Chapter 5: Choice of Entity and Tax Issue Entity Formations

¶ 501 WELCOME

This chapter discusses the business advantages and disadvantages of different types of business entities, including C corporations, S corporations, limited liability companies, partnerships, and sole proprietorships. It also covers the tax advantages and disadvantages of each entity type. Finally, it addresses the tax treatment and potential pitfalls involved in forming each type of entity.

¶ 502 LEARNING OBJECTIVES

Upon completion of this chapter, you will be able to:

- Identify the business advantages and disadvantages of various business entity structures
- Identify the tax advantages and disadvantages of various business entity structures
- Recognize the treatment of formation transactions for C corporations, S corporations, LLCs, and partnerships
- Describe potential current and future pitfalls of forming each entity type

¶ 503 INTRODUCTION

Choosing which type of entity to use to form and organize a new business can be challenging. One must weigh the costs and benefits today versus those in the future, without knowing what the future will bring. Often, business concerns suggest one type of entity, while tax concerns suggest another. These decisions are also affected by the Tax Cuts and Jobs Act of 2017 (TCJA), which provide a new 20 percent pass-through deduction and a lower tax rate for C corporations.

¶ 504 OVERVIEW OF ENTITY TYPES

The most common forms for operating businesses include the sole proprietorship, general partnership, limited partnership, limited liability company (LLC), corporation, and S corporation. The following sections discuss each type of entity in more detail.

Sole Proprietorship

A sole proprietorship is an unincorporated business that is owned and operated by one individual, with no legal distinction between the business and the owner. The owner is entitled to all the profits of the business and responsible for its debts, losses, and liabilities, unless otherwise modified by contract. Sole proprietorship is the default status applied to a business that has a sole owner and takes no action to form an entity. Some owners choose to register a trade name to create a commercial identity for the business, but a sole proprietorship may exist even if the business is conducted under a trade name.

The business is not taxed separately from its owner. Generally, the owner reports business income on Schedule C, and sometimes on other related schedules, to the owner's Form 1040. The owner is taxed on the profits of the business whether or not the profits remain in the business, and the owner can access the cash in the business at any time without tax consequences.

The advantages of a sole proprietorship include the following:

- Setting up and maintaining a sole proprietorship is typically inexpensive.
- The business has all the tax advantages of a pass-through entity (i.e., there is no second level of tax). (The tax treatment of pass-through entities is discussed later in this chapter.)

This form of business entity also presents some disadvantages. Because there is no separate legal entity, sole proprietorships do not offer protection from personal liability. Therefore, it is generally not a good idea to operate a business that may result in exposure for contract or tort liability as a sole proprietorship, because the owner will be personally liable.

Some sole owners will form a single member LLC to operate the business, which offers limited liability but is disregarded for tax purposes. The result is the same tax treatment as a traditional sole proprietorship.

General Partnership

A general partnership is a business with more than one owner, and the owners are partners. Any time two or more owners create a business and do not form any other type of legal entity, their business will default to a general partnership structure. The partners are personally liable for all business liabilities, jointly and severally, and they can be sued individually for the actions of another partner. Because most business owners prefer not to have unlimited liability, a full general partnership is fairly uncommon. By partnership agreement or under state law, a partner may have a right of contribution from other partners if he or she becomes liable to third parties for partnership liabilities.

Partners contribute capital (money or property, including know-how) or "sweat equity" (services) to the partnership in return for a share of the profits and losses in agreed-upon percentages or other sharing arrangements. Any partner can bind the business with his or her actions, and thus subject the partnership to liabilities. The partnership may try to alter this by agreement, but that may not be enough to bind third parties.

A general partnership results in pass-through treatment for tax purposes. The partnership files a Form 1065 annual partnership return and issues Schedule K-1 information returns to each partner showing their share of partnership losses, gains, and other tax attributes. The partnership itself will not pay any tax at the partnership level, but there will be an annual partnership return and the individual items will pass through to the partners, in accordance with their percentage interest or with special allocations set forth in the partnership agreement.

This form of business offers several advantages:

- A general partnership business structure is easier to form and less expensive to maintain than a corporation, LLC, or limited partnership.
- There is no need for a legal filing; a general partnership can exist through an oral agreement. However, it is generally a good idea to clarify the agreement between the partners with a written partnership agreement.

- The economic arrangement is flexible in terms of how the partners share profits and losses. Priority of payments can be specified so that certain partners can be repaid before the other partners begin to share the profits. However, this specification requires a written partnership agreement, which can be complicated and expensive to draft.
- Because the partners share financial commitments, they are all invested in the entity's success.
- General partnerships enjoy the tax advantages of pass-through entities.

Several disadvantages are associated with this type of entity as well. For example, the partners have joint and several liability, and each partner can bind the business. As mentioned earlier, partnership agreements can be complex and expensive to draft, even for "simple" 50-50 partnerships.

Limited Partnership

A limited partnership has at least one general partner subject to general liability and one or more limited partners. The limited partners, sometimes called *silent partners*, enjoy limited liability but cannot be very involved in the business. The general partners, on the other hand, control and run the business but end up with unlimited liability.

Limited partnership status generally requires a state law filing and a written partnership agreement that spells out the status and role of the general and limited partners. Like a general partnership, this type of entity enjoys the advantages of pass-through taxation, with multiple owners.

> **COMMENT:** One of the key tax differences between a general partnership and a limited partnership structure relates to the passive activity rules. If there is material participation, an activity is not passive; it is active. Therefore, it is more difficult for limited partners to meet the material participation test because they are not very involved with the business.

Limited Liability Company

An LLC is a hybrid business entity that provides the limited liability advantages of a corporation with pass-through tax treatment and flexible operational and governance features. The owners of the LLC are "members," and they all have limited liability. Depending on the state law, an LLC may have a single member or have multiple individuals, corporations, or other LLCs as members. All members have limited liability.

An LLC offers flexibility as to which members are involved in the business and its management, and how the governance structure will work. For example, an LLC can be used to create limited liability for a sole proprietorship. The "check-the-box" rules (discussed later in this chapter) allow a single-member LLC to be a disregarded entity for tax purposes.

LLCs are pass-through entities with the tax attributes of a partnership, or of a sole proprietorship if there is only one owner. Some states may impose state-level taxes on the LLC at the entity level. The advantages and disadvantages of this business type are listed below.

Advantages:

- Limited liability for members.
- Flexibility in economic arrangements (the various members' economic interests) and governance (which members are managing members, and what decision-making authority members have).
- Pass-through taxation unless the owners decide to "check the box" to treat the LLC as a corporation for tax purposes.

Disadvantages:

- State filing as an LLC is required, and filing fees may be collected.
- Limited liability is dependent on observing and maintaining "corporate" formalities required by state law.
- The LLC agreement (often called the *operating agreement*) can be complex, depending on the economics and governance arrangements the members agree upon.
- The LLC may be subject to state or local entity tax.

Corporation

A corporation is an independent legal entity that is owned by shareholders. The shareholders purchase stock of the corporation with money or other assets, and the corporation uses this money for operational purposes. The corporation is a legal "person" and is held legally liable for its actions, debts, and taxes. It is a separate taxpaying entity.

Under the "check-the-box" rules, a business corporation defaults to a corporation for tax purposes and is often referred to as a *C corporation* because it is governed by Subchapter C of the Internal Revenue Code. If eligible, a corporation can elect to be an S corporation that is treated as a modified form of pass-through entity.

C corporations are easy to form but potentially difficult and expensive to get out of, thanks to their double taxation. (C corporations pay corporate-level tax, and their shareholders pay tax on dividends.) Exiting the corporation requires paying a corporate-level tax on any appreciated assets or the business as a whole, unless the business is acquired in a tax-free reorganization.

The advantages of choosing this type of entity include the following:

- Shareholders have limited liability.
- Documentation and governance are typically more straightforward than partnership and LLC operating agreements, but less flexible. The economic arrangement is easier to understand.
- Corporations can raise capital more easily than other entities through sale of stock to shareholders (including public shareholders).
- The corporate tax rate is lower than the top individual tax rates, especially after the TCJA.
- There are no self-employment taxes. The corporation pays the employer's share of employment tax for shareholder-employee.
- It is easier to attract investments from non-U.S. persons and tax-exempt investors who do not typically want U.S. pass-through income.
- Corporations can be acquired in tax-free reorganizations and stock-for-stock exchanges, with no tax to the corporation or shareholders. The rules are generally easier to meet than the requirements for tax-free acquisitions of pass-through entities.
- Unlike other pass-through entities, if the entity plans to go public, it is already organized as a corporation.

However, this form of business entity is not without disadvantages. Perhaps the most obvious is double taxation. In addition, the incorporation process takes time and money. A corporation must file with the secretary of state, and minimum taxes may be imposed at the state level. Also, it is not as flexible as a partnership or LLC to allow complex, non-pro-rata economic arrangements.

One advantageous feature of corporations is qualified small business stock (QSBS). QSBS is stock in a domestic corporation that does not have more than $50 million in assets as of the date the stock was issued and immediately after the issuance. The corporation's assets must be used in an active trade or business. Shareholders that sell QSBS can exclude a portion of the gain on the sale from their federal income if they acquired the stock as part of an original issue (not on secondary market) and they have held it for at least five years when sold. The remaining gain is taxed as capital gain. The excludable percentage ranges from 50 to 100 percent, depending on the rule in place in the year of issuance.

S Corporation

For state law purposes, an S corporation is a corporation that elects to be treated as an S corporation under the Internal Revenue Code. For legal purposes, an S corporation is no different from a C corporation. If an election is made at the outset, the S corporation will generally be treated as a pass-through entity for tax purposes. An S corporation's profits and losses flow through to shareholders and are taxed at the shareholder level, whether or not any cash or property is distributed to them.

One of the benefits of this type of business entity is that distributions of cash generally are not taxed. The rules for basis adjustments for undistributed profits and losses are similar to those for other pass-through entities. Among the disadvantages of this entity type are the restrictions on the ability to make and maintain S corporation status.

- S corporations are allowed to have only a single class of stock, which can be voting and nonvoting, but preferred stock or distribution preferences for certain shareholders are not allowed.
- Ownership is generally restricted to U.S. citizens, estates, and certain types of trusts.
- S corporations generally cannot have more than 100 shareholders.
- Inadvertent violations of these requirements can result in the termination of S corporation status and treatment as a C corporation.
- An S corporation that was formerly a C corporation must keep track of built-in gains at the time of conversion and is subject to corporate-level tax.

STUDY QUESTIONS

1. Which of the following is a *disadvantage* of a general partnership business structure?
    a. The partners share financial commitments.
    b. There is no need for a legal filing.
    c. The actions of any partner can bind the business.
    d. The owners are considered partners.
2. Which of the following is an *advantage* of an LLC business structure?
    a. The owners of the LLC are "members."
    b. An LLC must file with the state in which it will do business.
    c. An LLC can determine how its governance structure will work.
    d. The LLC's operating agreement is typically complex.

¶504

3. Which of the following statements is true regarding silent partners?

    a. A general partnership must have one or more silent partners.

    b. Silent partners cannot be involved in the organization's business.

    c. Silent partners have joint and several liability.

    d. The responsibilities of silent partners are outlined in IRC Subchapter C.

4. A(n) _____ is an independent legal entity owned by shareholders.

    a. Corporation

    b. LLC

    c. General partnership

    d. Limited partnership

¶ 505 EMPLOYMENT TAXES AND EMPLOYEE BENEFITS

This section explains how employment taxes and employee benefits work in the context of different types of entities.

Owner-Employees

Determining whether an owner who provides substantial services to a business entity is also an employee can be difficult. It is often more likely for owners who provide services to a corporation to be treated as employees than for owners of pass-throughs to be treated this way.

A C corporation may offer advantages in this respect, such as employer-provided health insurance that is deductible to the company and not taxable to the employee. Group-term life insurance and other tax-deductible fringe benefits are easy to implement through a C corporation. Owners of pass-through entities, on the other hand, generally cannot receive health benefits and other fringe benefits tax-free. Pass-through owners are generally subject to self-employment tax, whereas a corporate employee is generally liable for only the employee's share of Social Security and Medicare taxes. (The other half is paid by the employer as a deductible expense.) Pass-throughs that are partnerships for tax purposes offer opportunities for service providers to receive equity interests that receive capital gain treatment (profits interests).

In a corporation, officers are paid a salary that is subject to employment taxes. Dividends of retained earnings are subject to income tax (perhaps at capital gain rates) at the shareholder level. In an S corporation, officers are also paid a salary that is subject to employment taxes, but dividends of retained earnings are *not* subject to income tax at the shareholder level, provided there is a sufficient shareholder basis.

In a partnership or LLC, the partners are not employees; amounts that are paid out are considered to be distributions of earnings, unless they qualify as guaranteed payments (partnership profits issued in exchange for services with a partnership-run LLC). Self-employment taxes are imposed on the general partners' share of income. No tax is imposed on distributions, provided there is sufficient outside basis.

Fringe Benefits

In a corporation, nontaxable fringe benefits are available to all shareholders who are also employees. Such benefits cannot be discriminatory in favor of highly compensated employees. With regard to S corporations, shareholders who own 2 percent or more of the business are required to include the value of fringe benefits in their gross income. Similarly, in partnerships and LLCs, all partners are required to include the value of any fringe benefits in their income.

Employment Taxes

Self-employed individuals are required to pay a self-employment tax equivalent to the Federal Insurance Contributions Act (FICA) tax rate. While certain amounts are nontaxable (e.g., rental and dividend income), most earnings are taxable at a rate of 12.4 percent for Social Security tax and 2.9 percent for Medicare tax.

S corporations have a distinct advantage when it comes to self-employment taxes: neither the corporation nor the shareholder has to pay self-employment taxes on *distributions to the owner*. The corporation must withhold payroll taxes from amounts deemed to be wages for any employee-shareholder based on the value of that employee's services. However, the remainder of any distribution is not subject to self-employment or payroll taxes. This can save significant taxes for the owners.

For a single-member LLC, the individual owner is treated as the sole proprietor (unless the entity has elected corporate treatment). For self-employment tax purposes, this means that the entire amount of profits of the LLC is subject to the self-employment tax (limited by the caps on the Social Security portion).

For multimember LLCs and partnerships, the situation is more complicated. Under proposed regulations, the IRS treats LLC members as partners in a limited partnership. Generally, for purposes of the self-employment tax, only the income a limited partner receives for services rendered is taxable. Although there are several exceptions, a member of an LLC typically is treated as a limited partner as long as he or she avoids personal liability for the company, works fewer than 500 hours for the LLC, and avoids general power to contract in the name of the LLC. This situation is much more likely to exist in a "manager-managed" LLC.

Stock Options

One way a corporation can reward its employees is with stock options. Stock options allow employees to share in the growth in value of a company. They also encourage employees to meet the company's goals, and align the employees' interests with those of the shareholders. The following definitions are helpful in understanding stock options:

- **Vesting:** A requirement that an employee works for certain length of time or meets certain performance goals before stock options become exercisable.

- **Strike price:** The price at which an option holder may purchase a share of stock using the option.

- **Spread** or **in-the-money:** The spread is the difference between the strike price and the fair market value of stock on the date of exercise. If a stock option is "in-the-money," the strike price is lower than the fair market value so it looks to be economically sensible to exercise the option.

Code Sec. 83 applies when a taxpayer receives property in exchange for the performance of services. According to Code Sec. 83(a), a taxpayer includes in income the difference between the fair market value of the property and the amount paid, on the date that the property becomes transferable or is no longer subject to a substantial risk of forfeiture. Code Sec. 83 does not consider an option to be "property," so an employee is not taxed until the option is *exercised*. Upon exercise, the employee has property (the stock he purchased). The spread between the strike price and the fair market value on the date of exercise is compensation income.

Profits Interests in Partnerships and LLCs

A profits interest is an interest in the future profits and appreciation of a partnership or LLC; it is not an interest in any liquidating proceeds that would be distributed at the time the interest is granted (Rev. Proc. 93-27).

As long as a service provider is only getting a profits interest, there is no current taxation, and future appreciation is generally capital gain. Note that a profits interest is different from a capital interest. A capital interest is an interest that would give the holder a share of the proceeds if the partnership's assets were sold at fair market value and then the proceeds were distributed in a complete liquidation of the partnership. This determination generally is made at the time of receipt of the partnership interest (Rev. Proc. 93-27).

There used to be a significant difference in treatment between the taxation of capital interests received in exchange for the performance of services, and of profits interest received in similar manner. The taxation now depends on whether the interest is vested or unvested at the time of receipt. Basically, the treatment works the same way as with respect to restricted stock under Code Sec. 83.

Fair market value. One issue that arises in these contexts is fair market value. To calculate the amount of income recognized by the service provider and the corresponding deduction to the partnership, the fair market value of the partnership interest must be determined. This only applies for an interest that is transferred to a service provider by such partnership in connection with services provided to the partnership either in the past or future. Also, a partnership interest will not qualify if it: (1) relates to a substantially certain and predictable stream of income from partnership assets, such as income from high-quality debt securities or a high-quality net lease; (2) is transferred in anticipation of a subsequent disposition; or (3) is an interest in a publicly traded partnership. See Rev. Proc. 93-27, Notice 2005-43 (proposed rules).

Carried interests. Many private equity and hedge fund managers are paid a set percentage management fee, plus a 20 percent "carried interest," which is a profits interest. Thanks to the profits interest rules, they are able to pay tax at a capital gain rate on these carried interests, even though they are arguably receiving the interest in exchange for their management services. Many people have argued that this "loophole" should be closed to require fund managers to pay tax at the ordinary rate on this type of income. President Trump argued for closing this loophole during his campaign, but the TCJA does not do much to address it.

STUDY QUESTION

5. Which of the following statements about self-employment tax is true?

    a. Single-member LLCs are not subject to self-employment tax.

    b. Limited partnerships are not subject to self-employment tax.

    c. S corporations must pay self-employment tax on distributions.

    d. Sole proprietorships must pay self-employment tax.

¶ 506 ENTITY CLASSIFICATION AND CONVERSION

This section explores the rules for entity classification, and how a business entity can convert to another type of business entity if needed.

¶506

Overview

The tax rules for classifying business entities are largely, but not entirely, independent of state law categories. For example:

- A partnership under state law may or may not be a partnership for tax purposes.
- An LLC under state law will never be an LLC for tax purposes; there is no such thing.
- However, a corporation under state law is *generally* always a corporation for tax purposes.

If the tax classification rules seem confusing, remember that there are only three major classifications: corporation, partnership, and nothing (i.e., disregarded entity, which is actually an important category). Before 1997, LLCs were classified as partnerships or corporations. If an LLC lacked two or more of the following four "corporate" characteristics (the "Four-Factor Test"), it was classified as a partnership:

- Continuity of life
- Centralized management
- Limited liability (liability for entity debts limited to entity property)
- Free transferability of interests

Check-the-Box Rules

In 1997, the IRS released a set of regulations (Treas. Reg. §§ 301.7701-1 to -4) designed to alleviate much of the complexity and unpredictability of classifying an entity using the Four-Factor Test. The regulations authorized many business entities, generally including LLCs, to choose whether to be taxed as corporations or partnerships (or sometimes as nothing). The choice is made by checking the appropriate box on IRS Form 8832, *Entity Classification Election.*

Most businesses tend to be satisfied with their "default" classification (the classification they are assigned if they do not file Form 8832), and therefore never literally "check the box."

Important questions to consider with respect to entity classification include the following:

- Is there an entity?
- If there is an entity, is it a business entity or a trust?
- If it is a business entity, is it an eligible entity?
- If it is an eligible entity, what is its "default" classification?
- Has it properly elected a classification other than the "default"?

Is There an Entity?

Making this determination can be tricky because there are no clear rules spelling out whether an entity exists. "Whether an organization is an entity separate from its owners for federal tax purposes is a matter of federal tax law and does not depend on whether the organization is recognized as an entity under local law" (Reg. § 301.7701-1(a)(1)).

Certain joint undertakings give rise to entities for tax purposes that are not entities under state business law, and certain state business law entities are not entities for tax purposes. Absence of a state law entity is *not* dispositive. An entity cannot avoid the complexities of partnership tax merely by refusing to form a state law entity. Presence of a state law entity is *not* dispositive. Especially in tax shelter situations, the courts may refuse to recognize the existence of a tax entity despite the existence of a valid state law entity.

As mentioned previously, there are no hard-and-fast rules for determining if an entity exists. Many relationships can involve some economic sharing, and may or may not be "entities"; for example:

- Debtor/creditor
- Employer/employee
- Lessor/lessee
- Licensor/licensee
- Cost-sharing
- Co-ownership
- Joint production

COMMENT: "The question is . . . whether, considering all the facts—the agreement, the conduct of the parties in execution of its provisions, their statements, the testimony of disinterested persons, the relationship of the parties, their respective abilities and capital contributions, the actual control of income and the purposes for which it is used, and any other facts throwing light on their true intent—the parties in good faith and acting with a business purpose intended to join together in the present conduct of the enterprise" (***Comm'r v. Culbertson,*** 337 US 733 (1949)).

Is It a Business Entity or Trust?

One of the questions that arises is whether something is a business entity or a trust. A *trust* is not one of the business entities discussed in this chapter; instead, it is "an arrangement created either by a will or by an inter vivos declaration whereby trustees take title to property for the purpose of protecting or conserving it for the beneficiaries" (Reg. § 301.7701-4(a)). A trust's purpose is "to vest in trustees responsibility for the protection and conservation of property for beneficiaries who cannot share in the discharge of this responsibility and, therefore, are not associates in a joint enterprise for the conduct of business for profit" (Reg. § 301.7701-4(a)).

A trust is almost like a disregarded entity for tax purposes in that, essentially, everything is taxed to the trust's owner. A *non-grantor trust* is subject to trust tax rates under federal income tax rules. An *investment trust* is a trust if there is a single class of ownership interests, representing undivided beneficial interests in the trust's assets, and there is no power to vary the investment. An investment trust with multiple classes of ownership interests is likely to be a business entity. A *business trust* (sometimes called a *Massachusetts business trust*) is likely to be a business entity.

Is It an "Eligible" Entity?

An eligible entity can select its classification under the check-the-box regulations. It is defined as any business entity other than one that is ineligible. Entities that are ***usually*** eligible include:

- LLCs
- Limited liability partnerships (LLPs)
- Limited liability limited partnerships (LLLPs)
- Limited partnerships
- General partnerships

State law versus tax law. State law partnerships are not necessarily classified as partnerships for tax purposes; in some instances they may be classified as corporations or disregarded entities. LLCs and state law partnerships (limited partnerships, general partnerships, LLPs, LLLPs) are usually considered eligible entities, but not always.

> **OBSERVATION:** One cannot determine the tax classification of an eligible entity just by looking at its characteristics. When buying or selling an LLC or partnership, the tax classification should always be verified in the purchase agreement.

Partnership versus S corporation. The main similarity between partnerships and S corporations is that they are both pass-through entities and are *not* taxed as corporations. However, despite this similarity, there are also some differences. For example:

- S corporations are subject to many of the same Subchapter C tax rules that apply to C corporations. For example, S corporations are subject to the rule that the contributors of property in a tax-free contribution must have 80 percent control of the corporation (Code Sec. 351).

- Entities taxed as partnerships are subject to Subchapter K and *not* to Subchapter C. For example, the contributors of property to a partnership do not need to meet the 80 percent control requirement in order to get tax-free treatment (Code Sec. 721).

Which entities are not eligible? All entities taxed as partnerships have one thing in common: they are not state law "corporations." If an entity has *Inc.* in its name, it is *not* taxed as a partnership. However, if an entity is unincorporated (i.e., is not a state law corporation), one cannot assume that it will be taxed as a partnership.

Corporations under state law are ineligible entities. If an entity is called a corporation under state statute, it is ineligible, regardless of the characteristics of the entity. Other ineligible entities include:

- Insurance companies and banks
- Most publicly traded partnerships, unless 90 percent or more of the gross income is passive (Code Sec. 7704)
- Foreign entities listed in the regulations
- Exempt organizations and government entities
- Specialized forms such as mutual funds and real estate investment trusts (REITs)

Most partnerships are safe under a regulatory "private placement" safe harbor if no interests are required to be registered under the Securities Act of 1933, and there is a 100 partner maximum. Outside of several regulatory safe harbors, the definition of *publicly traded* is unclear.

What Is the Entity's Default Classification?

Once the eligibility of an entity has been determined, its default classification should be considered. A domestic eligible entity is never classified as a corporation by default. If it has two or more members, its default classification is partnership. If it has one member, the default classification is disregarded entity.

Note that a tax advisor's concept of member (or partner) does not always correspond to that under state law. The tax concept is closer to what a business lawyer might call an "economic interest holder" (or owner of an equity interest). For example, a "bankruptcy remote" LLC can be disregarded for federal tax purposes when one of its two members is present simply to prevent bankruptcy filing and has no economic interest (IRS Private Letter Ruling 200201024, October 5, 2001).

¶506

Foreign eligible entities (formed after 1996) are classified as corporations if all members have limited liability. If a foreign eligible entity has two or more members and not all members have limited liability, it is classified as partnership unless it elects otherwise. If there is only one member and that member does not have limited liability, it will be treated as a disregarded entity unless it elects otherwise.

Did the Entity Elect Out of Its Default Classification?

The next question to consider is whether the entity elected out of its default classification. Most domestic entities are happy with their default classification and rarely elect out. However, with the recent reduction of the corporate tax rate, more entities might want to elect out of their default classification and instead be treated as corporations. Because foreign eligible entities can be classified as corporations by default, it is much more common for them to elect out of that classification. Again, the election is made on Form 8832. An eligible entity almost always has the right to elect, on Form 8832, to be classified as an "association" (i.e., corporation). However, only one election is allowed every five years.

Consequences of Checking the Box

The tax consequences of changing an entity's classification by checking the box are generally the same as for entering into an actual transaction—changing classification can have the effect of a taxable transaction with high cost. Entities must be especially cautious before converting from a corporation to another type of entity.

- **Partnership to corporation.** When a partnership converts to a corporation, the partnership is deemed to contribute all of its assets and liabilities to the corporation in exchange for the corporation's stock. Immediately thereafter, the partnership is deemed to liquidate by distributing the stock of the corporation to the partners. These transactions may be tax-free, but check Code Secs. 351, 357(c), 704(c)(1)(B), 707(a)(2)(B), 731, and 737. State law conversions and state law mergers are usually deemed to be assets-over transactions (Rev. Rul. 2004-59, 2004-1 C.B. 1050; Treas. Reg. § 301.7701-3(g)(1)(i)).

- **Corporation to partnership.** When a corporation converts to a partnership, the corporation is deemed to distribute its assets and liabilities to its shareholders in liquidation. The shareholders are then treated as recontributing all the distributed assets and liabilities to the partnership. This conversion is often taxable, so entities must be careful and plan accordingly.

- **Corporation to disregarded entity.** When a corporation converts to a disregarded entity, the corporation is deemed to distribute all of its assets and liabilities to its sole owner in complete liquidation. There is no further deemed step; the sole owner is treated as continuing to own the assets and liabilities. This conversion can be taxable (except usually for corporate subsidiaries).

- **Disregarded entity to corporation.** When a disregarded entity converts to a corporation, the owner of the disregarded entity is deemed to contribute all of the assets and liabilities of the entity to the corporation in exchange for stock of the corporation. The deemed contribution generally will be tax-free if the requirements of Code Secs. 351 and 357(c) are met.

- **Change in number of members.** A disregarded entity becomes classified as a partnership when the entity begins to have more than one member. A partnership becomes a disregarded entity when the entity has only one member left.

Partnership Incorporation

The IRS respects three different forms in which a partnership incorporates (Rev. Rul. 84-111, 1984-2 CB 88):

- Assets-up form
- Assets-over form
- Interest-over form

The IRS respects these forms in the sense that it gives effect to the somewhat different tax consequences of each. Some differences arise because of:

- Disparities between inside basis (basis of the partnership in its assets) and outside basis (basis of the partners in their partnership interests)
- Disparities between inside holding period and outside holding.

An assets-up transaction sometimes offers an entity the opportunity to reduce taxable gain under Code Sec. 357(c) on incorporation. There are also other incidental tax consequences. Incorporation of a partnership into a corporation, under any of these three methods, is often (but not always) tax-free. The reverse is rarely tax-free; extreme caution should be exercised before changing a corporation (even an S corporation) to a partnership.

Generally, provided that the partners will continue to own at least 80 percent of the corporation, the incorporation is tax-free; there are possible exceptions under Code Secs. 357(c), 704(c)(1)(B), 731(c), 737, and 751(b). A taxpayer should choose the method of incorporating based on specific facts.

A partnership merger or conversion into a corporation is not respected as a distinct form but is likely deemed to be assets-over. For an assets-up or interests-over form, an entity should not use a state law merger or conversion.

STUDY QUESTIONS

6. The IRS released the "check-the-box" regulations to:

- **a.** Alleviate the complexity of classifying an entity.
- **b.** Introduce several new entity classifications.
- **c.** Mandate use of the Four-Factor Test.
- **d.** Require all businesses to take action to form an entity.

7. Which of the following statements is true regarding the determination of whether an entity exists?

- **a.** If an entity is determined to exist under state law, the entity exists for federal tax purposes.
- **b.** There are no firm rules for making this determination.
- **c.** Any relationship that involves economic sharing is deemed to be an entity.
- **d.** An entity exists if a business has a physical facility in the United States.

8. Entity AB is a domestic eligible business that has two members. It chooses **not** to classify its business structure. What is its default classification?

- **a.** Corporation
- **b.** Partnership
- **c.** Disregarded entity
- **d.** Trust

9. Which type of entity conversion is *most likely* to have tax consequences?

   a. Partnership to corporation

   b. Disregarded entity to corporation

   c. Corporation to partnership

   d. All of these conversions are taxable.

10. Which of the following entities is typically *eligible* to elect its tax classification?

   a. General partnership

   b. Corporation

   c. Foreign entity

   d. Government entity

¶ 507 CHOICE OF ENTITY EFFECTS ON INCOME TAXES AND OTHER CONSIDERATIONS

This section discusses how its choice of entity can affect a business's income taxes, as well as other considerations. The following simple scenarios illustrate the basic tax consequences in several situations.

EXAMPLE 1: C corporation: Double taxation example—ordinary income:

Business A has revenues of $200 and expenses of $100. Its net income is $100, and the corporate tax rate is imposed: 100×21 percent = $21. The amount of $79 is distributed to the shareholder. Tax of 23.8 percent (20 percent capital gain rate + 3.8 percent Medicare tax) is imposed on the dividend, = $18.80. $60.20 remains for the shareholder after both levels of tax.

Business A must consider the time value of money. Does the money have to be distributed to shareholders right away? What if Business A just pays the corporate-level tax of 21 percent and leaves the $79 there to grow, perhaps to put it to use in the business?

EXAMPLE 2: Pass-through entity: Single taxation example—ordinary income:

Business B has revenues of $200 and expenses of $100. Its net income is $100, and it has no entity-level tax. The full $100 passes through to the owner, whether or not it is distributed. Assuming a 37 percent tax rate, $63 remains for the owner: $100 – $37 = $63.

Recall that in Example 1, $60.20 remained for the shareholder. Here, the owner is left with $63, so the amounts are close. Note that this example does not account for the 20 percent potential deduction under Code Sec. 199A.

EXAMPLE 3: C corporation: Double taxation example—capital gain:

The amount realized from Business C's sale of a capital asset is $200. Business C's tax basis in the asset is $100, so it has a net gain of $100. Corporate tax of 21 percent ($21) is imposed, leaving $79 distributed to the shareholder. Subtracting the 23.8 percent tax on the dividend, $60.20 remains for the shareholder after both levels of tax: $79 – $18.80 = $60.20.

This example illustrates that for the corporation, there is no advantage to the fact that it held the capital gain; it will be taxed at $60.20, the same rate as in Example 1.

EXAMPLE 4: Pass-through entity: Single taxation example—capital gain:

The amount realized from Business D's sale of a capital asset is $200. Business D's tax basis in the asset is $100, so it has a net gain of $100. The $100 passes through to the owner. The capital gain tax rate is 20 percent, so $80 remains for the owner: $100 – $20 = $80.

Note: This example assumes active participation by the owner to avoid application of the 3.8 percent net investment income tax.

When considering the best choice of entity, a business must take into account how it will be making money, including whether it expects to have a large capital gain transaction from selling an asset.

Other Specialty Forms of Ownership

In addition to the business formats already discussed, there are other specialty forms of ownership. In some cases, people may not want to form an entity, particularly if there is a very limited purpose for which they are engaging in the venture. For example, they could own property as joint tenants or as tenants in common without forming a legal entity. This type of joint ownership is usually used for real estate or securities. Although it is easy to document, it offers no liability protection and is generally ignored for tax purposes.

A REIT is created to allow investors to invest in real estate funds that invest in real estate assets. In other words, rather than investing directly in those real estate funds, the investors can invest in a funded real estate asset. REITs are essentially tax advantageous pass-through structures. One downside is that there are many technical requirements. Generally, the income will pass through to investors, but the losses will not. There is a single level of tax just at the investor level. Any dividends will not be qualified dividends, so the ordinary rate will apply to those.

Pass-Through of Losses

When thinking about the choice of entity, a business should also consider pass-through of losses.

Pass-through entities typically will allow losses to pass through to the owners to the extent of their basis in the S corporation stock or LLC or partnership interest. LLCs and partnerships allow entity debt to count as basis, including a partner's share of nonrecourse debt. However, S corporations do not allow entity debt to count toward shareholder basis. For them, is will be either recourse debt for which the shareholder is personally liable or loans from the S corporation to the shareholder.

Outside Investors

C corporations can issue convertible preferred stock, which is the typical vehicle for a venture capital investment or private equity types of investment. Investors who do not want to be taxed on the entity's income (e.g., foreign investors or nonprofits) may refuse to invest through a pass-through. They will not want a Schedule K-1. Sometimes they invest in pass-through operating entities through a "blocker corporation" to block the pass-through income. The owners of the blocker corporation can essentially stay anonymous and not have to file any tax returns in the United States or whatever state they are trying to avoid.

¶507

Exit Strategy

Another factor that should be taken into account in terms of choice of entity is exit strategy. This can come into play, for example, if a business is planning to do an initial public offering and corporate status is necessary. Noncorporate entities are more flexible in terms of exit; many offer capital gain. Some can be tax-free if there is continuing investment.

C corporations, and S corporations for which an election has been revoked, may take part in tax-free mergers and acquisitions. If the business is a partnership or an LLC, doing so will be much more difficult. Noncorporate entities are easier to split apart.

Tax Distributions

Pass-through entities often need to make "tax distributions" of cash to allow owners to pay taxes. Even though there is no business-level tax with respect to pass-through entities, they may be pressured by their owners to do the equivalent of paying the tax, which is to make tax distributions to the members. This issue should be taken into account when forming a new LLC or partnership. The partnership agreement should spell out how tax distributions will be handled.

Because all the taxes are supposed to be paid out at the corporate level, C corporations do not get pressure from shareholders to do this. However, they do need to ensure that cash is available to pay the corporate-level tax.

Tax Complexity

When determining the right entity choice, businesses should consider the complexity of their tax returns and their investor/owners' appetite for complicated tax structure. Pass-through entities generally have more complicated structures, with consequences for owners. A level of sophistication is needed. For example, each investor will get a Schedule K-1, which typically requires professional tax preparation assistance. Also, reading and understanding the provisions regarding tax allocations may be confusing. Finally, changes to debts of pass-through entities may have consequences for owners.

Basis Step-Up

Basis step-up is a less apparent consideration when one thinks about choice of entity. It is easier to get a basis step-up in the "outside basis" in a partnership and LLC interest. There are provisions that allow one to make adjustments of the outside basis fairly easily. It is very difficult to change stock basis in C corporation.

Partnership rules allow "booking up" capital accounts to reflect changes in value upon entry of new partners and other events. Partners essentially can give themselves more basis credit as the partnership increases in value. A C corporation will have low inside basis as well, particularly if it has held its assets for a period of time or has depreciated those assets. However, those cannot be "booked up" as easily as with a partnership.

Other LLC Advantages

An LLC can allow special allocations of gain and loss to specific partners that can be different from their pro-rata ownership, offering a great deal of flexibility. Also, appreciated property can be distributed to owners without double taxation. And as mentioned earlier, profits interests allow equity compensation with capital gain treatment.

¶507

¶ 508 TAX CUTS AND JOBS ACT EFFECTS ON CHOICE OF ENTITY CONSIDERATIONS

The TCJA (P.L. 115-97), which became law on December 22, 2017, amended the Internal Revenue Code of 1986. Significant changes in the legislation that affect choice of entity considerations include the following:

Corporate tax rate reduction. The reduction, from a graduated scale of 15 percent to 35 percent in 2017, to a flat rate of 21 percent in 2018, makes double taxation less costly, especially for businesses that do not plan to make distributions to shareholders. And because the top individual tax rates are much higher, the corporate tax rate reduction might make a C corporation structure more desirable that than of a sole proprietorship. The reduction might also make corporations a much more attractive structure for businesses that have a tax-free acquisition plan as their exit strategy.

Pass-through deduction. This change can affect an entity's overall tax rate as well as its choice of business entity. The TCJA offers pass-through entities a significant benefit. Under the legislation, they can deduct 20 percent of their qualified business income (Code Section 199A). The deduction is subject to several limitations; three main exceptions are service businesses, W-2 and capital expenditures, and compensatory payments. The types of entities that are covered by Code Sec. 199A include sole proprietorships, disregarded entities/single-member LLCs, multimember LLCs and partnerships, any entity that is taxed as an S corporation, REITs, trusts and estates, and certain business cooperatives.

For a single taxpayer, the pass-through deduction starts to phase out at income of $157,500 and is completely phased out at $207,500. For married couples, it begins to phase out at $315,000 and is completely phased out at $415,000. If taxable income is below those thresholds, taxpayers will be able to take advantage of the deduction. Taxpayers in specified service trades or businesses (e.g., doctors, attorneys, accountants, actuaries and consultants, performing artists, paid athletes, people who work in the financial services or brokerage industry, and any trade or business where the principal asset is reputation or skill) are subject to a different income threshold.

> **EXAMPLE:** For example, assume a business has revenues of $200 and expenses of $100. Its net income is $100. The 20 percent pass-through deduction leaves the business with $80 in taxable income. The 37 percent tax rate results in tax of $29.60, with after-tax cash of $70.40 resulting to owner. (Contrast that with $63 under the old law and $60.20 with corporate tax.)

SALT deduction limit. Under the TCJA, the SALT deduction is limited to $10,000 for individuals, but corporations can deduct unlimited SALT and property taxes, which may affect the choice of entity decision for some entities. For example, for a business operating as a sole proprietorship that is paying a great deal in state taxes, those will be limited to what it can deduct on its federal return. But if the business is a C corporation, it will be able to deduct its SALT. This may encourage some sole proprietorships to convert to corporation status.

Repeal of corporate AMT. The TCJA repealed the corporate AMT for tax years beginning after December 31, 2017. It allows a corporation to use its prior AMT carryover credits to offset its current and future income tax. This is another change that may make the corporation a much more attractive entity choice than it used to be.

Bonus depreciation. The TCJA expanded the bonus depreciation percentage from 50 percent to 100 percent for qualified property. This allows immediate expensing of tangible personal property at 100 percent of the cost in the year in which it is placed into service. As a result, more businesses might be interested in a pass-through structure so they can immediately take that deduction themselves, especially in light of activity rules that might permit those losses. The change in bonus depreciation may mean that more businesses will be in a loss position for the next five years because they are getting large depreciation deductions. Starting in 2023, the bonus depreciation will be gradually phased out.

NOL deduction. Under the TCJA, most entities no longer have the option to carry back NOLs; they can only be carried forward. The new law limits the NOL deduction to 80 percent of taxable income. The limitations on the ability to deduct NOLs might affect choice of entity in terms of how a business takes advantage of those NOLs. The new excess business loss rules that apply to non-C corporation taxpayers limit their ability to consolidate business losses with income from other activities

Businesses have these developments as well as many other factors to consider regarding entity type. Other issues to consider when making an entity choice include the following:

- Whether the business generates many losses and, if so, whether those losses are useful when they pass through
- Code Sec. 1202 qualified small business stock and the 100 percent exclusion on the capital gain
- Financial investors' desire for preferred returns
- The business's exit strategy
- What the business wants in terms of equity-based compensation arrangements
- Capital generation of business: growth or dividends?
- Salary obligations
- Whether the business is an international businesses (if so, consider the international tax rules)

STUDY QUESTIONS

---

11. Which of the following statements is true about the SALT deduction under the TCJA?

    a. The new SALT deduction will encourage corporations to convert to sole proprietorships.

    b. Under the TCJA, a C corporation can deduct unlimited SALT.

    c. The TCJA repealed the SALT deduction for certain entities.

    d. The TCJA raised the SALT deduction for individuals to $100,000.

12. Which of the following statements about a real estate investment trust (REIT) is correct?

    a. A REIT is not a pass-through structure.

    b. REITs were established in 2017 by the TCJA.

    c. REITs are simple to set up and have few requirements.

    d. A REIT is not eligible to elect its entity classification.

MODULE 2: DEVLOPMENTS IMPACTING BUSINESS ENTITIES—Chapter 6: Sale of Closely Held Businesses

¶ 601 WELCOME

This chapter addresses common tax issues that arise in the sale of nonpublic companies and other closely held businesses, including the tax treatment of stock sales and asset sales, the election under Code Sec. 338(h)(10) and the allocation of purchase price, escrow arrangements and earnouts, and the tax treatment of intellectual property and intangible assets.

¶ 602 LEARNING OBJECTIVES

Upon completion of this chapter, you will be able to:

- Differentiate tax treatment between stock sales and asset sales
- Identify when a Code Sec. 338(h)(10) election should be made and describe its consequences
- Describe how earnouts and other contingent purchase price transactions are treated under tax rules
- Identify special rules regarding taxation of intangible assets
- Recognize the business consequences of a stock sale
- State which Internal Revenue Code section states that the buyer and seller shall allocate the purchase price in the manner prescribed in Code Sec. 338(b)(5)
- Identify which asset class is allocated last with respect to a purchase price allocation as required by Internal Revenue Code Sec. 1060
- Recognize which type of property is a capital asset
- Identify what is considered a related party under Internal Revenue Code Sec. 267(b)
- Recognize when Section 197 intangibles, which include covenants not to compete, are amortizable
- Differentiate Internal Revenue Code sections and how they apply to a sale of a business

¶ 603 INTRODUCTION

The sale of closely held businesses raises a large number of challenging tax issues. For example, some sales proceeds are taxed at ordinary income rates rather than capital gain. The structure of the sales transaction affects the buyer's depreciation and amortization going forward. And a purchaser may or may not be able to deduct transaction fees related to the acquisition.

For tax and business law purposes, the form of a transaction matters. An incorporated business can sell stock or have the corporation sell its assets. S corporations can also do stock sales but elect to treat them as asset sales. A limited liability company (LLC) can sell the LLC interests or sell its assets. Even though an LLC is not incorporated, it is similar to C corporations and S corporations in that either assets or interests can be sold.

¶ 604 STOCK SALE VERSUS ASSET SALE

From a business and legal standpoint, it is very easy to effectuate and implement a stock sale. A business would have a simple stock purchase agreement and get the shareholders to agree to sell the stock. There is typically no need to transfer any licenses, permits, or contracts.

For tax purposes, it is much more complicated to sell multiple assets than it is to sell stock. Therefore, an asset sale is much more complicated to effectuate than a stock sale. Generally, a purchase agreement covers multiple assets, but the assets must be listed and scheduled out. Many may require special real estate transfers of deeds, and other property may be difficult to transfer as well. In addition, real property may be subject to transfer taxes, so if a lot of real property is involved, an asset sale could be difficult.

An asset sale is generally good for the buyer but not as good for the seller. The seller must look at the character of the assets and treat each sale of an asset as its own individual sale with tax consequences.

The business and tax consequences of a stock sale and an asset sale include the following:

Stock Sale

- Business consequences
  - The sale is easy to implement with a simple purchase agreement.
  - There is no need to transfer licenses, permits, or contracts (which may be non-assignable).
  - The purchaser will be subject to all of the business's liabilities.
- Tax consequences
  - The sale will produce all capital gain for the seller (typically long-term capital gain). Certain "hot asset" rules may change this for LLC interests.
  - The buyer will not get a basis step-up in assets for the purchase price. Instead, it will have a high stock basis. However, the corporation's basis in its assets will stay the same.

Asset Sale

- Business consequences
  - It is more complicated to sell multiple assets.
  - Can have a purchase agreement covering multiple assets, but the assets must be listed and scheduled out
  - Real property will need deed transfers and may be subject to transfer and other taxes.
  - It may be difficult to transfer licenses, permits, or contracts (some of which may be non-assignable).
  - The purchaser may be able to leave old liabilities behind; however, some successor liability statutes make this difficult.
- Tax consequences
  - Typically, there are no asset sales of a C corporation because double taxation is too costly.
  - For S corporations and LLCs, the tax consequences will depend on the character of the underlying assets.

- Depreciation recapture, inventory, and accounts receivable will produce ordinary income that will pass through to the seller.
- The buyer will get a basis step-up in assets for the purchase price.
- The excess purchase price over the aggregate fair market value of other assets will be allocated to goodwill.
- The buyer will be able to depreciate using a new increased asset basis, and some assets may qualify for bonus depreciation.
- Goodwill may be amortized over 15 years.

EXAMPLE: Purchaser P wants to buy a business for $1 million based on a discounted cash flow price. The fair market value of the hard assets (real estate, equipment, and accounts receivable) is $250,000, and there is an additional $750,000 for goodwill. The real estate and equipment have zero basis.

If the purchaser buys stock, the business will not have depreciation deductions to increase its after-tax return. If the purchaser buys the assets, it can depreciate nearly $1 million of basis. The real estate will be depreciable over 39 years (assuming it is nonresidential real estate). The equipment will probably give immediate 100 percent bonus depreciation, and the goodwill will be amortized over 15 years. This will increase the after-tax return on the purchase of the business. The "cost" is that the tax on the asset sale will not all be capital gain.

If a "business" is sold in an asset sale (rather than stock of a corporation or a partnership or LLC interest), the "business" cannot be treated as a single asset. Instead, the total aggregate purchase price must be allocated among all of the assets, and the character of the gain or loss on each asset must be determined separately. This applies if an individual, a corporation, or a partnership sells its assets.

¶ 605 CODE SEC. 1060 PURCHASE PRICE ALLOCATION

Code Sec. 1060 states that the buyer and the seller shall allocate the purchase price in the manner prescribed in Code Sec. 338(b)(5). Treas. Reg. §1.338-6 and §1.338-7 provide more detail, as do the Treasury Regulations under Code Sec. 1060. In general, these regulations provide that the purchase price shall be allocated in order of certain asset classes, from the most liquid and easiest to value to the least liquid and hardest to value, in accordance with each asset's purchase price. The Code Sec. 1060 allocation order is as follows:

- Class I: Cash
- Class II: Actively traded personal property (readily tradeable securities) and certificates of deposit and foreign currency
- Class III: Assets the taxpayer marks to market and debt instruments (including accounts receivable)
- Class IV: Inventory
- Class V: Everything that is not in another class
- Class VI: Section 197 intangibles other than goodwill and going concern
- Class VII: Goodwill and going concern (whether amortizable or not). This ensures that the purchase premium is allocated to goodwill.

As already mentioned, the regulations require the buyer and seller to agree on an allocation of purchase price for an asset sale transaction. Both parties must file a statement setting forth the allocation with their tax returns for the year of sale. The parties are bound by such allocation, but the IRS is not, and it may challenge it if it wishes. Often, parties wait until it is time to file the tax returns to think about this agreement on purchase price allocation. At that point, the buyer has the business and the seller has his or her money, and no one has any incentive to negotiate. For this reason, tax practitioners should try to persuade clients to get at least a "big picture" agreement on purchase price allocation, as the consequences are important.

> **EXAMPLE:** Buyer B is purchasing all the assets of a dental practice and plans on allocating a large amount of the purchase price to dental imaging equipment that has been fully depreciated by the seller. Buyer B wants to take bonus depreciation in the year of purchase. However, the seller thinks that most of the purchase price should be allocated to goodwill, based on the large number of patients and business practices. Allocating to the imaging equipment would create ordinary income for the seller, rather than capital gain as the goodwill would.

> If the parties do not discuss this at the time of the transaction, it will be difficult for them to come to an agreement. At the time of the deal, other concessions can be made to compensate the "losing" party.

STUDY QUESTIONS

1. Which of the following is true regarding the business consequences of a stock sale?

    a. Liabilities may be left behind.

    b. Deed transfers for real property will be required.

    c. It is easy to implement.

    d. It is complicated to implement.

2. Which Internal Revenue Code section states that the buyer and seller shall allocate the purchase price in the manner prescribed in Code Sec. 338(b)(5)?

    a. 197

    b. 1060

    c. 1221

    d. 1222

3. With respect to a purchase price allocation as required by Code Sec. 1060, which of the following asset classes is allocated last?

    a. Cash

    b. Goodwill

    c. Inventory

    d. Section 197 Intangibles

¶ 606 CHARACTER OF BUSINESS ASSETS

In an asset sale or a deemed asset sale, the character of the assets will determine the tax consequences, and whether there is ordinary income or capital gain. Code Sec. 1222 defines *capital gain* as gain from the sale or exchange of a capital asset. Code Sec. 1221 defines a *capital asset* as property held by the taxpayer, *except* for the following:

- Inventory or property held for sale to customers in the ordinary course of business
- Depreciable or real property used in a trade or business

- Certain copyrights or literary properties
- Accounts or notes receivable acquired in the ordinary course of trade or business
- Certain U.S. government publications
- Certain commodity derivative financial instruments held by dealers
- Hedging transactions identified as such in advance
- Supplies of a type regularly used or consumed by the taxpayer in the ordinary course of business

All other assets are capital gain assets. Although Code Sec. 1221 purports to list all the exceptions to capital asset status, some judicial doctrines also carve certain assets out of capital asset treatment. The idea is that all "property" held by the taxpayer is a capital asset unless it meets one of the exceptions, but certain assets should not be considered "property." Therefore, the courts developed a doctrine that there is no capital gain treatment for "substitutes for ordinary income."

Sale of Contract Rights

To determine whether the sale of a contract right produces capital gain, one must consider whether all that is being sold is the "mere" right to receive income or profits, or whether the contract right also includes something more. In the law, these special rights are called *equitable rights* because they are so important that they cannot be protected or enforced with money alone. Examples of capital asset contract rights include the right to produce a play, the right to prevent the making of a film until the play has run for a period of time, a franchisee's right to an exclusive territory, or a right of first refusal. Examples of a "mere" right to receive profits and thus ordinary assets include the sale of mortgage service agreements, a payment to cancel a professor's tenure, and a right to a percentage of movie profits.

Patents

Even though a patent may be created largely through personal efforts (such as a copyright or artistic creation), it results in capital gain treatment as long as there is a sale and not just a license. A license results in ordinary income treatment, whereas a sale results in capital gain treatment. A sale has occurred if the holder transfers all substantial rights to the patent (in time, territory, and benefits and burdens of ownership). It does not matter if payment is received in lump sum or in royalty form; what matters is that all substantial rights are transferred. For example, if a patent holder sells the right to exploit a patent throughout the world other than in Asia, that is a license with ordinary income treatment because the patent holder did not transfer all substantial rights.

Covenant Not to Compete

Another type of asset that raises questions of character is a covenant not to compete. Covenants not to compete often exist in the context of a business. In the past, buyers wanted to allocate the purchase price of an asset sale to covenants not to compete so as to amortize the assets over the remaining useful life. However, sellers disliked this method because covenants not to compete produce ordinary income. Code Sec. 197 now treats covenants not to compete as Section 197 intangibles, amortizable over 15 years rather than over the term of covenant.

Now, however, both parties typically avoid allocating to covenant not to compete; sellers dislike doing so and buyers are indifferent. The IRS occasionally challenges this method, stating that some amount must be allocated to covenant not to compete. In some cases, the parties will have the seller enter into a "consulting agreement" to consult about business and also about covenant not to compete. This can be deducted currently by the buyer as it is paid, rather than being capitalized and amortized over 15 years.

Goodwill

The amount that a buyer of assets pays over the fair market value of the tangible assets will be allocated to intangible assets in Class VI and then to goodwill. A taxpayer does not generally capitalize costs incurred for self-created goodwill, but will allocate the purchase price for purchased goodwill. Pursuant to Code Sec. 197, goodwill may be amortized over 15 years. Note that it can be difficult to distinguish between contract rights (the sale of which produces ordinary income to the seller) and goodwill (which produces capital gain). Existing business relationships contribute to the value of goodwill, but existing contracts at particular prices that will produce specific amounts of revenue are ordinary income assets. Often, parties will attempt to place a low value on contract rights and a higher value on goodwill.

Medicare Tax

Also relevant to the discussion of the character of assets and capital gain or ordinary income is the 3.8 percent Medicare tax on unearned income, sometimes called the *net investment income tax*. Although it is phrased as a Medicare "contribution" of 3.8 percent, the tax is mandatory.

The Medicare tax applies to individuals, estates, and trusts. For individuals, it applies to the lesser of "unearned" net investment income or modified adjusted gross income (MAGI) greater than $200,000 ($250,000 for married taxpayers). MAGI is AGI increased by certain foreign source income, generally foreign source income excluded under Code Sec. 911. For trusts, the Medicare contribution applies to the lesser of undistributed net investment income or the excess of AGI greater than $11,950. Income that is distributed is taxed to beneficiaries. Grantor trusts are taxed to the owners.

Code Sec. 1411 imposes the 3.8 percent Medicare tax on net gain attributable to the disposition of property, other than property held in a nonpassive or nontrading trade or business. The "look-through" rule applies when selling an interest in a partnership or LLC. The taxpayer is treated as though the entity sold all of its assets and gain/loss passed through to the taxpayer. Many have criticized the regulations for adding too much complexity and administrative cost. The rules reference the passive activity rules in Code Sec. 469 to determine if the assets sold (or deemed sold) are held in a nonpassive trade or business. This makes the passive activity rules relevant for taxpayers who may not have worried about it before, because there are no losses.

STUDY QUESTIONS

4. Which of the following types of property is a capital asset?
    a. Real estate
    b. Inventory
    c. Certain U.S. government publications
    d. Notes receivable acquired in the ordinary course of a trade or business

5. With respect to the net investment income tax, which of the following statements with respect to individuals is true?

   a. Single filers will be subject to the tax if adjusted gross income is $200,000 or more.

   b. Individuals who file with the Married Filing Separate status will be subject to the tax if adjusted gross income is $150,000 or more.

   c. Couples filing Married Filing Joint will be subject to the tax if their modified adjusted gross income is $250,000 or more.

   d. Couples filing Married Filing Joint will be subject to the tax if their adjusted gross income is $275,000 or more.

6. Trusts are subject to the net investment income tax, which applies to the lesser of: (i) undistributed net investment income; or (ii) the excess of AGI that is greater than _____.

   a. $11,950

   b. $12,750

   c. $37,000

   d. $125,000

¶ 607 SECTION 338(h)(10) ELECTION: DEEMED ASSET SALE

In some cases, a buyer might want the ease and business advantages of stock transaction, but the basis step-up from an asset purchase. Code Sec. 338(h)(10) allows the buyer and seller to elect to treat a transaction as an asset sale for tax purposes, even though it is a stock sale in the "real world." The Section 338(h)(10) election can only be made for a "qualified stock purchase" (at least 80 percent of stock) by one corporation of another corporation. The election must be made on Form 8023 by the 15th day of the 9th month following the acquisition.

This election is rarely made for C corporations because double taxation makes it prohibitive—unless the C corporation has net operating losses to absorb gain from the deemed asset sale. However, the election is often made for S corporations because they offer pass-through taxation. Typically, the only difference in tax to the selling shareholders is the difference between capital gain and ordinary income on any ordinary income assets. For tax purposes, it is treated as though the S corporation sold all of its assets to a fictional new S corporation in exchange for the transaction consideration.

The gain from such asset sale flows through to the shareholders, and the character will depend on which assets were sold. The gain that flows through will increase the shareholders' basis in their S corporation stock. Then, the original S corporation is considered to have liquidated, distributing whatever it received to the shareholders in redemption of their stock. Any gain on this piece would be capital gain to the shareholders. However, there might not be gain on this piece depending on the shareholders' basis.

¶ 608 DEFERRED PAYMENTS IN SALE OF BUSINESS: INSTALLMENT SALES AND EARNOUTS

An installment sale is a disposition of property in which at least one payment will be received in a taxable year beyond the year of sale. The recognition of gain may be deferred under the "open transaction doctrine" or the installment sale rules under Code Sec. 453.

Consider a taxpayer that sells all of the stock in his business for a note for $1,000,000 due in five years. If the fair market value of the note is ascertainable, the taxpayer must calculate and recognize gain in the year of sale, even if he could only sell the note to a bank for $.50 on the dollar (or not at all). According to Treas. Reg. § 1.1001-1(g), the fair market value of the note will be presumed to be $1,000,000. How will the taxpayer pay the tax? How will he actually collect on the note?

Code Sec. 453 and the installment sale rules are Congress's compromise position. The taxpayer can wait to report gain until he actually collects on the note, *but* he must allocate basis ratably between all payments rather than recovering all basis first, as in so-called open transaction treatment, which applies only in rare circumstances. The installment method automatically applies unless the taxpayer elects out under Code Sec. 453(d).

How to Apply the Installment Method

The installment method is applied by following three basic steps:

1. If the note does not bear adequate stated interest, the taxpayer must apply the original issue discount (OID) rules under Code Sec. 1274 to determine if there is any hidden interest in the purchase price.
2. Compute the taxpayer's gain on the transaction, and the ratio of the gain to the total amount received; this is the gross profit ratio.
3. Apply that gross profit ratio to each payment to be received, to determine the amount of gain in each payment.

EXAMPLE: A sells stock to B for $100,000, with $10,000 payable at closing and the remainder in equal installments over the next nine years. The transaction is evidenced by a note with adequate stated interest. A's basis in the stock is $40,000. The gain, or gross profit, equals $60,000 ($100,000 – $40,000). The contract price, or total amount received, is $100,000.

The gross profit ratio equals $60,000/$100,000, or 60 percent. Thus, of every payment received, 60 percent ($6,000) will be gain, and 40 percent ($4,000) will be basis recovery.

What if a taxpayer sells all of the stock in her business for $3 million plus an earnout payment equal to 5 percent of the business's net income for the next four years? Assume her stock basis is $500,000. Although the open transaction doctrine allows the taxpayer to wait to report gain until she has collected her entire basis, the IRS regulations provide that the open transaction doctrine is only available in rare and extraordinary cases in contingent sale transactions in which the fair market value of the contingent payment right cannot reasonably be ascertained. Instead, the taxpayer should use the contingent payment installment sale regulations.

The treatment of contingent payment sales under the installment sale rules is described in Temp. Reg. § 15a.453-1(c)(2). If the contract provides a maximum sales price, it is treated as the contract price in computing the gross profit ratio (e.g., $3 million + 5 percent of sales up to a maximum of $500,000). If there is no maximum selling price, but a fixed term, the basis should be allocated ratably over the fixed term (i.e., $3 million + 5 percent of sales each year for the next four years). If there is neither a maximum selling price nor a fixed term, the basis should be allocated ratably over 15 years.

EXAMPLE: Taxpayer S sells all the stock in her business for $3 million plus 5 percent of net income for the next four years. Her stock basis is $500,000. Under the contingent payment installment sale rules, the taxpayer must spread her basis over a total of five years, which equals $100,000 per year. She will have $2.9 million of gain in the year of sale. If Taxpayer S collects nothing else under the earnout, she can then take a loss for the $400,000 of unrecovered basis.

EXAMPLE: Taxpayer T sells all of the stock in his business for $3 million plus 5 percent of income in perpetuity. His stock basis is $500,000. Under the contingent payment installment sale rules, Taxpayer T must spread his basis over a total of 15 years because there is no fixed price or fixed time period. His basis will be $33,333 per year. Taxpayer T will have $2.966 million of gain in the year of sale. If he collects nothing else under the earnout, he can then take a loss for the $466,666 of unrecovered basis after 15 years.

Lesson: Taxpayers should not add a contingent earnout piece to their sale unless they think it will earn them something. Otherwise, taxpayers are just pushing basis recovery into the future.

Limitations on the Use of the Installment Method

Use of the installment method is limited to certain situations. The installment method may *not* be used to defer gain on:

- Publicly traded property (Code Sec. 453(k)).
- Dealer dispositions (including real property held for sale in ordinary course of trade or business). There are some exceptions if the taxpayer elects to pay an interest charge on the deferral.
- Inventory of personal property, including bulk sales of inventory in the context of sale of a business.
- Depreciation recapture. There is no installment sale treatment for the portion of gain that must be recaptured as ordinary income under Code Sec. 1245.

Note that these exceptions apply in the context of a "bulk sale," such as the sale of all of the assets of a business.

Interest Charge on Large Installment Sales

Under Code Sec. 453A, a taxpayer must pay interest on tax deferred under the installment method if:

- The sale price of the property is greater than $150,000, and
- Outstanding installment obligations that arose during the year and are outstanding during the year exceed $5 million.

Interest is calculated at the underpayment rate under Code Sec. 6621.

EXAMPLE: Taxpayer Q sells stock in his company for $30 million, with $10 million to be paid at the date of sale and $20 million to be paid in 5 years' time. The note bears adequate stated interest, and the stock basis was $5 million. The gross profit ratio equals 25/30, or 83 percent. The taxpayer has $8.3 million of gain in the year of sale, and $16.6 million of gain in 5 years.

Code Sec. 453A imposes an interest charge on $3.3 million of tax on the deferred gain at the capital gain rate of 20 percent, times the "applicable percentage" of the excess installment note. Here, 15/20 is the excess installment note, so 75 percent of the 3.3 million tax is subject to the interest charge, $2.5 million. Interest is charged each year on $2.5 million at the underpayment rate.

Installment Sale Rules Applied to the Sale of a Business

In a sale of stock by shareholders, the treatment is fairly straightforward: simply apply the installment method to the shareholder gain on the sale of the stock. But how is the installment method applied to a sale of multiple assets, especially when some of them are ineligible for the installment method (e.g., depreciation recapture and inventory)? Does the taxpayer have to allocate cash and installment note pro rata to each asset? Or,

¶608

can the taxpayer choose to recognize low taxed capital gain (i.e., on goodwill) and defer higher taxed gain (such as unrecaptured depreciation on real estate taxed at 25 percent)? Consider the following example.

EXAMPLE: Seller M sells his business for $3 million, with $1 million paid in cash and $2 million in a note (bearing adequate stated interest) due in three years. The transaction is structured as a true asset sale. (Alternatively, it could be an S corporation stock sale with a Code Sec. 338(h)(10) election.)

The taxpayer's tangible assets are as follows:

- Accounts receivable: $200,000 basis, $250,000 fair market value
- Inventory: $100,000 basis, $250,000 fair market value
- Trucks: $50,000 basis, $250,000 fair market value ($150,000 prior depreciation deduction)
- Building: $200,000 basis, $1 million fair market value ($500,000 prior depreciation deduction)

The taxpayer must allocate the $3 million purchase price among all assets in accordance with fair market value (per the instructions in Code Sec. 1060).

- The $50,000 gain on receivables is ordinary income.
- The $150,000 gain on inventory is ineligible for the installment method.
- $150,000 of the $200,000 gain on trucks is ineligible for the installment method.
- $500,000 of the $800,000 gain on the real estate will be taxed at the 25 percent rate.
- $1.250 million of the purchase price will be allocated to goodwill with zero basis.
- This will be taxed at the 20 percent capital gain rate.

How much choice does the taxpayer have in allocating the $1 million cash and $2 million note among the assets? Does each asset have to be one-third cash and two-thirds note? The installment sale rules are silent on this matter. There is nothing that says that the taxpayer may not allocate the cash and note in the manner that is most beneficial to the taxpayer. There is an IRS publication that says the taxpayer "should" allocate the cash and note between the assets in accordance with fair market values. Still, some commentators think that allocating the note in the most beneficial manner is fine.

In general, the taxpayer should allocate the note to the real estate (high taxed, yet still eligible for the installment method) or the goodwill—and not to the inventory, accounts receivable, or trucks.

Sale of a Business

Representations and warranties. In a purchase agreement, the seller typically makes numerous representations to the buyer about the financial condition of the business, the disclosure of all potential liabilities, compliance with regulations and laws, and so on. The seller also provides warranties and covenants about what the seller will do and refrain from doing between the time the agreement is signed and the sale closes. The representations are statements, and the warranties are promises to do or not do something.

"Baskets." If the seller "breaches" these representations and warranties (i.e., has not told the truth in its representations or has not done what it promised to do) and the buyer is harmed, the buyer can collect under the purchase agreement on the theory that he overpaid for the business due to these breaches. Often there are caps on how much a buyer can claim due to breaches of representations and warranties, and sometimes there are "baskets" with certain amounts allocated to different sections of the agreement or different types of liabilities. For example, the "environmental" basket could have a cap of $250,000, and the "taxes" basket could have a cap of $250,000.

Escrow accounts. To protect the buyer and make it easier for him to collect under these representations and warranties if necessary, the parties may create an escrow account. Typically, the buyer "holds back" some amount of the purchase price. Instead of giving it to the seller, the buyer places it in an escrow account, to be released to the seller at the expiration of the period under which the buyer can collect under the representations and warranties.

This raises a question: Should this "cash" that is set aside be treated as cash proceeds to the seller, even though the seller cannot get it now, or should it be treated more like a note, taxed when the seller receives it?

As long as the escrow account serves a "bona fide" business purpose of the buyer (i.e., to protect the ability to collect on the representations and warranties) and there are "substantial restrictions" on the seller's ability to receive the cash, the amounts in escrow will not be taxed to the seller until they are released from the escrow (IRS Private Letter Ruling 200521007; Rev. Rul. 79-91). This is to distinguish between a situation where cash is placed in an escrow account for the seller's benefit. In that case, the seller would be taxed on the money at the time of sale under the economic benefit theory, as long as the eventual receipt of the money was unconditional

What is a "substantial restriction"? Typically, the seller will not receive the funds until the buyer notifies the escrow agent that the representations and warranties have not been breached; only then will the funds be released. Problems may arise if the escrow is overly broad compared to the representations and warranties—for example, the representations and warranties expire after 18 months, but the escrow stays in place for three years. Or, the cap on collecting under the representations and warranties is $2 million, but the amount in the escrow is $3 million. In cases like these, it may appear that the seller is trying to defer tax without any credit risk from the buyer.

STUDY QUESTIONS

7. Form 8023 is used when:

    a. Reporting a related party installment sale

    b. Making an election under Code Sec. 338(h)(10)

    c. Remitting interest owing on tax deferred under the installment method

    d. Reporting the net investment income tax

8. ABC Corporation sells stock to XYZ, Inc. for $200,000, with $20,000 payable at closing and the remainder in equal installments over the next 9 years. Assume the transaction is evidenced by a note with adequate stated interest, and that ABC Corporation's basis in the stock is $80,000. The gross profit ratio is:

    a. 10 percent

    b. 25 percent

    c. 40 percent

    d. 60 percent

9. Continuing on the basis of the facts stated in Question 8, of every installment payment received, how much will be characterized as basis recovery?

    a. $2,000

    b. $2,500

    c. $8,000

    d. $12,000

10. Which of the following provides that if there are substantial restrictions on the seller's receipt of cash in escrow, and the account serves a bona fide business purpose of the buyer, the amounts in escrow will *not* be taxed to the seller until they are released from escrow to the seller?

    a. Revenue Ruling 79-91

    b. Revenue Ruling 72-172

    c. Revenue Procedure 2011-29

    d. Anti-*INDOPCO* Regulations

¶ 609 SALES TO RELATED PARTIES

There are special rules relating to the disposition of an installment note after a sale from a related party. They include a disallowance of losses on sale or exchanges of property between related parties, a disallowance of deductions between related parties in certain circumstances, and the recharacterization of gain on the sale of depreciable property between related parties.

Related Party Installment Sales

If a related party purchases property with an installment note and then sells the property within two years of the original related party sale, the amount realized on disposition is treated as payment to the original related party seller, to the extent of the installment obligation outstanding. This ends the deferral on the theory that the related party unit has cashed out.

> **EXAMPLE:** A mother sells business assets to her son for $400,000 cash plus a $1,600,000 note. Her basis is $1,000,000. Therefore, the gross profit is $1,000,000 and the contract price is $2,000,000, for a gross profit ratio of 50 percent. Each payment from the son will be a 50 percent gain to the mother.
>
> One year later, the son sells the property to a third party for $2,000,000 cash. According to Code Sec. 453(e), the mother has to treat the $2,000,000 that the son receives as payment on the son's note (accelerating the gain and ending deferral under the installment method). However, it is limited to the $1,600,000 outstanding obligation, so it is treated as though the mother received a $1,600,000 payment, with an $800,000 gain (based on 50 percent) gross profit ratio.

Code Sec. 267 Loss Disallowance

Another provision that comes up frequently in the context of closely held businesses and related parties is the special Code Sec. 267 rule on loss disallowances. Code Sec. 267 disallows a deduction in respect of any loss from the sale or exchange of property, directly or indirectly, between related persons (as defined in Code Sec. 267(b)). This affects numerous transactions, and applies to transactions that are conducted at arm's length. The loss disallowance applies automatically.

If Code Sec. 267(a)(1) applies and the transferee later sells or otherwise disposes of such property at a gain (or of other property the basis of which in his hands is determined directly or indirectly by reference to such property), then such gain shall be recognized only to the extent that it exceeds so much of such loss as is properly allocable to the property sold or otherwise disposed of by the transferee.

EXAMPLE: A father sells to his daughter stock in his closely held corporation for $500,000. The father's basis in the stock was $800,000. The loss of $300,000 is not allowable to the father (Code Sec. 267(a)(1) and Reg. § 1.267(a)-1).

The daughter later sells this stock for $1,000,000. Although the daughter's realized gain is $500,000 ($1,000,000 – $500,000 [her basis]), her recognized gain under Code Sec. 267(d) is only $200,000, the excess of the realized gain of $500,000 over the loss of $300,000 not allowable to her father. In determining capital gain or loss, the daughter's holding period commences on the date of the sale from father to daughter.

However, if the daughter later sold her stock for $300,000 instead of $1,000,000, her recognized loss would be $200,000, not $500,000, because Code Sec. 267(d) applies only to the nonrecognition of gain and does not affect basis.

Section 267(a)(2) Deduction Deferral

If by reason of a payment recipient's method of accounting (cash versus accrual), the amount thereof is not includible in the gross income of that recipient and at the close of the taxable year of the payor, the amount would be deductible, both the payor and the related person are 267(b) related persons, then any deduction allowable in respect of such amount shall only be allowable as of the day in which the amount is includible in the recipient's gross income.

If two parties are counterparties in a transaction, and one is on the cash method and one is on the accrual method, it does not really matter if the timing matches up. The cash method recipient does not have to take the deduction into account until he actually receives the income. The accrual method payor might be able deduct it in the earlier year. Different methods of accounting have different timing rules. However, if the two parties are related parties, their treatment must be matched under Code Sec. 267(a)(2). The deduction is deferred until the time when it should be included in income for the recipient.

Even if the deduction would normally be allowed in the earlier year if the related party recipient will not be taking the income into account until the later year, the payor cannot take the deduction until that time.

This could apply to payments between a company and a seller if the seller retains some stock in the company so they are still related, or if the seller and the company are related indirectly, because a family member of the seller owns the company.

Section 267(b) Related Party Definitions

Related party is defined under both Code Sec. 318 and Code Sec. 267. For related party installment sales, the Code Sec. 267 definition applies, but for some of the other related party provisions, either the Code Sec. 267 or 318 definitions are applicable.

Code Sec. 267(b) defines related parties as follows:

- Members of a family
- An individual and a corporation if the individual holds more than 50 percent (value) of the stock
- Two corporations that are members of the same controlled group

¶609

- A grantor and a fiduciary of any trust
- A fiduciary of a trust and a fiduciary of another trust, if the same person is a grantor of both trusts
- A fiduciary of a trust and a beneficiary of such trust
- A fiduciary of a trust and a beneficiary of another trust, if the same person is a grantor of both trusts
- A fiduciary of a trust and a corporation more than 50 percent in value of the outstanding stock of which is owned, directly or indirectly, by or for the trust or by or for a person who is a grantor of the trust
- A person and an organization to which Section 501 applies and that is controlled directly or indirectly by such person or (if such person is an individual) by members of the family of such individual
- A corporation and a partnership if the same persons own (a) more than 50 percent in value of the outstanding stock of the corporation, and (b) more than 50 percent of the capital interest, or the profits interest, in the partnership
- An S corporation and another S corporation if the same persons own more than 50 percent (value) of the stock of each corporation
- An S corporation and a C corporation, if the same persons own more than 50 percent (value) of the stock of each corporation
- Except in the case of a sale or exchange in satisfaction of a pecuniary bequest, an executor of an estate and a beneficiary of such estate

Section 1239: A Recharacterization Rule

Section 1239 states that in a sale or exchange of property, directly or indirectly, between related parties, any gain that is recognized to the transferor is treated as ordinary income if that property is depreciable property under Code Sec. 167. Therefore, a related party sale of depreciable property will be recharacterized as ordinary income. This applies to asset sales and Code Sec. 338(h)(10) transactions with respect to depreciable property. It can also apply in an LLC context with respect to look-throughs to underlying LLC assets.

Code Sec. 1239 has its own definition of related parties:

- A person and all entities that are controlled entities with respect to such person,
- A taxpayer and any trust in which such taxpayer (or his spouse) is a beneficiary, unless such beneficiary's interest in the trust is a remote contingent interest (within the meaning of Section 318(a)(3)(B)(i)), and
- Except in the case of a sale or exchange in satisfaction of a pecuniary bequest, an executor of an estate and a beneficiary of such estate.

Controlled entities include:

- A corporation with more than 50 percent of the value of the outstanding stock of which is owned, directly or indirectly, by or for such transferor
- A partnership with more than 50 percent of the capital or profits interests in which is owned, directly or indirectly, by or for such transferor
- Two corporations if more than 50 percent of the voting power or value of the stock of which is owned, directly or indirectly, by the same person
- A corporation and a partnership if the same persons own, directly or indirectly, more than 50 percent in value of the outstanding stock of the corporation and more than 50 percent of the capital or profits interests in the partnership

- Two S corporations, if the same persons own, directly or indirectly, more than 50 percent in value of the outstanding stock of each corporation

- An S corporation and C corporation, if the same persons own, directly or indirectly, more than 50 percent in value of the outstanding stock of each corporation

   EXAMPLE: A father sells all the stock in his S corporation to his daughter, and they decide to make a Code Sec. 338(h)(10) election. Under Code Sec. 1239, all property that will be depreciable for the daughter (real estate, depreciable personal property, Section 197 intangibles) will result in ordinary income to the father.

   EXAMPLE: A husband and wife sell their interests in a partnership to a controlled corporation. The portion attributable to the depreciable assets of the partnership is treated as ordinary income to the husband and wife (Rev. Rul. 72-172).

¶ 610 DISPOSITIONS OF UNWANTED ASSETS PRIOR TO THE SALE OF A BUSINESS

In some cases, a business owner may want to dispose of unwanted assets prior to the sale of a business. Perhaps the purchaser wants only some of the assets. A spin-off or split-off may be an option.

Section 355 Spin-Offs and Split-Offs

Suppose a brother and sister operated a closely held software design business (a C corporation). The business has both an off-the-shelf software design business and a custom software design and consulting business. The brother and sister have operated the business together for years, but now they want to take the business in different directions. The brother wants to keep operating the off-the-shelf software business, while the sister wants to operate the custom consulting line of the business.

The owners can split the business into two separate corporations, distributing the stock of one of the lines of the business to the brother and one to the sister. Suppose the corporation drops the off-the-shelf assets into a new corporation (Shelfco) and distributes Shelfco to the brother in redemption of his Oldco stock. Several general requirements must be met:

- Immediately before the distribution, "distributing" must control "controlled."

- There must be two separate active businesses, each with a five-year active history, and each must be active after the distribution.

- The spin-off must have a business purpose and not be a device for distributing earnings and profits.

- Shareholders of the distributing and controlled must retain their interests after the spin-off.

Now suppose instead that the business is wholly owned by the brother. A strategic buyer wants to buy the custom software design business only, as it has many hospital and healthcare clients and that is a growth business. The brother wants to keep operating the off-the-shelf software business. In this case, the general requirements are as follows:

- Immediately before distribution, "distributing" must control "controlled."

- There must be two separate active businesses, each with a five-year active history, and each must be active after the distribution.

- The spin-off must have a business purpose and not be a device for distributing earnings and profits.
- Shareholders of the distributing and controlled must retain their interests after the spin-off.

Note that this scenario will cause problems with the requirement that both lines be operated by shareholders after the transaction. Code Sec. 355(e)'s anti-Morris Trust rules specifically prohibit the brother splitting the business into two and then selling one part.

After the spin-off, shareholders are prohibited from selling or otherwise disposing of the business for two years. Thus, this will only work if the shareholders prepare long in advance of the potential acquisition.

If a business is in S corporation, unincorporated, or LLC form, the acquirer can choose which assets to acquire and leave others behind. If the business is a C corporation, doing a taxable asset sale may be too costly with the corporate-level gain. However, this may work if the corporation has net operating losses it can use to absorb the gain.

STUDY QUESTION

11. Under Internal Revenue Code Sec. 267(b), which of the following is considered a related party?

   a. An S corporation and another S corporation, if the same persons own more than 33 percent (by value) of the stock of each corporation

   b. An S corporation and another S corporation, if the same persons own more than 60 percent (by value) of the stock of each corporation

   c. A fiduciary of a trust and a fiduciary of another trust, if the same person is a grantor of both trusts

   d. An individual and a corporation if the individual holds more than 50 percent in voting power of the stock

¶ 611 CAPITALIZATION OF TRANSACTION COSTS

Transaction costs are very important to the sale of closely held businesses.

Costs Related to Acquisitions and Dispositions of Assets

Generally, expenses incurred to acquire or dispose of assets (other than inventory) must be capitalized. Examples include legal fees, professional fees for appraisals and valuations, zoning fees, and sales commissions. Costs that relate to acquiring the asset are capitalized into the basis of the asset, and costs incurred to dispose of an asset reduce the amount realized, thereby reducing gain on sale. Expenses paid or incurred in defending or perfecting title to property, in recovering property, or in developing or improving property, constitute a part of the cost of the property and are not deductible expenses.

> **EXAMPLE:** Moe owns a restaurant that has a patio and an outdoor parking lot. The neighboring restaurant owner repaves Moe's parking lot and builds a wall. Moe discovers that the neighboring wall encroaches on his land, and he hires a lawyer to make the neighbor remove the wall. Moe's legal fees must be capitalized into the basis of the property.

INDOPCO and the Anti-*INDOPCO* Regulations

For many years, taxpayers only capitalized costs relating to the acquisition of a "separate and distinct asset." This included intangible property such as stock and other financial instruments, in addition to tangible property.

In *INDOPCO Inc. v. Commissioner* (503 U.S. 79 (1992)), the taxpayer incurred legal and investment banking fees to fend off a hostile takeover attempt. The fees were large amounts, and the taxpayer deducted them in the year incurred. The IRS challenged the deduction and said the fees must be capitalized. The problem was that there was no "asset" in which to capitalize the fees since the taxpayer had not purchased an asset. Thus, requiring capitalization would essentially deny the deduction, because there was not a good way for the taxpayer to recover those costs. On the other hand, the costs were large, one-time expenses, so deducting them in one year would be distortive.

The Supreme Court held for the IRS, concluding that the taxpayer had to capitalize the fees because they created a "significant future benefit." The Court said no "separate and distinct asset" was necessary to require fee capitalization.

Taxpayers and their advisors panicked, worrying that any expense with a significant future benefit might have to be capitalized. The IRS soon issued regulations to clarify the rules, essentially overriding the Supreme Court decision. The "anti-*INDOPCO*" regulations generally adopt the "separate and distinct asset" test, requiring that a separate asset exist to capitalize transaction costs. Costs incurred to acquire stock are added to the stock basis, and costs incurred to acquire assets are added to the asset basis.

In a multi-asset acquisition of the entire business, the transaction costs are likely added to goodwill, which takes the residual purchase price allocation under Code Sec. 1060. In a nontaxable asset acquisition such as a tax-free reorganization, the fees are capitalized but cannot be recovered until the entity is dissolved. Simplifying conventions provide that employee compensation and overhead do not have to be allocated and capitalized, even if they relate to an acquisition.

Costs incurred prior to the acquisition do not have to be capitalized, but they may be deducted. The regulations provide that the costs incurred prior to signing a letter of intent are "investigative" costs that may be deducted. Any costs that are "facilitative" to the acquisition must be capitalized. (Contingent fees that are conditioned on a successful acquisition are generally capitalized as "facilitative.") The burden is on the taxpayer to show what portion of the fees, if any, are investigative, prior to the letter of intent. There is also a safe harbor under which the taxpayer may treat 30 percent of contingent fees as investigative and thus deductible (Rev. Proc. 2011-29).

STUDY QUESTION

12. In which of the following did the IRS assert that a taxpayer must capitalize fees if they created a significant future benefit even where there was no separate and distinct asset acquired?

    a. *Gregory*

    b. Revenue Ruling 79-91

    c. Revenue Ruling 72-172

    d. *INDOPCO*

MODULE 2: DEVLOPMENTS IMPACTING BUSINESS ENTITIES—Chapter 7: The Tax Cuts and Jobs Act: Impact on Reasonable Compensation for S Corporation Shareholder-Employees

¶701 WELCOME

This chapter discusses reasonable compensation, including how it works within the context of S corporation planning, how it fits in with the qualified business income deduction (QBID) under Code Sec. 199A, and planning strategies.

¶702 LEARNING OBJECTIVES

Upon completion of this chapter, you will be able to:

- Recognize how to determine "reasonable compensation" for S corporation shareholders
- Identify and apply the reasonable compensation rules in specific settings
- Recognize characteristics of the new QBID deduction
- Explain how to maximize S corporation shareholders' QBID
- Name the factors the courts have taken into account in determining reasonable compensation
- Identify the steps in calculating the cost of lost Social Security benefits
- Describe planning strategies with regard to reasonable compensation for S corporation shareholders

¶703 INTRODUCTION

To be tax deductible, compensation must be "reasonable." Reasonable compensation is never an exact number, so there are circumstances where practitioners may want to push a taxpayer toward the high end of reasonable compensation (discussed later in this chapter). There are also situations where a taxpayer's reasonable compensation should be on the lower side of reasonable compensation, perhaps partly for payroll tax purposes and also to increase the QBID, which will be discussed in more detail later in this chapter.

Historically, the profession most frequently involved in reasonable compensation litigation has been CPAs. Other frequent litigators include construction contractors, veterinarians, attorneys, and trucking companies.

In 2008, the IRS released a fact sheet listing the factors it uses to determine if compensation is reasonable. That list includes the following:

- Training and experience
- Duties and responsibilities
- Time and effort devoted to the business
- Dividend history

- Payments to non-shareholder employees
- Timing and manner of paying bonuses to key people
- What comparable businesses pay for similar services
- Compensation agreements
- The use of a formula to determine compensation

The most important of these factors is what comparable businesses pay similar people for similar services. If a company fails to pass the reasonable compensation test, it can end up with a tax assessment for underpaid payroll taxes. Reasonable compensation is a critical issue for some S corporations. According to the IRS, S corporations should not try to reduce or avoid paying employment taxes by having their officers treat their compensation as cash distributions, payments of personal expenses, or loans rather than as wages.

In order to increase compensation income (and therefore payroll taxes) of a S corporation's shareholder, the IRS must have some payment to "recharacterize." Recharacterization requires an *actual payment* to the shareholder or payment for the benefit of the shareholder that was not initially treated as compensation (IRS FS 2008-25). The instructions for IRS Form 1120-S state: "Distributions and other payments by an S corporation to a corporate officer must be treated as wages to the extent the amounts are reasonable compensation for services."

¶704 REASONABLE COMPENSATION: CASE LAW

Over the years, the courts have provided a great deal of guidance on reasonable compensation. A few of the more interesting cases are discussed in the following sections.

Barron v. Commissioner (TC Summary Opinion 2001-10)

Wiley Barron, a CPA, owned 100 percent of the stock of an S corporation. He was the only CPA working in the firm. Barron paid himself $2,000 in wages in 1994 and took $56,352 in distributions. He soon realized that his wages were too high and that he had grossly overpaid himself, so in order to "catch up," he paid himself zero wages in 1995 and 1996. Over the course of three years, he included wages of only $2,000 on his Form W-2, and in two of those three years, he did not issue himself a W-2 at all.

During those three years, he took significant distributions, even though his W-2 wages were almost zero. The IRS brought in an expert to review Barron's compensation, but the expert did not argue that the entire amount of Barron's distribution should be wages. In fact, for 1996, $83,341 had originally been distributed, but $49,000 of that was recharacterized as wages. In other words, even after the IRS adjustment, approximately $24,000 passed to Barron without payroll tax. Barron was likely building up goodwill. Goodwill is not an asset that shows up on the books, but it is still property, and the value of Barron's services did not include the value of the property of the corporation. The goodwill likely increased the value of the practice and increased the distributions Barron should have received as a shareholder, but it did not affect his reasonable compensation.

Wiley Barron, CPA			
	W-2	Distributions	Reasonable Compensation
1994	$2,000	$56,352	$45,000
1995	$0	$53,257	$47,500
1996	$0	$83,341	$49,000

Herbert v. Commissioner (TC Summary Opinion 2012-124)

Patrick Herbert tried to live the American dream but unfortunately was a casualty of the 2008 Great Recession. He worked for a delivery service company, Gopher Delivery Services, as manager and a salesperson. In 2004, he and his wife took out a home equity line of credit to purchase the company through an S corporation. In 2009, however, Gopher Delivery Services went out of business and, to make matters worse, the bank foreclosed on the couple's home.

In 2007, Herbert had deposited $60,000 from the S corporation into his personal bank account but treated only $2,400 of it as wages. Some distributions were used to pay business expenses. The IRS decided to audit Herbert, and it argued that his reasonable compensation was the full amount of cash he had taken out of the S corporation ($60,000).

However, citing **Mayson Mfg. Co. v. Commissioner (178 F.2d 115 (6th Cir. 1949))**, the Tax Court looked at Herbert's average annual wages for the period from 2002 to 2006, which were $30,445. Those earnings were less than his earnings in the year before he bought the business ($46,498). The Court noted that the IRS was not challenging the reasonableness of prior compensation. The court found that Herbert's reasonable compensation was $30,445. It is intriguing that the amount of reasonable compensation the court came up with was less than what Herbert had earned prior to becoming an owner of the S corporation. This seems to indicate that reasonable compensation is a range rather than a precise amount.

Glass Blocks Unlimited v. Commissioner (TC Memo 2013-180)

In some cases, utilizing an S corporation can backfire. The old saying "You can't get blood out of a turnip" has been at issue in a number of cases. What if an S corporation loses money, but a shareholder still takes some cash out? Can the IRS argue that the cash was really reasonable compensation and drive the S corporation into a large loss by recharacterizing distributions or loan repayments to the shareholder? As we will discover, it turns out that sometimes you can get blood out of a turnip, and sometimes you cannot.

Glass Blocks Unlimited v. Commissioner is an interesting case on this topic. Fred Blodgett was the sole shareholder and a full-time employee of Glass Blocks. In court, he claimed that he worked only 20 hours per week, but the company's website indicated it was open from 8:00 a.m. to 5:00 p.m. Monday through Friday. Glass Blocks' net income was $877 in 2007 and $8,950 in 2008. Fred admitted that he took loan repayments of approximately $30,000 from the corporation in both 2007 and in 2008, but he claimed that money was not compensation; rather, he said, it was used to repay loans.

The court disagreed, noting because there was no collateral, no promissory note, and no interest for the loans, they did not appear to be "real" loans. In determining Blodgett's amount of reasonable compensation, the Tax Court stated that whether the S corporation has net income as a result is irrelevant. The court believed Blodgett had lied about the number of hours he worked per day, and that he actually worked eight or nine hours per day. It argued that his "loan repayments" were really salary, and that after recharacterizing the $30,000 a year as reasonable compensation, they drove the S corporation into the negative by about $30,000. Blodgett paid far more in payroll taxes than if he had simply filed a Schedule C. So in this case, he paid more payroll taxes than if he had simply remained a sole proprietor.

Scott Singer Installations v. Commissioner (TC Memo 2016-161)

Scott Singer was a 100 percent owner of Scott Singer Installations, Inc., a company that repaired and modified recreational vehicles. His company was growing rapidly, and he needed money. Singer decided to take out a home equity line of credit of $646,000 in his own name and then re-loan the money to the S corporation. Then came the Great Recession, and his business grinded to a halt.

In an attempt to maintain his business and keep his employees, Singer obtained more money through a loan from his mother and in turn re-lent that money to the S corporation. The IRS noted that Singer had no loan documents, no interest, and no maturity date for his so-called shareholder loans, but Singer noted that he reported them as loans on Form 1120-S and on the corporation's general ledger.

In this case, the court agreed with Singer—that the money *did* qualify as loan repayments and not as wages. Unlike in *Glass Blocks*, here the court basically stated that you *cannot* get blood out of a turnip. It accepted that the $646,000 home equity loan was indeed a loan, but that the money Singer borrowed from his mother and then loaned to Scott Singer Installations looked more like equity.

Goldsmith v. Commissioner (TC Memo 2017-20)

Goldsmith v. Commissioner is another "blood out of a turnip" case. Scott Goldsmith was a successful attorney who had worked for several large firms. Eventually, he started his own S corporation to operate his law practice. He admitted that his poor managerial skills led to his financial problems. In an attempt to salvage his firm, he flew to Florida for a big case but came out on the losing side. Singer found himself stuck in a motel in Tampa with no money to fly home. Finally, a week or so later, a friend wired him the money to pay for a flight back to his home in Minnesota.

In the six years he was in business, Goldsmith made money in only one year—an $880,000 contingent fee. He lost an enormous amount of money in five of the six years he was in business and borrowed money against his home at an interest rate of up to 60 percent per year. He later went to prison for failing to account for and deposit payroll taxes.

After he was released from prison, the IRS conducted a civil tax audit on Goldsmith. The IRS contended that when Goldsmith took a distribution from the S corporation, it was a return of capital, not wages. Therefore, the IRS found that you *can* squeeze blood out of a turnip, but the Tax Court disagreed.

J&D Associates v. United States (No. 3:04-cv-59, DC North Dakota 2006)

Another reasonable compensation case is that of Jeff Dahl. Dahl grew up on a farm and later worked for a Big 8 accounting firm. Eventually, he formed his own accounting firm, JD & Associates, of which he was the sole shareholder, president, vice president, secretary, and treasurer. The firm did taxes, bookkeeping, and financial statement reviews, and its revenues grew steadily. Dahl was working hard, taking sole responsibility for the firm's personnel hiring and retention decisions, overall management, marketing, and review of others' work.

The IRS audited Dahl's firm and raised the issue of reasonable compensation. The IRS expert used Risk Management Associates data to compare JD & Associates' salaries to publicly available salary data and noted that based on the firm's sales, Dahl should have been paid an annual salary in the range of $69,000 to $79,000 over three years in the late 1990s. For that period, his actual salary was only $19,000 to $30,000 per year. The IRS's expert also computed the amount of "fair" wages as set forth below.

Payments to Jeff Dahl				
Year	W-2 Wages	Dividends	Total (Wages + Dividends)	IRS "Fair" Wages
1997	$19,000	$47,000	$66,000	$61,817
1998	$30,000	$50,000	$80,000	$63,672
1999	$30,000	$50,000	$80,000	$65,582

The court homed in on the fact that in 1997, Dahl paid a lower-level employee (Linda) more than he paid himself, which was an indication he was not taking reasonable compensation.

	Jeff Dahl's Wages	Linda's* Wages
1997	$19,000	$22,000**
1998	$30,000	$23,266
1999	$30,000	$27,448

* Employee of JD & Associates, Inc.; not an officer and not involved in management or marketing.
** Estimated from the case.

The court also remarked that it was curious that JD & Associates had inordinately high profit margins. Industry data showed that the average bottom-line profit for most accounting firms was only about 11 percent, whereas JD & Associates' was approximately 40 percent—an indication that the firm was not paying enough compensation.

Profitability		
	J&D Associates	Average Accounting Firm
1997	43%	14.1%
1998	38%	11.3%
1999	37%	7.7%

Ultimately, Dahl's compensation was found to be unreasonable.

Watson v. Commissioner (668 F.3d 1008, 8th Cir. 2012)

As illustrated by these cases, to determine what is reasonable, the courts tend to look at independent data, such as salary surveys and the compensation of others in the same company. The case involving David Watson further clarifies how courts determine reasonable compensation.

David Watson is a highly qualified CPA with a graduate degree in tax. Watson advertised that his firm was an expert in S corporations, including reasonable compensation. Through his S corporation, he was paid a very low amount of wages, only $24,000 annually in 2002 and 2003. He voluntarily raised that amount to $48,000 after his IRS audit began, but for the years in question he was taking compensation of only $24,000 per year.

Th IRS's expert (the same expert who participated in the *JD & Associates* case) noted that because an accountant straight out of college makes at least $40,000 per year, Watson's salary seemed unreasonably low. In 2002, Watson's gross billings and gross distributions were each about $200,000 for the year. The IRS believed that $200,000 was "begging" to be recharacterized into reasonable compensation.

The expert claimed that according to the *Almanac of Business and Industrial Financial Ratios*, Watson's firm was much more profitable than its peers. The IRS also referred to a study by consulting firm Robert Half that indicated a director or manager of an accounting firm who has more than 11 years of experience typically has wages ranging from the mid-$60,000s to $90,000 per year, which was much higher than Watson's compensation. In addition, the IRS expert noted that according to the National

¶704

MAP (Management of an Accounting Practice) Survey, the average reasonable compensation for a director (i.e., an employee who has skills similar to a partner, but who does not own an equity interest) of a CPA firm was $70,000. The expert then increased this $91,044 to take into account that partners have higher billing rates than directors. Therefore, Watson's compensation was not reasonable.

Most significantly, the expert did not argue that Watson's reasonable compensation should be the same as total income for most CPA firm owners; that appears to be due to the fact that an owner's income has two components: wages and return on capital. It appears that a reasonable return on capital should not be included in the determination of reasonable compensation. Reasonable compensation should be based upon the value of services alone.

Sean McAlary Ltd. Inc. v. Commissioner (TC Summary Opinion 2013-62)

The McAlary case also illustrates how reasonable compensation is determined. Sean McAlary had worked in the computer industry but was not making enough money, so he decided to switch careers and sell real estate instead. In his first year in real estate sales, he had cash flow of $240,000 and paid out $240,000, resulting in zero wages for himself. The question became *how* to determine McAlary's reasonable compensation.

The court looked at the average hourly wage for real estate agents in California ($48.44/hour) and said that because McAlary was a novice, his hourly rate should be lower, at $40 per hour. It held that McAlary's reasonable compensation should be $83,200 per year ($40 per hour at 2,080 hours per year).

Lessons Learned

There are several takeaways from these cases for determining reasonable compensation:

- Take into account the wages paid to non-shareholders, such as less experienced workers and recent college graduates (as illustrated in *JD & Associates*).
- Review public compensation information, including information from the U.S. Department of Labor, state data, surveys, and online sources such as salary.com.
- Consider if the company in question is more profitable than others in its industry. This might indicate that employees are undercompensated.
- Property matters, including goodwill. There should be a return on the fair market value of property owned by an S corporation.

STUDY QUESTION

---

1. Which of the following cases found that reasonable compensation may be a range based on certain prior years?

    a. *Goldsmith v. Commissioner*

    b. *Scott Singer Installations v. Commissioner*

    c. *Patrick Herbert v. Commissioner*

    d. *Glass Blocks v. Commissioner*

¶705 QUALIFIED BUSINESS INCOME DEDUCTION

The Code Sec. 199A qualified business income deduction (QBID), also called the 20 percent pass-through deduction, is one of the biggest tax changes in decades. Under the TCJA, it has a shelf life of eight years (2018 through 2025). At its core, the QBID is fairly simple: a qualifying business can take a deduction of 20 percent of its income. Therefore, if its income is $100,000, its QBID will be $20,000. Although that is a bit of an oversimplification, it is broadly how the QBID works.

Wage/Property Caps

There are two income-dependent caps on the QBID—(1) a specified service trade or business (SSTB) cap and (2) a wage or wage and property cap (the "wage cap"). These limitations apply to higher income ("caviar") taxpayers, which drives strategy in the S corporation area. SSTBs include any trade or business whose principal asset is the reputation or skill of one or more of its employees. Examples include businesses that provide accounting, health, law, or consulting services.

For both caps, married taxpayers filing jointly with pre-QBID taxable income equal to or less than $315,000 can deduct 20 percent of QBID on all of their SSTB income. Further, these taxpayers are not subject to the wage requirement. For those with taxable income of $315,000 or more, the QBID on SSTB income begins to slowly phase out; at $415,000 it is entirely phased out. For non-SSTB businesses (like restaurants, wholesale businesses, real estate agents, etc.), taxpayers will begin to lose the QBID unless the business generates sufficient amounts of wages or property. To simplify this discussion, a "hamburger" taxpayer is one with $315,000 of taxable income or less (married filing jointly). A "caviar" taxpayer is one with taxable income of $415,000 or more.

A taxpayer who files married filing jointly has no wage cap at up to $315,000 in income and gets the full QBID for SSTB income. Between income of $315,000 and $415,000, that taxpayer starts losing the QBID for SSTB income. For those who file as single, head of household, or married filing separately, the limits are exactly half that of married filing joint taxpayers—the limits do not apply if their income is $157,000 or less.

	Wage and Wage/Property Caps: Phase-In		
Tax Filing Status	**Threshold Amount (No Wages or Property Required)**	**Phase-In Range**	**Full Phase-In ("Caviar" Rule; Need Wages/Property)**
Single, Head of Household, Married Filing Separately	$157,500	$50,000	$207,500
Married Filing Jointly	$315,000	$100,000	$415,000

Wages and property are central to the S corporation planning area. For "caviar" taxpayers, the QBID is capped at (1) 50 percent of Form W-2 wages or, if it produces a better result, (2) 25 percent of wages plus 2.5 percent of a property factor. If such taxpayers do not have wages or property, their QBID will be limited. Because higher income taxpayers have a wage or wage property requirement, sometimes the S corporation will need to pay them more in wages so they get the full benefit of the QBID.

Higher income taxpayers with rental real estate usually pick the second of the two cap options because they typically do not have wages, and the wages and property factor usually breaks out better for them. W-2 wages include *both* of the following:

- Wages to the owner: Consider bonuses to S corporation shareholder/employees (if the taxpayer has insufficient wages). It must be reasonable compensation.
- Wages to everyone else.

Note that paymaster issues can arise. For example, consider a management company that acts as the common paymaster for S corporation A, which operates a restaurant, and S corporation B, which also operates a restaurant. Those wages are treated as being paid by the common law employers, which in this case are S corporation A and S corporation B, not the common paymaster—even though the common paymaster will issue the W-2s.

There are three ways to determine wages (Rev. Proc. 2019-11), but most taxpayers use the approach provided in the final regulations:

- Box 1 wages (including medical insurance shown on a 2 percent shareholder's W-2), plus
- Elective deferrals (e.g., 401(k) deferrals and simple deferrals).

For tax planning purposes, one must understand how this works in the phase-in territory. For example, a married taxpayer filing jointly with an income of $315,000 does not need any wages at all, but one with an income of $415,000 may need a great deal of wages. The calculation has two steps: first, compute the loss of QBID as if the taxpayer were a "caviar" taxpayer and apply the full 50 percent of wages limit. And then, multiply that by the percentage that represents how "deep" the taxpayer is into phase-in territory. For example, if the taxpayer has $325,000 in taxable income, it would be 10 percent into the phase-in range ($325,000 – $315,000 = $10,000; and the total phase-in range occurs over $100,000, between $315,000 and $415,000). Then multiply the QBID that would be lost as if it were a "caviar" taxpayer, by 10 percent.

Assume a "caviar" taxpayer would lose $5,000 in QBID because of the wage cap. If it were 10 percent of the way into the phased-in range—in other words, its taxable income was $325,000, it would multiply that 10 percent by the $5,000 cap as if it were a "caviar" taxpayer and would reduce the QBID by $500.

In the example below, assume the taxpayers are married filing jointly and have pre-QBID taxable income of $335,000 (i.e., they are 20 percent deep into the phase-in range).

Phase-In: "Steak Hit" (Taxable Income = $335,000; Not SSTB)			
Step 1 (What Would Full "Caviar Hit" Be?)			
Preliminary QBID for S Corporation Pass-Through ($100,000 × 20%)			$20,000
Wage Limit (Wages $30,000 × 50%)			$15,000
"Caviar hit" ($20,000 QBI vs. $15,000)			$5,000
Step 2 (How Deep into Phase-In Territory?)			
Taxable Income	$335,000		
Threshold	$315,000		
Wage Phaseout Effect	$20,000		
Phaseout Range	$100,000		20%
"Steak Hit" ($5,000 "Caviar Hit" × 20% Deep)			($1,000)
QBID After Phased-In Wage Cap			$19,000

Guaranteed Payments

Guaranteed payments received by a partner do not qualify for the QBID (Code Sec. 199A(c)(4)(B)). Further, a partnership's deduction of guaranteed payments reduces QBI. In the area of LLCs and single-member LLCs, there is no such thing as the concept of reasonable compensation. The idea for these entities, therefore, is to reduce guaranteed payments without affecting the amount of cash each partner gets.

¶705

EXAMPLE: Bob and Jeb are each 50 percent owners of an LLC. Historically, Bob has taken a guaranteed payment of $100,000, and Jeb has taken $50,000. If Bob's guaranteed payment is reduced by $50,000 and Jeb's is reduced by $50,000, each, as a 50 percent member, will get $50,000 more in distributions.

The guaranteed payments of each will be reduced by $50,000 (which will be exactly offset by the increased amount of distributions). So, the economics stays on track and the qualified business income will increase to $300,000, and therefore the QBID will increase to $60,000.

Guaranteed Payments: Planning		
	Without Planning	With Planning
Pre-guaranteed Payment Income	$350,000	$350,000
Guaranteed Payment–Bob (50% member)	($100,000)	($50,000)
Guaranteed Payment–Jeb (50% member)	($50,000)	($0)
Qualifying Business Income	**$200,000**	**$300,000**
Tentative QBID (@20%)	**$40,000**	**$60,000**

The idea is that entities outside the S corporation vehicle sometimes come out ahead, at least with respect to the QBID.

Aggregating Businesses

The wage/property cap is a business-by-business limit, so if a client owns one S corporation that has a barber shop and one that owns a coffee shop, this wage calculation is generally separate for each. However, the regulations allow individuals to aggregate certain businesses for purposes of applying the wage cap. The final regulations also allow entities themselves to aggregate businesses at the S corporation and the partnership level. Once an individual or entity elects to aggregate businesses, it must consistently group them unless there is a material change in facts. Note that individuals and entities are not required to aggregate all of their businesses that qualify. Each business to be aggregated must meet all of the following conditions:

- The businesses must be under common control (50 percent or more; 50 percent is sufficient, and it includes indirect ownership). The Code Sec. 267 definition of attribution applies to determine ownership. This common control must exist for the majority of the year and on the last day of the year. Any number of persons may be counted for the 50 percent or more test, as long as they own at least some interest in all the entities sought to be aggregated.

- The businesses must report on the same taxable year (however, an exception is provided for businesses with short taxable years).

- None of the aggregated businesses can be a SSTB.

- The businesses must meet certain reporting requirements every year (discussed later in this chapter).

- The businesses must meet at least two of three factors:

  — They must have the same products, property, or services. For example, a restaurant and a food truck would meet this requirement because the product for both is food. In the alternative, this first hurdle can be satisfied if the products, property, or services are customarily provided together (e.g., a gas station and a car wash).

  — They must share facilities *or* share significant centralized business elements (e.g., common personnel, accounting, legal, purchasing, human resources,

IT, advertising, etc.). For example, if the restaurant and the food truck have the same accountants and the same lawyer, they should be able to clear this second hurdle.

— They must be operated in coordination with or reliance on other aggregated businesses. A classic example is a supply chain. If S corporation A manufactures widgets, and S corporation B sells the same widget, that would be an interdependency and the businesses would clear this hurdle.

EXAMPLE: Bob manages two apartment buildings and arranges purchasing and repairs for both. Ownership is as shown below. The businesses share common significant centralized business elements (management and purchasing) and involve the same type of property (residential real estate). They are also under common control. Not only can Bob and John aggregate, but Carl can also aggregate. The entities' combined income is limited by its combined property if it elects to aggregate.

	ABC, LLC	XYZ, LLC
Bob	40%	40%
John	40%	40%
Carl	10%	20%
Jerry	10%	0%
Total	100%	100%

Aggregation is beneficial if one business is limited by wages or by wages and property and the other has more wages than it needs. However, aggregation can backfire when:

- One business uses the wage limit and the other uses wage/property.
- Each business can barely cover its own limit.

S corporations and partnerships that aggregate also must make an annual disclosure. Each year, they must attach an aggregation statement to each Schedule K-1 identifying the businesses aggregated. The following must be reported:

- A description of each business
- The name and employer identification number (EIN) of the entity
- Information on any business that was formed, discontinued, acquired, or disposed of in the year
- Information on any aggregated business of a passthrough entity in which the entity holds ownership interest
- Any other information required by forms

If an individual or entity has an interest in a partnership or an S corporation and fails to attach the aggregation statement to its Schedule K-1, the IRS can disaggregate the businesses and keep the individual or entity from re-aggregating for the next three years.

STUDY QUESTIONS

2. Each of the following is a characteristic of the new QBID deduction, *except:*

     a. It is a 20 percent deduction of qualifying business income.

     b. It is one of the most profound tax changes in decades.

     c. It has a shelf life of 10 years.

     d. It phases out for certain businesses.

3. Which of the following identifies the 2018 full phase-in amount for the QBID for those individuals filing as single?

    a. $157,500

    b. $207,500

    c. $315,000

    d. $415,000

4. The new Code Sec. 199A QBID deduction allows for a _____ percent deduction on qualifying business income.

    a. 10

    b. 15

    c. 20

    d. 25

¶ 706 PLANNING STRATEGIES

There are some strategies "caviar" non-SSTB taxpayers can use regarding wages. To find the optimal amount of wages for a "caviar" taxpayer, divide the taxpayer's pre-wage income by 3.5. For a taxpayer with pre-wage income of $350,000, dividing by 3.5 results in $100,000, the optimal amount of wages. If the taxpayer pays $100,000 in combined wages to the owner and all employees, it is at the perfect balancing point. If the taxpayer pays *more* than $100,000 in wages, however, it ends up paying extra payroll taxes and has a reduced QBID. The $100,000 provides just enough W-2 limits so that the taxpayer qualifies for the full QBID. Of course, compensation must be reasonable.

Proof		
Net income (before wages)		$350,000
Optimal wages		$100,000
Net income		$250,000
QBID (net income × 20%)		$50,000
Wages (to owner and nonowners)	$100,000	
50% wage limit	50%	$50,000

Sole Proprietorship or S Corporation?

For tax planning, sometimes the question becomes whether to have a S corporation at all. S corporations are required to pay reasonable compensation, which can reduce QBID. On the other hand, sole proprietorships (including single-member LLCs taxed as sole proprietorships) and multimember LLCs have no QBID adjustment for the value of the owner's services, making these entity types a better choice than an S corporation in some situations.

    EXAMPLE: Frederick is trying to decide between operating his business as a sole proprietorship or as an S corporation. He expects to make $150,000 net income before any wages. Assume that if he chooses to operate as an S corporation, he will have to pay himself $100,000 in wages, because that is the reasonable amount of compensation. That $100,000 will move income from the Schedule K-1 (where it qualifies for the QBID) to the W-2 (where it does not qualify for the QBID), reducing his qualified business income to $50,000 and resulting in a $10,000 QBID. With a sole proprietorship, the QBID would be $30,000.

Sole Proprietorship vs. S Corporation		
	Sole Proprietorship	S Corporation
Pre-Wage Business Income	$150,000	$150,000
Reasonable Compensation	N/A	($100,000)
Qualifying Business Income	$150,000	$50,000
Tentative QBID (QBI × 20%)	$30,000	$10,000

The general rule is that a sole proprietorship is the better choice if the taxpayer is a "hamburger" taxpayer and has a higher reasonable compensation requirement. However, if a taxpayer has a very low reasonable compensation requirement, the S corporation is more advantageous because the taxpayer will save more in payroll taxes than it would benefit from the QBID.

The following table assumes the taxpayer is a "hamburger" taxpayer who is not subject to the wage/property requirements. These two scenarios present two very different taxpayers. In Scenario 1, we have a semi-retired owner who works only on Fridays (reasonable compensation would be only $25,000 if an S corporation were chosen). In this scenario, the S corporation will screen a considerable amount of payroll taxes, and a very small amount of income ($25,000) will be dragged from Schedule K-1 (where it qualifies for the QBID) to the W-2 (where it will not qualify for the QBID). Therefore, the S corporation provides a much lower overall tax liability.

In Scenario 2, a highly skilled, hard-charging insurance broker works 2,800 hours per year. (Reasonable compensation would be very high if an S corporation were chosen.) In this scenario, choosing an S corporation would be a mistake: the S corporation would screen very little in payroll taxes (since reasonable compensation is so high) and an S corporation would move almost all the income to Form W-2 (which does not qualify for the QBID). In Scenario 2, the taxpayer is better off with a sole proprietorship (which includes single-member LLCs that are disregarded for federal income tax purposes).

Total Payroll and Income Taxes					
	Reasonable Compensation	Pass-through Income	Total Income	Sole Proprietorship	S Corporation
Scenario 1: Semi-retired	$25,000	$150,000	$175,000	$37,250	**$21,903**
Scenario 2: Insurance Broker	$150,000	$25,000	$175,000	**$37,250**	$42,041
Note that the benefits are even greater if one considers increased Social Security benefits in the future.					

Planning for "Caviar" One-Man Bands

A "one-man band" in this discussion means a taxpayer who makes a great deal of money but does not pay anybody else—for example, real estate agents or insurance brokers who work alone and have no employees. This type of taxpayer might be a sole proprietorship that does not pay the taxpayer any wages, or maybe it is a single-member LLC. Converting to an S corporation can result in huge savings for these types of taxpayers. This is intended to illustrate the principle that in some cases, high-income taxpayers are better off using S corporations because they can pay wages to themselves (from their S corporations) to help meet the W-2 wage limit.

> **EXAMPLE:** Client A is a single "caviar" taxpayer with non-SSTB income. The client's problem is that it has no wages at all. Therefore, both its wage cap and its QBID are 0.

¶706

One-Man Band: Sole Proprietorship		
Sole Proprietorship (Schedule C) Income	$350,000	
Tentative QBID	20%	$70,000
Wages	$0	
Wage factor	50%	
Hard cap (caviar taxpayer)		$0
QBID (limited by wage cap)		$0

What if client A converts to a S corporation? Of the $350,000 in income from its Schedule C, $250,000 will be pass-through income and $100,000 will go on the W-2. Multiplying $250,000 by 20 percent results in a $50,000 QBID. The client has $100,000 in wages. By switching from a sole proprietorship to an S corporation, Client A's QBID rose from zero to $50,000 because it created its own wage cap by paying the owner wages.

One-Man Band: S Corporation		
S Corporation Passthrough Income	$250,000	
Tentative QBID	20%	$50,000
Wages	$100,000	
Wage factor	50%	
Hard cap (caviar taxpayer)		$50,000
QBID (limited by wage cap)		$50,000

Lost Social Security Benefits

While S corporations can benefit from paying less in compensation, if they pay less than reasonable compensation in the long term, the result is typically less in Social Security benefits. The following theoretical computation explains the relationship between payroll taxes and Social Security benefits:

- Step 1: What are your historical social security wages?
- Step 2: Convert those historical wages to *the current dollar equivalent.* (The Index Factors for Earnings are available at www.ssa.gov/oact/cola/awifactors.html.)
- Step 3: Get the monthly average (high 35-year indexed Social Security wages) ÷ 420 (35 years × 12 months/year = 420 months).
- Step 4: Plug the inflation-adjusted high 35-year wage average into the Average Indexed Monthly Earnings (AIME) table. This is the Social Security benefit at normal retirement age (age 67 if born in 1960 or later). The benefit is decreased if drawn *before* normal retirement age.

The actual computations are a bit more complex.

EXAMPLE: If Sheila retires at age 67, she will compute her AIME using the tables in effect in the year she turned 62, and then index for inflation. For the first $11,112 in earnings, Sheila will get a 90 percent payout, so for every dollar of earnings she will get $0.90, but she only had to pay in 15.3 percent if she had her own S corporation.

For up to $67,000 in wages, she would pay 15.3 percent for 35 years and get 32 percent back for her life expectancy. Finally, if Sheila had more than $67,000 in annual earnings, she will pay 15 percent for 35 years, but only get 15 percent back for her life expectancy.

¶706

Relationship: Social Security Earnings and Benefits	
Average Indexed Annual Earnings (High 35-Year Average)	Annual Social Security Benefit (at Full Retirement Age)
$0–$11,112	90%
$11,112–$66,996	32%
$66,996–$128,400	15%
> $128,400	0%

STUDY QUESTIONS

5. Which of the following identifies the first step in calculating the cost of lost Social Security benefits?

   a. Adjust historical wages to get current dollars.

   b. Determine the amount of historical Social Security wages.

   c. Determine the monthly average of historical Social Security wages.

   d. Plug the inflation-adjusted high 35-year wage average into the AIME table.

6. Which of the following identifies the annual Social Security benefit at full retirement age with averaged indexed annual earnings of less than $11,112?

   a. 15 percent

   b. 32 percent

   c. 43 percent

   d. 90 percent

CPE NOTE: When you have completed your study and review of chapters 4-7, which comprise Module 2, you may wish to take the Final Exam for this Module. Go to **cchcpelink.com/printcpe** to take this Final Exam online.

¶ 10,100 Answers to Study Questions
¶ 10,101 MODULE 1—CHAPTER 1

1. a. *Incorrect.* Property placed in service during 2024 is eligible for bonus depreciation. The bonus depreciation for property placed in service during 2024 is 60 percent.

b. *Incorrect.* Property placed in service during 2025 is eligible for bonus depreciation. The bonus depreciation for property placed in service during 2025 is 40 percent.

c. *Incorrect.* Property placed in service during 2026 is eligible for bonus depreciation. The bonus depreciation for property placed in service during 2026 is 20 percent.

d. *Correct.* **Property placed in service during 2027 is not eligible for bonus depreciation. This compares to property placed in service during 2026 where the bonus depreciation is 20 percent.**

2. a. *Incorrect.* This is not the maximum depreciation (not including bonus) for passenger automobiles assuming qualified business use in the second taxable year after December 31, 2017.

b. *Correct.* **This is the maximum depreciation for passenger automobiles assuming qualified business use in the first taxable year after December 31, 2017. Instead, if this was the first taxable year, the maximum depreciation would only be $10,000.**

c. *Incorrect.* This is the maximum depreciation in the third taxable year after December 31, 2017, not the second taxable year. If bonus depreciation is taken, the maximum amount would exceed this amount.

d. *Incorrect.* This is not the maximum depreciation for passenger automobiles assuming qualified business use in the second taxable year after December 31, 2017. Instead, this is the maximum depreciation in succeeding years in the recovery period after the third taxable year.

3. a. *Correct.* **Land improvements are not eligible for Section 179 expense treatment both before and after the TCJA. This compares with qualifying leasehold improvements, which were eligible prior to 2018, and after 2018 are not.**

b. *Incorrect.* Qualifying leasehold improvements are eligible for Section 179 expense treatment when placed into service prior to 2018. However, if they are placed into service after 2017, they are not eligible.

c. *Incorrect.* Nonresidential roofs (placed into service after the building) are eligible for Section 179 expense treatment when placed into service after to 2017. However, if they are placed into service before 2018, they are not eligible.

d. *Incorrect.* Non-residential HVAC is not eligible for Section 179 expense treatment when placed into service prior to 2018. However, if it is placed into service after 2017, it is eligible.

4. a. *Incorrect.* This is not the maximum Section 179 expense amount for 2018. Instead, this is the maximum Section 179 expense amount for 2017.

b. *Correct.* **This is the maximum Section 179 expense amount for 2018. This is an increase from $500,000, which was the maximum amount for 2017.**

c. *Incorrect.* This is not the maximum Section 179 expense amount for 2018. Instead, this is the beginning of the phaseout for 2017.

d. *Incorrect.* This is not the maximum Section 179 expense amount for 2018. Instead, this is the beginning of the phaseout for 2018.

5. a. *Incorrect.* Land would not be eligible for Section 179 deduction. Section 179 allows taxpayers to elect to deduct the cost of certain types of property on their income taxes as an expense, rather than requiring the cost of the property to be capitalized and depreciated

b. *Incorrect.* The building would not be eligible for Section 179 deduction. Real property (except qualified real property improvements) does not qualify for the Section 179 deduction. Real property is typically defined as land, buildings, permanent structures, and the components of the permanent structures (including improvements not specifically covered on the qualifying property page).

c. *Correct.* Personal property used for lodging first qualified for a Section 179 deduction in 2018.

d. *Incorrect.* Land improvements would not be eligible for Section 179 deduction. Section 179 was enacted to help small businesses by allowing them to take a depreciation deduction for certain assets (capital expenditures) in one year, rather than depreciating them over a longer period of time. Land improvements are not among those assets.

6. a. *Correct.* In addition to having book conformity, taxpayers without audited financial statements need an accounting policy for financial purposes which can be unwritten. For taxpayers with audited financial statements, this policy must be written.

b. *Incorrect.* Taxpayers with audited financial statements cannot elect up to $10,000 per invoice. Instead, they can only elect up to $5,000 per invoice (or per item if substantiated by an invoice).

c. *Incorrect.* Taxpayers without audited financial statements cannot elect up to $5,000 per invoice. Instead, they can only elect up to $2,500 per invoice as prescribed by IRS Notice 2015-82.

d. *Incorrect.* Taxpayers with audited financial statements are required to have a written accounting policy. Alternatively, taxpayers without audited financial statements are not required to have a written policy but should have a policy even if not written.

7. a. *Incorrect.* Buildings are not considered placed in service when paid or incurred. Instead, they are considered placed in service when a certificate of occupancy is received. See the *Stine* case.

b. *Correct.* Replacement improvements are considered placed into service when paid or incurred. This compares with improvement additions, which are considered placed into service when work is completed, as long as the taxpayer does not take a partial disposition election for the property replaced

c. *Incorrect.* Ready-to-go equipment is not considered placed in service when paid or incurred. Instead, it is considered placed in service when it is in the taxpayer's possession.

d. *Incorrect.* Unfinished equipment is not considered placed in service when paid or incurred. Instead, it is considered placed in service when it is actually suitable for the taxpayer's assigned function.

¶10,101

8. a. *Correct.* **Additions are considered placed into service when work is completed. This compares with improvement replacements, which are considered placed into service when paid or incurred.**

b. *Incorrect.* Buildings are not considered placed in service when work is completed. Instead, they are considered placed in service when a certificate of occupancy is received.

c. *Incorrect.* Ready-to-go equipment is not considered placed in service when work is completed. Instead, it is considered placed in service when it is in the taxpayer's possession.

d. *Incorrect.* Unfinished equipment is not considered placed in service when work is completed. Instead, it is considered placed in service when it is actually suitable for the taxpayer's assigned function..

9. a. *Incorrect.* Electing out of bonus depreciation does require electing out of all property in a class. In this case, class generally refers to recovery period under Section 168(e).

b. *Incorrect.* The surgical approach entails achieving the optimal amount of Section 179, not bonus depreciation.

c. *Incorrect.* It is possible to revoke a Section 179 election. This is achieved through the filing of an amended return. Additionally, it is possible to revoke only a part or all of the original Section 179 deduction.

d. *Correct.* **This is a correct statement. The surgical approach entails achieving the optimal Section 179 deduction. To accomplish this, a taxpayer must elect out of bonus depreciation unless bonus depreciation is not available.**

10. a. *Correct.* **The Section 179 active business income limit provides the opportunity to freeze deductions for future years at a higher tax rate. However, the active business income limit does not apply to C corporations.**

b. *Incorrect.* The active business income limit does apply to individuals. However, it's important to note that bonus and *de minimis* do not offer the same ability.

c. *Incorrect.* The active business income limit does apply to partnerships. The Section 179 active business income limit provides opportunity to freeze deductions for future years at a higher tax rate.

d. *Incorrect.* The active business income limit does apply to S corporations. While the Section 179 active business income limit provides opportunity to freeze deductions for future years at a higher tax rate, this advantage is not provided by bonus and *de minimis*.

11. a. *Correct.* **The freeze and thaw method involves revoking a prior Section 179 election. This type of method works if the taxpayer is unexpectedly in a lower tax rate in the following years. This is in contrast to the thaw and freeze method.**

b. *Incorrect.* A taxpayer does not take the bonus initially with respect to the freeze and thaw method. Instead, this is the approach deployed for the thaw and freeze method.

c. *Incorrect.* It does not work if a taxpayer is unexpectedly in a higher tax rate in later years. This is a characteristic of the thaw and freeze method. Instead, the freeze and thaw method works if a taxpayer is unexpectedly in a lower tax rate in the following years.

d. *Incorrect.* The freeze and thaw method does not involve making a late Section 179 election. Instead, making a late Section 179 election is a characteristic of the thaw and freeze method.

12. a. *Correct.* ***De minimis* does apply to assets outside the United States. However, both bonus and Section 179 depreciation do not apply to assets outside the United States.**

b. *Incorrect.* Bonus is not allowed even if a taxpayer is required to use ADS depreciation. However, Section 179 and *de minimis* are allowed even if a taxpayer is required to use ADS depreciation.

c. *Incorrect.* Bonus depreciation is not available for residential real property improvements, other than land improvements. Alternatively, it is available with respect to *de minimis*.

d. *Incorrect.* *De minimis* does not apply to Section 743 step-ups. This is also the case with Section 179. However, for bonus depreciation, it does apply.

¶ 10,102 MODULE 1—CHAPTER 2

1. a. *Incorrect.* Section 263A's uniform capitalization rules do not address the duplication of income.

b. *Incorrect.* Section 451 provides rules for determining the taxable year of inclusion and does not offer a solution to the double-counting of income.

c. *Incorrect.* Section 471 addresses general rules for inventories. It does not cover duplication of income after an accounting method change.

d. *Correct.* **A Section 481(a) adjustment can offset the double-counting of revenues and therefore solve the problem.**

2. a. *Incorrect.* Under the TCJA, small businesses that were using the accrual method can now switch to the cash method of accounting.

b. *Correct.* **Under the TCJA, small businesses no longer must account for inventory; they now can use an accounting method that either treats inventories as nonincidental materials and supplies or conforms to their financial accounting treatment of inventories.**

c. *Incorrect.* Under the TCJA, small businesses are now exempt from the Section 263A uniform capitalization rules.

d. *Incorrect.* The TCJA defines small businesses as those with average annual gross receipts of $25 million or less; under prior law, that amount was $10 million.

3. a. *Incorrect.* Under IRS Notice 2015-82, the *de minimis* capital expenditures threshold for such taxpayers is up to $5,000. For taxpayers with no audited financial statements, the amount is up to $2,500.

b. *Incorrect.* The *de minimis* threshold is applied either at the invoice level or, if multiple items appear on a single invoice, at the item level. This is true for taxpayers with and without audited financial statements.

c. *Incorrect.* The *de minimis* election has not been eliminated by the tax reform legislation.

d. *Correct.* **A written accounting policy for financial purposes is required for taxpayers who have audited financial statements. Taxpayers without audited financial statements also must have an accounting policy, but it can be unwritten.**

4. a. *Incorrect.* The TCJA provision that relieves small businesses of complying with the complex uniform capitalization rules is considered favorable to those taxpayers.

b. *Correct.* **Under the TCJA, small businesses with audited financial statements that recognize income sooner on their financial statements than they normally would on their tax return must now match them up and accelerate the income on the tax return under Code Section 451(b).**

c. *Incorrect.* The TCJA change to accounting for inventory is considered small business friendly because it allows such businesses to avoid complicated inventory accounting.

d. *Incorrect.* The TCJA long-term contracts provision allows small businesses to use the completed-contract method, which simplifies their accounting.

5. a. *Incorrect.* The TCJA did not supersede Rev. Proc. 2004-34; instead, it incorporated the revenue procedure's rules into Code Section 451(c).

b. *Incorrect.* Rev. Proc. 2004-34 applies to accrual method taxpayers with audited financial statements.

c. *Correct.* **Rev. Proc. 2004-34 gives taxpayers the option to defer including certain advance payments in income instead of including the full amount in the year of receipt.**

d. *Incorrect.* The goods and services covered under Rev. Proc. 2004-34 include the sale, lease, or license of computer software; use of intellectual property; gift cards; online databases and subscriptions; and more.

6. a. *Incorrect.* A preparer should file Form 3115 in duplicate: the original form should be attached to the return and a copy mailed to the IRS.

b. *Incorrect.* A taxpayer can file Form 3115 to request an accounting method change up to extended due date of tax return.

c. *Correct.* **A taxpayer need not wait for the IRS's consent after the Form 3115 is filed.**

d. *Incorrect.* The opposite is true; the IRS probably will require taxpayers to file Form 3115 to request a change in accounting method.

¶ 10,103 MODULE 1—CHAPTER 3

1. a. *Incorrect.* This is not the new standard deduction for head of households. Instead, this amount represents the new standard deduction for single filers, which is a significant increase from the prior year.

b. *Incorrect.* This is not the new standard deduction for head of households. Instead, this amount represents the previous standard deduction for those individuals who are married and filing jointly.

c. *Correct.* **This is the new standard deduction for head of households. This is nearly a doubling of the previous standard deduction, which for 2017 was $9,350. This near doubling was also the case for other tax filings statuses.**

d. *Incorrect.* This is not the new standard deduction for head of households. Instead, this amount represents the new standard deduction for those individuals who are married and filing jointly.

2. a. *Correct.* **Based on the new rules effective 2018 through 2025, home equity indebtedness is not deductible. Additionally, acquisition indebtedness incurred after December 15, 2017, is limited to $750,000.**

b. *Incorrect.* Acquisition indebtedness up to $1 million is not deductible after December 15, 2017. Instead, the limit has been lowered. For acquisition indebtedness incurred after December 15, 2017, it is limited to $750,000.

c. *Incorrect.* There was no change in tax related matters with respect to second homes. However, the new limits related to acquisition indebtedness do apply to the purchase of second homes.

d. *Incorrect.* While acquisition indebtedness of $750,000 is deductible on or before December 15, 2017, the limit is actually $1 million during this time period. However, after December 15, 2017, acquisition indebtedness is limited to $750,000.

3. a. *Incorrect.* $5,000 is not the new limit on property tax deduction based on the new tax rules for those taxpayers filing married jointly. Instead, this is the limit for those taxpayers who file as married filing separately.

b. *Correct.* **$10,000 is the new limit on property tax deduction based on the new tax rules for those taxpayers filing married jointly. Note that deductible amounts include domestic property taxes (real and personal) as well as the greater of sales tax or state and local income taxes.**

c. *Incorrect.* $12,000 is not the new limit on property tax deduction based on the new tax rules for those taxpayers filing married jointly. Instead, this amount represents the standard deduction for those individuals who are using the single filing status.

d. *Incorrect.* $18,000 is not the new limit on property tax deduction based on the new tax rules for those taxpayers filing married jointly. Instead, this amount represents the new standard deduction for those individuals filing as head of household.

4. a. *Incorrect.* Unreimbursed employee expenses are one of the most prominent miscellaneous itemized deductions that have been suspended through 2025. An additional deduction in this category includes union dues.

b. *Incorrect.* Investment advisory fees are one of the most prominent miscellaneous itemized deductions that have been suspended through 2025. An additional deduction in this category includes excess deductions on termination of a trust.

c. *Correct.* **Gambling losses are not one of the most prominent miscellaneous itemized deductions that have been suspended through 2025. Instead, examples of these include, but are not limited to, hobby loss expenses, excess deductions on termination of a trust, and union dues. Gambling losses can still offset gambling income.**

d. *Incorrect.* Tax preparation fees are one of the most prominent miscellaneous itemized deductions that have been suspended through 2025. An additional deduction in this category includes hobby loss expenses.

5. a. *Incorrect.* Contributions to HSAs are not deductible below-the-line. Instead, they are deductible above-the-line.

b. *Incorrect.* With respect to HSA accounts, Code Sec. 223(b)(7) prescribes that no contributions are allowed after the first month in which the taxpayer is entitled to Medicare.

c. *Incorrect.* Deduction limits are not the same for self-only and family coverage. In 2018, the deduction limits for self-only and family coverage are $3,450 and $6,900, respectively.

d. *Correct.* In order to have contributions to an HSA account deductible (above-the-line), the taxpayer is required to have both a HDHP plan as well as an HSA account. Many companies use HDHP plans and also make contributions to their employees' HSAs.

6. a. *Incorrect.* This is not one of the proposed state workarounds regarding the $10,000 deduction limit. Instead, one of the workarounds is to impose a tax on S corporations and partnerships.

b. *Correct.* This is one of the state tax workarounds with respect to the $10,000 deduction limit. In this situation, you would have a charitable contribution to the state, not taxes. However, the IRS issued Treas. Reg. §1.170A-1(h)(3) indicating that this was not possible (with an exception for state tax credits of 15 percent or less).

c. *Incorrect.* Personal exemptions were eliminated as a result of the TCJA. The concept of personal exemptions is not a state issue that can be changed on an individual's taxes.

d. *Incorrect.* A 529 plan is a tax-advantaged savings plan designed to help pay for education. Originally designed to pay post-secondary education costs, it was expanded to also cover K-12 education under the Tax Cuts and Jobs Act.

¶ 10,104 MODULE 2—CHAPTER 4

1. a. *Incorrect.* The new deduction allows for a larger percentage deduction on QBI. The deduction is available to any taxpayer other than a C corporation.

b. *Incorrect.* The new deduction allows for a larger percentage deduction on QBI. Additionally, the deduction is limited to the greater of (1) 50 percent of the W-2 wages with respect to the trade or business, or (2) the sum of 25 percent of the W-2 wages, plus 2.5 percent of the unadjusted basis immediately after acquisition of all qualified property (generally, tangible property subject to depreciation under Code Sec. 167).

c. *Correct.* Code Sec. 199A allows taxpayers other than corporations a deduction of 20 percent of QBI earned in a qualified trade or business, subject to certain limitations.

d. *Incorrect.* The new deduction allows for a smaller percentage deduction on QBI. Furthermore, QBI is the net amount of qualified items of income, gain, deduction, and loss with respect to a qualified trade or business that is effectively connected with the conduct of a business in the United States.

2. a. *Correct.* Code Sec. 751 income on sale of partnership interest based on Treas. Reg. §1.199A-3(b)(1)(i) is included within QBI. However, long-term capital gains and losses on investments are not included.

b. *Incorrect.* Guaranteed payments are not included in QBI.

c. *Incorrect.* Wages are not included in QBI. Additionally, interest income on working capital is not included in QBI.

d. *Incorrect.* Interest income from investment of working capital is not included in QBI.

3. a. *Incorrect.* This is not the full phase-in amount for QBID for those individuals filing as single. Instead, this represents the threshold amount for single filers, that is, where "hamburger" territory ends and the phase-in begins.

b. *Correct.* **This is the full phase-in amount for QBID for those individuals filing as single. For taxpayers who file as married filing jointly, the full phase-in amount is $415,000.**

c. *Incorrect.* This is not the full phase-in amount for QBID for those individuals filing as single. Instead, this represents the threshold amount for taxpayers who file as married filing jointly.

d. *Incorrect.* This is not the full phase-in amount for QBID for those individuals filing as single. Instead, this represents the full phase-in amount for taxpayers who file as married filing jointly.

4. a. *Incorrect.* This is a correct statement. In addition, there must be common ownership, meaning a 50 percent or more ownership (direct and indirect with attribution).

b. *Incorrect.* This is a correct statement. The aggregated business must meet two of three factors. These factors are outlined within Prop. Reg. § 1.199A-4.

c. *Correct.* **This is an incorrect statement. Service and nonservice businesses are not required to be aggregated.**

d. *Incorrect.* It might be easier for an entity to aggregate rather than each shareholder or partner. If an S corporation aggregates, shareholders must also follow the aggregation made by the entity.

5. a. *Incorrect.* Having separate books and records for each enterprise is one of the requirements in order to use the safe harbor as it relates to rental real estate.

b. *Correct.* **This is not one of the requirements. Instead, there must be greater than 250 hours, not 500 hours, of rental services per year in the enterprise.**

c. *Incorrect.* Having contemporaneous records is one of the requirements in order to use the safe harbor as it relates to rental real estate. The contemporaneous record-keeping requirement begins with 2019 tax returns; contemporaneous record keeping is not required for 2018 tax returns.

d. *Incorrect.* Having separate bank accounts for each enterprise is one of the requirements in order to use the safe harbor as it relates to rental real estate. The safe harbor can be utilized by individuals and RPEs.

6. a. *Incorrect.* This statement is true. A landscape design business qualifies as a SSTB under the final regulations, and thus its income is SSTB income.

b. *Incorrect.* This statement is true. According to the final regulations, assisted-living centers do not constitute health SSTBs when healthcare professionals bill separately for the medical services provided.

c. *Incorrect.* This statement is true. A surgical center in which doctors/nurses bill separate for medical services does not qualify as a health SSTB under the final rules.

d. *Correct.* **This statement is false. Commission-based sales of insurance are not considered "investing" and do not produce SSTB income.**

¶ 10,105 MODULE 2—CHAPTER 5

1. a. *Incorrect.* Because they share financial commitments, the partners are invested in the entity's success. This is an advantage, not a disadvantage.

b. *Incorrect.* It is true that a general partnership can exist through an oral agreement and does not require a legal filing. However, this not considered a disadvantage.

c. *Correct.* **The fact that the actions of any partner can subject the general partnership to liabilities is a major disadvantage of this type of structure.**

d. *Incorrect.* The simple fact that the owners of a general partnership are partners does not create a detriment or disadvantage.

2. a. *Incorrect.* The fact that an LLC's owners are called "members" is neither an advantage nor a disadvantage.

b. *Incorrect.* This is considered a disadvantage because state filing typically involves paying a fee.

c. *Correct.* **The flexibility to determine which members are involved in the business and its management, and how the governance structure will work, are considered advantages of this business type.**

d. *Incorrect.* Such complexity is considered a disadvantage rather than a benefit.

3. a. *Incorrect.* Silent partners are found in limited partnerships, not general partnerships.

b. *Correct.* **General partners control and run the business, but the silent partners do not take part in the business's dealings.**

c. *Incorrect.* Silent partners have limited liability; they are not subject to general liability.

d. *Incorrect.* Subchapter C governs C corporations; it does not address the duties of silent partners.

4. a. *Correct.* **Shareholders purchase stock of the corporation with money or other assets, and the corporation uses this money for operational purposes. The corporation is a separate entity.**

b. *Incorrect.* An LLC is owned by members who all have limited liability.

c. *Incorrect.* A general partnership is a business entity owned by one or more partners; there is no separate legal entity.

d. *Incorrect.* A limited partnership is controlled by at least one general partner. It has no shareholders.

5. a. *Incorrect.* In this type of entity, the individual owner is treated as the sole proprietor, which means that the entire amount of profits of the LLC is subject to the self-employment tax.

b. *Incorrect.* Generally, for purposes of the self-employment tax, only the income a limited partner receives for services rendered is taxable. However, there are several exceptions.

c. *Incorrect.* In an S corporation, neither the corporation nor the shareholder has to pay self-employment taxes on distributions to the owner.

d. *Correct.* **Sole proprietorships must pay a self-employment tax equivalent to the Federal Insurance Contributions Act (FICA) tax rate.**

6. a. *Correct.* **The IRS issued Treas. Reg. §§301.7701-1 to -4 to alleviate both the complexity and unpredictability of classifying an entity using the methods that were in place.**

b. *Incorrect.* The regulations did not introduce any new entity classifications.

c. *Incorrect.* The Four-Factor Test was used to classify entities as partnerships prior to the release of the check-the-box regulations.

d. *Incorrect.* The IRS does not require all businesses to take such action; those that do not choose an entity classification are assigned a default classification.

7. a. *Incorrect.* The tax rules for classifying business entities are largely independent of state law categories. Some state business law entities are not entities for tax purposes.

b. *Correct.* **Although currently there is some guidance for making such a determination, there are no clear rules that indicate whether an entity exists.**

c. *Incorrect.* These types of relationships may or may not be determined to be "entities."

d. *Incorrect.* A physical U.S. location does not prove the existence of a business entity.

8. a. *Incorrect.* A domestic eligible entity is never classified as a corporation by default.

b. *Correct.* **A domestic eligible business with two or more members is classified as a partnership by default.**

c. *Incorrect.* If Entity AB had one member, its default classification would be disregarded entity. Because it has two members, it is classified differently.

d. *Incorrect.* A trust is not one of the default classification categories.

9. a. *Incorrect.* When a partnership converts to a corporation, the partnership is deemed to contribute all of its assets and liabilities to the corporation in exchange for the corporation's stock. This type of conversion is typically tax-free.

b. *Incorrect.* When a disregarded entity converts to a corporation, the owner of the disregarded entity is deemed to contribute all of the assets and liabilities of the entity to the corporation in exchange for stock of the corporation. The deemed contribution is generally tax-free.

c. *Correct.* **Entities must be especially cautious before converting from a corporation to a partnership because of the tax implications.**

d. *Incorrect.* This statement is incorrect. Some of the entity conversions listed are tax-free transactions.

10. a. *Correct.* **A general partnership typically has the option to choose its entity classification for federal tax purposes.**

b. *Incorrect.* Corporations under state law are typically considered ineligible entities and cannot make the election.

c. *Incorrect.* Foreign entities listed in the regulations are considered ineligible for the election.

d. *Incorrect.* Government entities are among the entities ineligible to elect their tax classification under the regulations.

11. a. *Incorrect.* The tax legislation will not encourage this conversion, but it may encourage the opposite: sole proprietorships converting to corporations.

b. *Correct.* **The unlimited SALT deduction and the resulting savings can make a corporation structure a more attractive entity choice.**

c. *Incorrect.* The tax legislation changed the deduction but did not eliminate it.

d. *Incorrect.* The TCJA instead capped the deduction limit for individuals at $10,000.

12. a. *Incorrect.* In a REIT, income will pass through to the investors.

b. *Incorrect.* REITs are a type of entity created long ago by Congress.

c. *Incorrect.* The opposite is true; REITs are complex and have many technical requirements.

d. *Correct.* **Specialized entities such as mutual funds and REITs do not have the option to elect their classification for tax purposes.**

¶ 10,106 MODULE 2—CHAPTER 6

1. a. *Incorrect.* One of the features of an asset sale is that liabilities of the entity may be left behind.

b. *Incorrect.* When there is an asset sale, deed transfers for real property will be required.

c. *Correct.* **A stock sale is relatively easy to implement, requiring only a stock purchase agreement.**

d. *Incorrect.* An asset sale is more complicated to implement, requiring a purchase agreement that must identify and schedule each individual asset covered by such agreement.

2. a. *Incorrect.* Code Sec. 197 designates certain assets as intangible assets.

b. *Correct.* **Code Sec. 1060 provides that the buyer and seller must allocate the purchase price as provided in Code Sec. 338(b)(5).**

c. *Incorrect.* The term *capital asset* is defined in Code Sec. 1221.

d. *Incorrect.* Code Sec. 1222 defines the term *capital gain*.

3. a. *Incorrect.* The purchase price is allocated to cash first.

b. *Correct.* **The last class of assets to which the purchase price is allocated is goodwill.**

c. *Incorrect.* Inventory is Class IV property, which is not allocated last.

d. *Incorrect.* The purchase price is allocated to Code Sec. 197 intangibles second to last.

4. a. *Correct.* **Real estate is a capital asset.**

b. *Incorrect.* Inventory is not a capital asset.

c. *Incorrect.* Code Sec. 1222 defines a capital asset as property held by the taxpayer but specifically excludes certain U.S. government publications.

d. *Incorrect.* Notes receivable that are acquired in the ordinary course of a trade or business are not considered a capital asset.

5. a. *Correct.* **Single filers will be subject to the net investment income tax if adjusted gross income is $200,000 or more.**

b. *Incorrect.* Individuals who file with Married Filing Separate status will be subject to the tax if adjusted gross income is $125,000 or more.

c. *Incorrect.* The net investment income tax applies to adjusted gross income, not modified adjusted gross income, and the threshold for married couples filing a joint return is not $250,000.

d. *Incorrect.* The appropriate threshold for married couples filing a joint return is less than $275,000.

6. a. *Correct.* **The excess of AGI over $11,950, if it is less than undistributed net investment income, will be subject to the net investment income tax.**

b. *Incorrect.* Trusts reach the highest income tax bracket when income reaches $12,750.

c. *Incorrect.* The amount on which a trust's adjusted gross income will be subject to the net investment income tax is less than $37,000.

d. *Incorrect.* The amount on which a trust's adjusted gross income will be subject to the net investment income tax is less than $125,000.

7. a. *Incorrect.* The reporting of a. related party installment sale is not done via Form 8023

b. *Incorrect.* Form 8023, *Elections Under Section 338 for Corporations Making Qualified Stock Purchases,* is used when making a Code Sec. 338(h)(10) election.

c. *Correct.* **Form 8023 is not used when remitting interest owing on tax deferred under the installment method.**

d. *Incorrect.* The net investment income tax is calculated and reported using an individual's tax return (Form 1040).

8. a. *Incorrect.* The gross profit ratio is higher than 10 percent.

b. *Incorrect.* The gross profit ratio is not calculated by dividing the amount payable at closing ($20,000) over the basis of the stock ($80,000).

c. *Incorrect.* The gross profit ratio is not calculated by dividing the basis in the stock ($80,000) by the contract price ($200,000).

d. *Correct.* **The gross profit ratio is 60 percent, calculated by first calculating the gain (gross profit equals $200,000 – $80,000, which is $120,000). The contract price (or total amount received) is $200,000. The gross profit ratio equals $120,000/$200,000, or 60 percent.**

9. a. *Incorrect.* The basis recovery amount of each installment payment is more than $2,000.

b. *Incorrect.* $2,500 is not the amount of the basis recovery for each installment payment.

c. *Correct.* **$8,000 of each installment payment will be the amount of the basis recovery.**

d. *Incorrect.* The basis recovery amount of each installment payment is less than $12,000.

10. a. *Correct.* Revenue Ruling 79-91, as well as IRS Private Letter Ruling 200521007, provide that as long as the escrow account serves a bona fide business purpose of the buyer and there substantial restrictions on the seller's receipt of the cash, the amounts in escrow will not be taxed to the seller until they are released from escrow.

b. *Incorrect.* Revenue Ruling 72-172 addresses the characterization of the sale of partnership interests as depreciable assets.

c. *Incorrect.* With respect to costs incurred in connection with an acquisition, Revenue Procedure 2011-29 provides a safe harbor under which a taxpayer may treat 30 percent of contingent fees as investigative and, therefore, deductible.

d. *Incorrect.* The anti-*INDOPCO* regulations address the capitalization of fees incurred in a transaction in which there was no separate and distinct asset acquired.

11. a. *Incorrect.* Under Code Sec. 267(b), with respect to an S corporation and another S corporation, the ownership interest (by value) of the stock of each corporation required to confer related party status is higher than 33 percent.

b. *Incorrect.* Under Code Sec. 267(b), an S corporation and another C corporation, will be considered related parties if the same persons own more than 50 percent (by value) of the stock of each corporation.

c. *Correct.* If a grantor is the grantor of two different trusts, the grantor is a related party of both trusts.

d. *Incorrect.* The relevant metric is not the voting power of the stock.

12. a. *Incorrect.* The *Gregory* case did not address the capitalization of fees.

b. *Incorrect.* Revenue Ruling 79-91 addresses the issue of whether assets in escrow are constructively received.

c. *Incorrect.* Revenue Ruling 72-172 addresses the characterization of the sale of partnership interests as depreciable assets where Section 1239 applies to the transaction.

d. *Correct.* The *INDOPCO* case asserted that taxpayers must capitalize fees if they created a significant future benefit.

¶ 10,107 MODULE 2—CHAPTER 7

1. a. *Incorrect.* In this case, the taxpayer started a law firm and operated it through an S corporation. The taxpayer was a self-proclaimed poor manager with money problems.

b. *Incorrect.* In this case, the court agreed with the taxpayer (Singer) that his loans *did* qualify as loan repayments and not as wages.

c. *Correct.* Herbert was the owner of Gopher Delivery Services. In 2009, the company went out of business and the bank foreclosed on his home. In this case, the court indicated that reasonable compensation is a range rather than a precise amount.

d. *Incorrect.* This case involved Fred Blodgett, who was the sole shareholder and full-time employee of an S corporation. The court noted that whether the S corporation had net income was irrelevant. The critical fact was whether payments were actually for employment.

2. a. *Incorrect.* This is a correct statement with respect to the QBID. Additionally, there are income-based caps, for "hamburger" and "caviar" taxpayers.

b. *Incorrect.* This is a correct statement with respect to the QBID. There are differences depending on whether the business is an S corporation or an LLC.

c. *Correct.* This is an incorrect statement with respect to the QBID. It has a shelf life of 8 years (2018 through 2025).

d. *Incorrect.* This is a correct statement with respect to the QBID. These certain businesses include, but are not limited to, doctors, lawyers, and CPAs.

3. a. *Incorrect.* This is not the full phase-in amount for QBID for those individuals filing as single. Instead, this represents the threshold amount for single filers.

b. *Correct.* This is the full phase-in amount for QBID for those individuals filing as single. For married taxpayers filing jointly, the full phase-in amount is $415,000.

c. *Incorrect.* This is not the full phase-in amount for QBID for those individuals filing as single. Instead, this represents the threshold amount for married taxpayers who file jointly.

d. *Incorrect.* This is not the full phase-in amount for QBID for those individuals filing as single. Instead, this represents the full phase-in amount for "caviar" taxpayers whose tax status is married filing jointly.

4. a. *Incorrect.* The new deduction allows for a larger percentage deduction on qualifying business income. The deduction is available to any taxpayer other than a C corporation.

b. *Incorrect.* The new deduction allows for a larger percentage deduction on qualifying business income. Additionally, the deduction is limited to the greater of (1) 50 percent of the W-2 wages with respect to the trade or business, or (2) the sum of 25 percent of the W-2 wages, plus 2.5 percent of the unadjusted basis immediately after acquisition of all qualified property (generally, tangible property subject to depreciation under Code Sec. 167).

c. *Correct.* Code Sec. 199A allows taxpayers other than corporations a deduction of 20 percent of qualified business income earned in a qualified trade or business, subject to certain limitations.

d. *Incorrect.* The new deduction allows for a smaller percentage deduction on qualifying business income. Furthermore, qualified business income is the net amount of qualified items of income, gain, deduction, and loss with respect to a qualified trade or business that are effectively connected with the conduct of a business in the United States.

5. a. *Incorrect.* Adjusting historical wages to determine the current dollars is not the first step in the process. Instead, this is the second step in the process.

b. *Correct.* This is the first step in the process of calculating the cost of lost Social Security benefits. Once this step is performed, you should adjust the historical wages to get current dollars.

c. *Incorrect.* Determining the monthly average of historical Social Security wages is not the first step in the process. Instead, this step should be performed after the historical wages are adjusted to get current dollars.

d. *Incorrect.* Plugging the inflation-adjusted high 35-year wage average into the AIME table is not the first step in the process. Instead, it is the last step in the process.

6. a. *Incorrect.* This percentage represents the annual Social Security benefit at full retirement age for average indexed earnings between $66,996 and $128,400.

b. *Incorrect.* This percentage represents the annual Social Security benefit at full retirement age for average indexed earnings between $11,112 and $66,996.

c. *Incorrect.* This is not one of the percentages of the annual Social Security benefit at full retirement age. Instead, the percentages are either 0 percent, 15 percent, 32 percent, or 90 percent.

d. *Correct.* **This is the percentage of the annual Social Security benefit at full retirement age for average indexed earnings less than $11,112. For averaged indexed earnings in excess of $128,400, the percentage is 0.**

Index

References are to paragraph (¶) numbers.

¶ 10,200 Glossary

Accrual method: An accounting method in which income is generally recognized when it is earned.

Alternative depreciation system: A system the IRS requires to be used in special circumstances to calculate depreciation on certain business assets (depreciable assets).

Alternative minimum tax: A supplemental income tax imposed by the U.S. federal government required in addition to baseline income tax for certain individuals, corporations, estates, and trusts that have exemptions or special circumstances allowing for lower payments of standard income tax.

Average Indexed Monthly Earnings (AIME): A calculation used to determine a taxpayer's primary insurance amount, which is then used to calculate the amount of Social Security benefits the taxpayer will receive.

Bonus depreciation: A valuable tax-saving tool for businesses that allows them to take an immediate first-year deduction on the purchase of an eligible business property, in addition to other depreciation.

Book-tax conformity: The association between financial accounting income and taxable income.

C corporation: A corporation that is governed by Subchapter C of the Internal Revenue Code.

Capital asset: A type of asset that has a useful life of more than one year and that is not intended to be for sale in the ordinary course of business.

Capital gain: Gain (income) realized upon the sale of property.

Capital interest: An interest that would give the holder a share of the proceeds if the partnership's assets were sold at fair market value and then the proceeds were distributed in a complete liquidation of the partnership.

Carried interest: A share of the profits of an investment paid to the investment manager in excess of the amount that the manager contributes to the partnership, specifically in alternative investments (private equity and hedge funds).

Cash method: An accounting method in which income is generally recognized in the year cash is received and deductions are generally taken into account in the year an expense is paid.

Check-the-box election: An entity classification election that is made using IRS Form 8832, *Entity Classification Election*. An entity makes the election by checking a box on the form.

Corporation: An independent legal entity that is owned by shareholders.

Cost segregation: The process of identifying personal property assets that are grouped with real property assets and separating out personal assets for tax reporting purposes.

De minimis: A Latin expression meaning "about minimal things."

Depreciation: An accounting method of allocating the cost of a tangible asset over its useful life. It is used to account for declines in value over time.

Disregarded entity: A business entity with one owner that for tax purposes is not recognized as an entity distinct from its owner.

Donor advised fund: A fund operated by a Code Sec. 501(c)(3) organization that is composed of the contributions of individual donors. When donors contribute to a donor-advised fun, they can generally take an immediate tax deduction.

Fair market value: An estimate of the market value of a property, based on what a knowledgeable, willing, and unpressured buyer would probably pay to a knowledgeable, willing, and unpressured seller in the market.

General partner: A person who, along with another, comes together to form a business. The general partner bears the responsibility for the daily management of the business, can legally bind the business, and has personal liability for the business's debts and obligations.

General partnership: A business with more than one owner, and the owners are partners. The partners are personally liable for all business liabilities, jointly and severally, and they can be sued individually for the actions of another partner.

Goodwill: The established reputation of a business, which is regarded as a quantifiable asset.

Guaranteed payment: A payment determined "without regard to the income of the partnership" under Code Sec. 707(c); it is not dependent on entrepreneurial risk.

Internal structural framework: Includes all load-bearing internal walls and any other internal structural supports, including columns, girders, beams, trusses, spandrels, and all other members essential to the stability of a building.

Itemized deductions: Eligible expenses that individual taxpayers can claim on federal income tax returns and which decrease their taxable income, and are claimable in place of a standard deduction, if available.

Leasehold improvement: An improvement made to a leased building by a department that has the right to use this leasehold improvement over the term of the lease.

Limited liability company (LLC): A hybrid business entity that provides the limited liability advantages of a corporation with pass-through tax treatment and flexible operational and governance features.

Limited partner: A partner who does not have total liability for the debts and obligations of a partnership. In other words, the partner's liability is limited to the amount invested in the company. However, limited partners also receive limited profits.

Limited partnership: A partnership that has at least one general partner and one or more limited partners.

Member: An owner in a limited liability company (LLC).

Net investment income tax: The 3.8 percent Medicare tax on unearned income. Also called *the Medicare tax*.

Net operating loss (NOL): A loss taken in a period where a company's allowable tax deductions are greater than its taxable income.

Personal exemption: An amount a taxpayer can deduct from his or her income for every taxpayer and most dependents claimed on his or her return.

Personal property: Generally, movable property, or property that is not real property.

Phaseout: The gradual reduction of a tax credit that a taxpayer is eligible for as the taxpayer's income approaches the limit to qualify for that credit.

Profits interest: An interest in the future profits and appreciation of a partnership.

Qualified business income: Ordinary, non-investment income of a business.

Qualified business income deduction (QBID): A deduction allowed by Code Sec. 199A of up to 20 percent of qualified business income, applied at the individual level, and subject to certain limitations. Also known as the *Section 199A deduction* or the *20 percent pass-through deduction*.

Qualified restaurant property: Any Code Section 1250 property that is a building or an improvement to a building placed in service during the tax year.

Qualified small business stock: Stock in a domestic C corporation that does not have more than $50 million in assets as of the date the stock was issued and immediately after the issuance.

Qualified trade or business: For purposes of Code Sec. 199A, any trade or business other than a specified service trade or business, or a trade or business of performing services as an employee.

Real estate investment trust (REIT): A company that owns, operates, or finances income-producing real estate.

S corporation: A closely held corporation (or, in some cases, a limited liability company or a partnership) that makes a valid election to be taxed under Subchapter S of Chapter 1 of the Internal Revenue Code.

Specified service trade or business (SSTB): According to the IRS, "a trade or business involving the performance of services in the fields of health, law, accounting, actuarial science, performing arts, consulting, athletics, financial services, investing and investment management, trading, dealing in certain assets or any trade or business where the principal asset is the reputation or skill of one or more of its employees or owners."

Ready-to-go equipment: Equipment that can be placed in service as soon as it is purchased, even if it is not being used.

Real property: Fixed property; generally refers to land and buildings.

Reasonable compensation: The normal compensation for an employee for the work performed or duties entailed.

Roth IRA: A special retirement account that a taxpayer funds with post-tax income. All future withdrawals that follow Roth IRA regulations are tax-free.

Section 179: The Internal Revenue Code section that allows taxpayers to elect to deduct the cost of certain types of property on their income taxes as an expense, rather than requiring the cost of the property to be capitalized and depreciated.

Small business: For purposes of the Tax Cuts and Jobs Act of 2017, a business that (1) has average annual gross receipts of $25 million or less in the three prior tax years and (2) is not a tax shelter.

Sole proprietorship: An unincorporated business owned and operated by one individual, with no legal distinction between the business and the owner.

Spin-off: A transaction in which the parent company forms a subsidiary corporation, then transfers relevant assets (typically, a division of the parent company or a separate line of business of the parent company) to that subsidiary.

Split-off: An exchange offer in which the shareholders of the parent company exchange their stock in the parent company for stock in the new entity.

Spread: The difference between the strike price and the fair market value of stock on the date of exercise.

Standard deduction: A dollar amount that non-itemizers may subtract from their income before income tax is applied.

Strike price: The price at which a option holder may purchase a share of stock using the option.

Tax Cuts and Jobs Act of 2017: P.L. 115-97, major tax reform legislation that was signed into law on December 22, 2017, and amends the Internal Revenue Code of 1986. Major elements of the changes include reducing tax rates for businesses and individuals; and a personal tax simplification by increasing the standard deduction and family tax credits, but eliminating personal exemptions and making it less beneficial to itemize deductions.

Tax shelter: According to Internal Revenue Code Section 6662(d), (1) a partnership or other entity (such as a corporation or trust), (2) an investment plan or arrangement, or (3) any other plan or arrangement, whose principal purpose is to avoid or evade federal income tax.

Unadjusted basis immediately after acquisition (UBIA): The amount a taxpayer paid for tangible depreciable property. Also known as the *property factor*.

Uniform capitalization (UNICAP) rules: Rules that require a taxpayer to capitalize all direct and indirect costs it incurs in producing real or tangible personal property that are allocable to that property. The rules are detailed in Section 263A of the Internal Revenue Code.

Vesting: A requirement that an employee work for a certain length of time or meet certain performance goals before options become exercisable.

¶ 10,300 Final Exam Instructions

To complete your Final Exam go to **cchcpelink.com/printcpe,** click on the title of the exam you wish to complete and add it to your shopping cart (you will need to register with CCH CPELink if you have not already). Click **Proceed to Checkout** and enter your credit card information. Click **Place Order** to complete your purchase of the final exam. The final exam will be available in **My Dashboard** under **My Account.**

This Final Exam is divided into four Modules. There is a grading fee for each Final Exam submission.

Online Processing Fee:	**Recommended CPE:**
$170.00 for Module 1	8 hours for Module 1
$255.00 for Module 2	12 hours for Module 2
$425.00 for all Modules	20 hours for all Modules
IRS Program Number:	**Federal Tax Law Hours:**
Module 1: 4VRWB-T-03435-19-S	8 hours for Module 1
Module 2: 4VRWB-T-03436-19-S	12 hours for Module 2
	20 hours for all Modules
CTEC Program Numbers:	
Module 1: 1075-CE-1633	
Module 2: 1075-CE-1634	

Instructions for purchasing your CPE Tests and accessing them after purchase are provided on the **cchcpelink.com/printcpe** website. **Please note, manual grading is no longer available for Top Federal Tax Issues. All answer sheets must be submitted online for grading and processing.**

Recommended CPE credit is based on a 50-minute hour. Because CPE requirements vary from state to state and among different licensing agencies, please contact your CPE governing body for information on your CPE requirements and the applicability of a particular course for your requirements.

Expiration Date: December 31, 2020

Evaluation: To help us provide you with the best possible products, please take a moment to fill out the course Evaluation located after your Final Exam.

Wolters Kluwer, CCH is registered with the National Association of State Boards of Accountancy (NASBA) as a sponsor of continuing professional education on the National Registry of CPE Sponsors. State boards of accountancy have final authority on the acceptance of individual courses for CPE credit. Complaints regarding registered sponsors may be submitted to the National Registry of CPE Sponsors through its website: www.learningmarket.org.

Additional copies of this course may be downloaded from **cchcpelink.com/printcpe.** Printed copies of the course are available for $3.99 by calling 1-800-344-3734 (ask for product 10024491-0007).

¶ 10,301 Final Exam Questions: Module 1

1. Under the new rules, a taxpayer can elect which percentage for bonus depreciation for property placed in service after September 27, 2017 but before December 31, 2017?

   a. 50 percent

   b. 60 percent

   c. 70 percent

   d. 80 percent

2. For eligible property acquired after September 27, 2017, the bonus depreciation is 60 percent if the property is placed into service in:

   a. 2021

   b. 2022

   c. 2023

   d. 2024

3. Assume that a taxpayer acquires a used duplex in 2018 and allocates the purchase price across land, building, land improvements, and personal property. Which of the following two items are eligible for bonus depreciation in this situation?

   a. Land and land improvements

   b. Land and personal property

   c. Land improvements and personal property

   d. Land improvements and building

4. Which of the following allocation methods/approaches uses little to no documentation and is based on a preparer's experience?

   a. Reproduction cost approach

   b. Reproduction cost less refurbishment approach

   c. Assessed value method

   d. Rule of thumb approach

5. With respect to bonus and Section 280(F) interaction, assuming 100% business use in the first year, the depreciation is the lesser of the cost of the car or:

   a. $18,000

   b. $15,000

   c. $12,000

   d. $10,000

6. Each of the following types of real property 15-year lives are eliminated as a result of the Tax Cuts and Jobs Act (TCJA), *except:*

   a. Qualified leasehold improvement property

   b. Qualified restaurant property

   c. Land improvements

   d. Qualified retail improvement property

7. Which of the following types of properties did *not* change as a result of the TCJA?

   a. Qualifying leasehold improvements

   b. Qualifying restaurant property

   c. Non-residential roofs

   d. Land improvements

8. Starting in 2018, the Section 179 expense phaseout begins at:

    a. $2,000,000

    b. $2,250,000

    c. $2,500,000

    d. $2,750,000

9. Each of the following is an exclusion related to qualified improvement property, *except:*

    a. Non-load-bearing interior walls

    b. Enlargement of a building

    c. Elevators and escalators

    d. Internal structural framework

10. Based on the TCJA amendments to Section 179, the author recommends which of the following approaches?

    a. Methodical approach

    b. Surgical approach

    c. Fair market value approach

    d. All-in approach

11. Which of the following identifies the *de minimis* election per invoice for taxpayers without audited financial statements?

    a. $2,500

    b. $5,000

    c. $7,500

    d. $9,000

12. Which of the following identifies the *de minimis* election per invoice for taxpayers that do *not* have audited financial statements?

    a. $2,500

    b. $5,000

    c. $7,500

    d. $9,000

13. Book conformity is required under:

    a. *De minimis* rules

    b. Bonus

    c. Section 179

    d. Section 280

14. There is no bonus depreciation for property with a recovery period greater than:

    a. 5 years

    b. 10 years

    c. 15 years

    d. 20 years

¶10,301

15. Which of the following types of property is considered placed in service when it is in the taxpayer's possession?

    a. Buildings

    b. Ready-to-go equipment

    c. Unfinished equipment

    d. Addition improvements

16. Which of the following identifies the correct sequence for basis reduction?

    a. *De minimis* > Section 179 > Bonus

    b. *De minimis* > Bonus > Section 179

    c. Section 179 > Bonus > *De minimis*

    d. Section 179 > *De minimis* > Bonus

17. When applying the surgical approach and electing out of bonus depreciation, the taxpayer should follow the instructions on:

    a. Form 4562

    b. Form 4568

    c. Form 6598

    d. Form 6554

18. The election out of bonus depreciation must cover _____ of the property in a class.

    a. At least 10 percent

    b. At least 50 percent

    c. At least 90 percent

    d. 100 percent

19. The Section 179 active business income limit provides the opportunity to freeze deductions for future years with:

    a. Higher tax rates

    b. Significantly lower tax rates

    c. Similar tax rates

    d. Marginally lower tax rates

20. Which of the following types of methods recapture on QRP allocates the selling price based upon the adjusted basis?

    a. Gain allocation method

    b. Pro rata method

    c. Fair value method

    d. Replacement cost method

21. The accounting method changes under the TCJA are effective for tax years beginning:

    a. After January 1, 2017

    b. After December 31, 2017

    c. After December 31, 2018

    d. On January 1, 2019

22. Which of the following will *not* require a Code Sec. 481(a) adjustment?

   a. Changing from the accrual to the cash method

   b. Using the completed contracts method

   c. Changing to the QuickBooks method of inventories

   d. Opting out of the Code Sec. 263A requirements

23. Accounting methods relate to _____ issues, such as depreciation, inventories, and cash versus accrual.

   a. Reporting

   b. Auditing

   c. Timing

   d. Deferral

24. Which of the following accounting methods is a tax shelter required to use?

   a. Accrual

   b. Uniform capitalization

   c. Completed contract

   d. Non-incidental treatment

25. Which of the following statements about accounting methods is true?

   a. Accounting methods involve permanently nondeductible expenses (like the nondeductible portion of meals expense).

   b. Accounting methods involve permanently nontaxable income (like municipal interest income).

   c. Accounting methods involve the timing of income and expenses (e.g., in what year an item of income or expense is reported).

   d. Once adopted, an accounting method may never be changed.

26. Which statement is true regarding the *de minimis* rule for improvements to property?

   a. It was implemented by the Tax Cuts and Jobs Act.

   b. It has been revoked by the Tax Cuts and Jobs Act.

   c. If a taxpayer uses the *de minimis* rule for tax, it does not have to use the rule for books.

   d. Its use has been clarified by the Tax Cuts and Jobs Act's broad waiver of Code Sec. 263A requirements.

27. For purposes of the Tax Cuts and Jobs Act, a tax shelter is defined as:

   a. An entity as defined by Code Sec. 6662(d)(2)(c)(ii)

   b. An entity whose interests have been offered for sale that is required to register with a state or federal agency under securities laws

   c. An entity that allocates more than 35 percent of its losses to a limited entrepreneur or limited partner

   d. All of the above

28. Under the Tax Cuts and Jobs Act, a small business taxpayer can use the cash method of accounting if it has:

    a. Average annual gross receipts of $25 million or less and is not a tax shelter

    b. More than $12 million in trailing average gross receipts and fewer than 50 employees

    c. Book conformity and written accounting procedures

    d. Audited financial statements and less than $25 million in annual gross receipts

29. Which of the following identifies the *de minimis* election maximum amount per invoice for taxpayers that have audited financial statements?

    a. $5,000

    b. $7,500

    c. $9,500

    d. $10,000

30. Which of the following is required under the *de minimis* rule for all taxpayers who do *not* have audited financial statements?

    a. Audited financial statements

    b. A *de minimis* election

    c. Book conformity

    d. A *de minimis* election, a *de minimis* policy, and book conformity

31. As a result of the TCJA, the 2018 standard deduction for taxpayers who are married filing jointly has been increased to what amount?

    a. $12,000

    b. $18,000

    c. $24,000

    d. $28,000

32. Which of the following tax deductions have been eliminated as a result of the TCJA?

    a. Personal exemptions

    b. Mortgage interest

    c. Charitable contributions

    d. Gambling losses

33. Based on the TCJA, mortgage interest is deductible for acquisition indebtedness incurred after December 15, 2017, up to what amount?

    a. $500,000

    b. $750,000

    c. $1,000,000

    d. $1,500,000

34. Deductible amounts related to property taxes include domestic property taxes plus the greater of sales tax or:

    a. State and local income taxes

    b. Federal income taxes

    c. Mortgage insurance taxes

    d. Excise foreign credit taxes

35. Which of the following types of funds can help some taxpayers "bunch" deductions to get greater benefit from charitable contributions for the period 2018–2025?

    a. Cause-specific

    b. General purpose

    c. Earmarked use

    d. Donor advised

36. Which of the following is an example of an unreimbursed employee expense that has been suspended by the TCJA from 2018 to 2025 for purposes of tax deduction?

    a. Transportation expense

    b. Investment advisory fees

    c. Tax preparation fees

    d. Union dues

37. Which of the following types of tax preparation fees can no longer be deducted above the line?

    a. Portion of fee allocable to Schedule C

    b. Portion of fee related to Schedule F

    c. Portion of fee related to Schedule E, Part 1

    d. Portion of fee related to Schedule A

38. Which of the following statements about health savings accounts (HSAs) is true?

    a. The TCJA made sweeping changes in regard to HSAs.

    b. HSA contributions are no longer deductible.

    c. HSAs are increasingly popular with taxpayers.

    d. HSAs appeal only to very low income taxpayers.

39. Which type(s) of gambler can take gambling losses in excess of wagering gains under the TCJA?

    a. All gamblers

    b. Professional gamblers only

    c. Casual gamblers with winnings of $5,000 or more

    d. Neither professional nor casual gamblers are allowed to take losses in excess of wagering gains.

40. The _____ is also known as the 20 percent pass-through deduction.

    a. Pease limitation

    b. QBID

    c. Charitable contribution deduction

    d. Interest expense deduction

¶ 10,302 Final Exam Questions: Module 2

1. Which of the following types of income is included in qualified business income (QBI)?

   a. Qualified real estate investment trust (REIT) ordinary dividends

   b. Capital gains

   c. Capital losses

   d. Wages

2. Which of the following areas is undecided as to whether it impacts the definition of QBI?

   a. Net operating losses (NOLs)

   b. Self-employed health insurance

   c. Interest expense on the purchase of S corporation stock

   d. Code Sec. 1231 losses

3. Which of the following identifies the "threshold" amount (the end of "hamburger" territory and the beginning of the phase-in range) for the QBID for individuals who file as married filing jointly?

   a. $157,000

   b. $207,500

   c. $315,000

   d. $415,000

4. Based on the final regulations, which of the following types of income would likely *not* be included in the SSTB classification?

   a. Insurance broker

   b. Mortgage broker

   c. Lobbyist

   d. Pharmacist

5. Which of the following entities would result in all income being treated as SSTB income?

   a. Exchange facilitator (5 percent of revenues from SSTB)

   b. Veterinarian and separate dog food sales businesses (two separate businesses)

   c. Veterinarian (S corporation) owning 98 percent of LLC (dog food sales business)

   d. Landscape design/lawn maintenance company with 15 percent of revenues from landscape design

6. Which of the following statements regarding aggregation and the impacts on QBID is correct?

   a. Aggregation is required for all entity types.

   b. Aggregation is permitted but not required for entities that clear all five hurdles.

   c. Aggregation is permitted only for partnerships.

   d. Aggregation is required only for only S corporations.

7. In which of the following cases did the court find that the rental real estate was a business?

    a. *Grier v. United States*

    b. *Balsamo v. Commissioner*

    c. *Union Bank of Troy*

    d. *Reiner v. United States*

8. Which of the following identifies an area that is "foggy" as it relates to rental real estate?

    a. Triple net leases, especially if the tenant is responsible for repairs

    b. Common control

    c. Aggregation

    d. Loss carryovers

9. Passive loss carryovers originating in _____ or before do *not* reduce QBI.

    a. 2016

    b. 2017

    c. 2018

    d. 2019

10. Which of the following identifies an area for which final QBID regulations did *not* differ from the proposed regulations?

    a. SSTB shared expenses *de minimis* rule.

    b. Wages being ineligible for the QBID

    c. The ability to make an aggregation choice on an amended return.

    d. 100 percent treatment as a SSTB if 80 percent of products provided to the SSTB are under common control.

11. The Tax Cuts and Jobs Act of 2017 _____ the corporate tax rate to _____ percent.

    a. Increased; 35

    b. Increased; 25

    c. Decreased; 21

    d. Decreased; 18

12. Which of the following entities is typically *ineligible* to elect its tax classification?

    a. LLC

    b. LLP

    c. Bank

    d. Limited partnership

13. An entity can "check the box" on _____ to elect its entity classification.

    a. Form 1040

    b. Form 1065

    c. Form 8832

    d. Schedule K-1

14. The Four-Factor Test for classifying an entity included (1) continuity of life, (2) centralized management, (3) limited liability and (4):

   a. Nonprofit status
   b. Exit strategy
   c. A detailed written agreement
   d. Free transferability of interests

15. Which type of entity does *not* offer protection from personal liability?

   a. LLC
   b. Limited partnership
   c. Corporation
   d. Sole proprietorship

16. A partnership becomes a disregarded entity when it:

   a. Acquires a third partner
   b. Has only one partner left
   c. Merges with another partnership
   d. Dissolves

17. Which type of entity files IRS Form 1065?

   a. C corporation
   b. Sole proprietorship
   c. Partnership
   d. Disregarded entity

18. Which type of entity can issue convertible preferred stock?

   a. C corporation
   b. LLP
   c. Limited partnership
   d. LLC

19. Which default status will be applied to a business that has one owner and takes no action to form an entity?

   a. LLC
   b. S corporation
   c. C corporation
   d. Sole proprietorship

20. A(n) _____ can have only a single class of stock.

   a. LLC
   b. C corporation
   c. S corporation
   d. Limited partnership

21. Which of the following statements correctly describes a difference between a C corporation and an S corporation?

    a. In a C corporation, dividends of retained earnings are subject to income tax at the shareholder level; in an S corporation they are not.

    b. In a C corporation, shareholders include the value of fringe benefits in their taxable income; in an S corporation, they do not.

    c. An S corporation must pay self-employment tax on distributions to the owner; a C corporation does not.

    d. An S corporation pays corporate-level income tax; a C corporation does not.

22. Which Code Section applies when a taxpayer receives property in exchange for the performance of services?

    a. Code Sec. 7704

    b. Code Sec. 721

    c. Code Sec. 199A

    d. Code Sec. 83

23. Partnerships and S corporations are similar in that they are both:

    a. Taxed as corporations

    b. Pass-through entities

    c. Subject to Subchapter C

    d. Subject to Subchapter K

24. Under the TCJA, pass-through entities can deduct up to ____ percent of their net business income from their income taxes.

    a. 20

    b. 21

    c. 50

    d. 80

25. Which of the following TCJA changes might put more businesses in a loss position for the next five years?

    a. Repeal of the corporate AMT

    b. 100 percent bonus depreciation

    c. SALT deduction limit

    d. New pass-through deduction

26. When did the IRS issue the "check-the-box" rules?

    a. 1997

    b. 2000

    c. 2007

    d. 2017

27. Which of the following is filed with the IRS to report a partner's share of the partnership's income?

    a. Schedule C

    b. Schedule K-1

    c. Form 1040

    d. Form 8832

28. For tax purposes, the three major entity classifications are:
   a. Corporation, partnership, and LLC
   b. Corporation, partnership, and disregarded entity
   c. Disregarded entity, sole proprietorship, and general partnership
   d. Limited partnership, corporation, and S corporation

29. Generally, an S corporation cannot have more than ____ shareholders.
   a. 50
   b. 75
   c. 100
   d. 250

30. What is a profits interest?
   a. An interest in liquidating proceeds that are distributed to partners
   b. An interest in the future profits and appreciation of a partnership or LLC
   c. An interest that gives shareholder a share of a corporation's proceeds
   d. An interest offered by financial institutions that is compounded over time

31. In an asset sale, the buyer may amortize goodwill over how many years?
   a. 10
   b. 15
   c. 27
   d. 39

32. When allocating the purchase price, which type of asset is a Class IV asset?
   a. Cash
   b. Readily tradeable securities
   c. Inventory
   d. Intangibles other than goodwill and going concern

33. Which of the following is an ordinary asset?
   a. Right to produce a play
   b. Right of first refusal
   c. Franchisee's right to exclusive territory
   d. Right to a percentage of movie profits

34. Section 197 intangibles, which include covenants not to compete, are amortizable over what period of time?
   a. 15 years
   b. 27 years
   c. Remaining useful life
   d. Period agreed to by the parties to the agreement

35. The net investment income tax, which is an additional Medicare tax on unearned income, is:
   a. 2.7 percent
   b. 3.8 percent
   c. 7.2 percent
   d. 11.65 percent

36. In which of the following Internal Revenue Code sections is the additional Medicare tax on net investment income found?

   a. Code Sec. 338

   b. Code Sec. 453

   c. Code Sec. 1221

   d. Code Sec. 1411

37. In which of the following Internal Revenue Code sections are the passive activity rules used to determine if assets sold (or deemed sold) are held in a nonpassive trade or business found?

   a. Code Sec. 197

   b. Code Sec. 338

   c. Code Sec. 453A

   d. Code Sec. 469

38. An election to treat a stock sale as an asset sale for tax purposes must be made no later than the _____ following the acquisition.

   a. 15th day of the 3rd month

   b. 15th day of the 6th month

   c. 15th day of the 7th month

   d. 15th day of the 9th month

39. Which of the following Internal Revenue Code sections addresses installment sales?

   a. Code Sec. 453

   b. Code Sec. 1001

   c. Code Sec. 1274

   d. Code Sec. 6621

40. With respect to the contingent payment installment sale rules, if there is neither a maximum sales price nor a fixed term, basis should be allocated ratably over _____ years.

   a. 5

   b. 7

   c. 11

   d. 15

41. Under Internal Revenue Code Sec. 453A, a taxpayer must pay interest on tax deferred under the installment method if: (i) the sales price of the property is greater than _____; and (ii) the outstanding installment obligations that arose during the year, and that are outstanding during the year, exceed $5 million.

   a. $100,000

   b. $125,000

   c. $150,000

   d. $200,000

42. The interest a taxpayer must pay on tax that is deferred under the installment method is the underpayment rate under Internal Revenue Code Sec. ____.

    a. 338

    b. 453A

    c. 1001

    d. 6621

43. If a related party purchases property with an installment note, and then sells the property within ____ year(s) of the original related party sale, the amount realized on disposition is treated as payment to the original related party seller, to the extent of the installment obligation outstanding.

    a. 1

    b. 2

    c. 3

    d. 4

44. Which Internal Revenue Code section provides that "in the case of a sale or exchange of property, directly or indirectly, between related persons, any gain recognized to the transferor shall be treated as ordinary income if such property is, in the hands of the transferee, of a character which is subject to the allowance for depreciation provided in section 167"?

    a. Code Sec. 338

    b. Code Sec. 355

    c. Code Sec. 453A

    d. Code Sec. 1239

45. With respect to the definition of a controlled entity under Code Sec. 1239, a corporation with more than _____ of the outstanding stock that is owned, directly or indirectly, by or for such transferor, will be considered a controlled entity.

    a. 33 percent of the value

    b. 50 percent of the value

    c. 40 percent of the voting rights

    d. 50 percent of the voting rights

46. Which Internal Revenue Code section sets forth the anti-Morris Trust rules?

    a. Code Sec. 355

    b. Code Sec. 911

    c. Code Sec. 1060

    d. Code Sec. 1239

47. After a spin-off, shareholders are prohibited from selling or otherwise disposing of the business for:

    a. One year

    b. Two years

    c. Three years

    d. Four years

48. Which of the following statements related to the acquisition and disposition of assets is true?

    a. Sales commissions paid upon the disposition of an asset is deductible.

    b. Legal fees incurred to dispose of inventory must be capitalized.

    c. Professional fees for appraisals are immediately deductible.

    d. Zoning fees are capitalized.

49. Which of the following costs may be deducted?

    a. Costs incurred prior to signing a letter of intent

    b. Costs that facilitate an acquisition

    c. Costs incurred upon closing of a transaction

    d. Costs incurred post-acquisition

50. Revenue Procedure 2011-29 sets forth a safe harbor under which a taxpayer may treat what percentage of contingent fees as investigative and, therefore, deductible?

    a. 10 percent

    b. 20 percent

    c. 30 percent

    d. 40 percent

51. Which of the following are commonly involved in litigation with respect to reasonable compensation?

    a. Teachers

    b. Biologists

    c. Veterinarians

    d. Doctors

52. Based on the IRS Fact Sheet, each of the following is a fact or circumstance considered with respect to reasonable compensation, ***except:***

    a. Financial outlook

    b. Duties and responsibilities

    c. Dividend history

    d. Payments to non-shareholder employees

53. The case of ***Herbert v. Commissioner*** dealt primarily with:

    a. Whether the shareholder was an employee

    b. The level of deductions taken by the taxpayer

    c. The assessment of reasonable compensation based on the prior year's range

    d. Classification of loans to an entity

54. In the ***McAlary Ltd.*** case, the taxpayer was a(n) _____ who took $240,000 in distributions but reported zero in wages.

    a. Real estate broker

    b. Attorney

    c. Geophysicist

    d. Appraiser

55. When calculating the cost of lost Social Security benefits that result from underpaying a shareholder-employee's compensation and resulting payroll taxes, after the historical wages are determined, you should next:

    a. Determine the monthly average.

    b. Plug the inflation-adjusted 35-year wage averaged into the AIME table.

    c. Apply a 2 percent premium adjustment.

    d. Adjust the historical wages using an inflation factor to get current dollars.

56. Social Security benefits at full age equal zero percent when 2018 indexed annual earnings are at least:

    a. $94,750

    b. $99,645

    c. $114,123

    d. $128,400

57. The new QBID deduction is in effect for _____ years unless otherwise extended.

    a. Six

    b. Seven

    c. Eight

    d. Nine

58. With respect to the new QBID deduction, the SSTB cap applies to each of the following professions, *except:*

    a. Teachers

    b. Doctors

    c. Lawyers

    d. CPAs

59. Which of the following identifies the threshold amount for QBID for those individuals whose tax status is married filing jointly?

    a. $157,000

    b. $207,500

    c. $315,000

    d. $415,000

60. Based on the requirements prescribed by Code Sec. 199A(c)(4)(B), guaranteed payments _____ qualify for QBID.

    a. Do not

    b. May

    c. Always

    d. Often

¶ 10,400 Answer Sheets

¶ 10,401 Top Federal Tax Issues for 2020 CPE Course: MODULE 1

(10014583-0008)

Go to **cchcpelink.com/printcpe** to complete your Final Exam online for instant results.

A $170.00 processing fee will be charged for each user submitting Module 1 to **cchcpelink.com/printcpe** for online grading.

Module 1: Answer Sheet

(10014583-0008)

Please answer the questions by indicating the appropriate letter next to the corresponding number.

1. ___	9. ___	17. ___	25. ___	33. ___
2. ___	10. ___	18. ___	26. ___	34. ___
3. ___	11. ___	19. ___	27. ___	35. ___
4. ___	12. ___	20. ___	28. ___	36. ___
5. ___	13. ___	21. ___	29. ___	37. ___
6. ___	14. ___	22. ___	30. ___	38. ___
7. ___	15. ___	23. ___	31. ___	39. ___
8. ___	16. ___	24. ___	32. ___	40. ___

Please complete the Evaluation Form (located after the Module 2 Answer Sheet). Thank you.

¶ 10,402 Top Federal Tax Issues for 2020 CPE Course: MODULE 2

(10014584-0008)

Go to **cchcpelink.com/printcpe** to complete your Final Exam online for instant results.

A $255.00 processing fee will be charged for each user submitting Module 2 to **cchcpelink.com/printcpe** for online grading.

Module 2: Answer Sheet

(10014584-0008)

Please answer the questions by indicating the appropriate letter next to the corresponding number.

1. ___	13. ___	25. ___	37. ___	49. ___
2. ___	14. ___	26. ___	38. ___	50. ___
3. ___	15. ___	27. ___	39. ___	51. ___
4. ___	16. ___	28. ___	40. ___	52. ___
5. ___	17. ___	29. ___	41. ___	53. ___
6. ___	18. ___	30. ___	42. ___	54. ___
7. ___	19. ___	31. ___	43. ___	55. ___
8. ___	20. ___	32. ___	44. ___	56. ___
9. ___	21. ___	33. ___	45. ___	57. ___
10. ___	22. ___	34. ___	46. ___	58. ___
11. ___	23. ___	35. ___	47. ___	59. ___
12. ___	24. ___	36. ___	48. ___	60. ___

Please complete the Evaluation Form (located after the Module 2 Answer Sheet). Thank you.

¶ 10,500 Top Federal Tax Issues for 2020 CPE Course: Evaluation Form

(10024491-0007)

Please take a few moments to fill out and submit this evaluation to Wolters Kluwer so that we can better provide you with the type of self-study programs you want and need. Thank you.

About This Program

1. Please circle the number that best reflects the extent of your agreement with the following statements:

		Strongly Agree				Strongly Disagree
a.	The Course objectives were met.	5	4	3	2	1
b.	This Course was comprehensive and organized.	5	4	3	2	1
c.	The content was current and technically accurate.	5	4	3	2	1
d.	This Course content was relevant and contributed to achievement of the learning objectives.	5	4	3	2	1
e.	The prerequisite requirements were appropriate.	5	4	3	2	1
f.	This Course was a valuable learning experience.	5	4	3	2	1
g.	The Course completion time was appropriate.	5	4	3	2	1

2. What do you consider to be the strong points of this Course?

3. What improvements can we make to this Course?

THANK YOU FOR TAKING THE TIME TO COMPLETE THIS SURVEY!